THE
MEMORY
OF ALL THAT

THE
MEMORY
OF ALL THAT

Love and Politics in New York,
Hollywood, and Paris

BETSY BLAIR

Alfred A. Knopf   New York   2003

THIS IS A BORZOI BOOK
PUBLISHED BY ALFRED A. KNOPF

Library of Congress Cataloging-in-Publication Data
Blair, Betsy, [date]
The memory of all that : love and politics in New York,
Hollywood, and Paris / Betsy Blair — 1st ed.
p.   cm.
ISBN 0-375-41299-9 (alk. paper)
1. Blair, Betsy, 1923–   2. Motion picture actors and actresses—United
States—Biography.   I. Title.
PN2287.B4549 A3 2003
791.43'028'092—dc21
[B]   2002029854

Manufactured in the United States of America
First Edition

For Kerry and Karel

Illustrations

Illustrations

THE
MEMORY
OF ALL THAT

By way of explanation . . .

GENE KELLY was eighty-three when he died. The death certificate signed by the doctor of his young third wife states the time of death as 8:15 Friday morning, February 2, 1996. I don't know how it was arranged that he could be cremated that same morning, but according to his widow, he was.

I knew Gene intimately for seventeen years, from when he was twenty-eight until he was forty-five. For almost sixteen of those years I was married to him, and we had a daughter, Kerry.

In private life he was lively, smart and funny, tender and loving, a natural teacher. (I admit he was old-fashioned and paternalistic, but then so were most men at that time). He loved life, he loved children, he loved games, he loved books and museums, he loved to travel, he loved to sit home and drink beer.

And he loved his work. He was great at it, and as you know, successful. But he never gave up trying to do more and do it better. Of course I'm talking of the seventeen years I lived with him and knew him well.

He had a lovely second wife, Jeanne Coyne, and two more children, Tim and Bridget. But Jeanne died of leukemia when they were only ten and eight. It was a great loss for all three of them.

Over the years, from Jeanne's death until his, I saw Gene once or twice a year. Whenever I was in Los Angeles, I'd go to Rodeo Drive for a cup of tea with him. Of course, it was different—the house was different, he was different. I was a visitor from the past—the past when musical comedies were flourishing and Gene was in his prime creative period.

In their coffee-table book *Gene Kelly: A Celebration,* Sheridan Morley and Ruth Leon describe how life changed in that house after I left and Gene married again. "Jeanne had never cared for the social gatherings around the volleyball court, or the endless games of charades . . . it was as if a fence had gone up all around the property."

In the late 1970s, Gene gave an interview to the *Beverly Hills Courier.* He talked, not about his work, but about how he'd been lucky in love. He was talking about his two marriages, to me and to Jeannie, and how his three children were now the joy of his life. He devoted himself to Bridget and Tim through the years of their childhood. Kerry was making her own life and career by then.

Gene married again a few years before his death. His new, very young wife was welcomed by his children as an intelligent companion for him. Sadly, she betrayed him and them. I believe she took a great deal away from him—first his pride and then his joie de vivre. And in the end, she had most of his fortune. It's hard for me to imagine that Gene, with his realistic attitude and his discerning insight, could have turned into a vain old man. But perhaps he did. He would not be the first man to believe that a clever young woman loved him for himself alone.

After his first stroke, Gene was in the hospital. Naturally, Kerry and Tim called and left messages of love and concern. They had the impression Gene didn't know about these calls. Bridget was told that her presence in the hospital was "embarrassing for him." But she could see the joy in his eyes when she arrived, so she just showed up every day. At the time of his second stroke, which left him paralyzed down one side, he was cut off from everything familiar: Lois, his secretary for fifty years, was no longer welcome in the house; the locks were changed; there was a new housekeeper. His doctor, his business manager, and his lawyer were fired and replaced. The telephone was never answered. Old friends who left messages over a period of months received no calls back. They assumed he was too ill and therefore incommunicado. Many asked me for news. I only knew what Kerry, who lived in Michigan, told me. She got bulletins from Bridget. And now Bridget was told not to drop in, to make an appointment. But she has her mother Jeannie's spirit—she could not be stopped, so she barged in anyway.

I'm sure he wanted no pity. I think he would have realized the irony of that active, athletic man, that dancer, being crippled. He never complained.

In 1995, when I was in Los Angeles for only three days, I had to insist that I too would not be stopped. I *was* coming to see Gene. When I succeeded, I thought it was because his new wife was somehow frightened of me.

We'd met two years earlier when I'd called on arrival and been invited, more formally than usual, to "tea at four o'clock on Friday." Gene was proud of his charming new wife, and tea was served to the three of us by a uniformed housekeeper from a beautiful Spode tea service—tiny sandwiches, fruit tarts, and cake. Clearly, I, the first wife, who now lived in London, was being shown that there was sophistication in Los Angeles too. But when he saw my empty cup, good old Gene said, with an Irish brogue, quoting his father and grandfather as he always had, "A little hot, hon?" He and I had a nostalgic little laugh as I offered my cup to the bride to be filled. She didn't take it. Instead, she reached across to a bell on the tea trolley and tinkled it. We waited in a slightly awkward silence as the housekeeper made her way from the kitchen and served me. And as the old wife, I couldn't tell the new one that even the queen of England pours the tea at her own table—unless of course, the Queen Mother is present.

At the end of our visit, Gene asked me that day in 1995, to come back the next day, and to bring our old friend Ted Reid. Gene's wife canceled our visit, leaving a message that it would be too much for Gene.

But the day before, during that last visit, the last time I saw him, he was lively and loving. All his old charm was there in a low-key way. We talked about the children and grandchildren, and the olden days. He brought up old jokes. He was wry and funny. When I was leaving, I kissed him good-bye on the cheek. We talked some more, and I said, "I'm going to kiss you good-bye again." Gene said, "Good—I don't get any of that." As I drove away I could hardly see through my tears. I didn't even know it was a final farewell; I just couldn't bear what that last sentence might mean. Of course, there was all the paraphernalia of round-the-clock nursing, but it seemed to me there was no love, no fun, no stimulation.

When I was fifty, I had finally gone to college. I became a speech therapist. I worked with stroke patients. Gene had no language or speech problems, but all such patients need affection, company, conversation. I think Gene was deprived of everything toward the end. I cannot forgive his widow, not because she got almost all of the children's inheritance, but because I don't think he had the happy ending he deserved.

On the Friday afternoon of the day Gene died, Kerry, Tim, and Bridget were notified in Michigan, New York, and Montana. Gene's widow told them there was so much to do that she couldn't have them stay at the house they had all grown up in. Besides, there was no reason to come—it was all over. They had to insist that they were flying in to Beverly Hills anyway. So it was conceded that they should come to the house at six o'clock Saturday evening.

And there, grief-stricken and in shock, they passed a most bizarre half hour. There were no friends, no food, no tears, and no embraces. They were given a tour of the flowers from famous people as if they were strangers.

Kerry later told me they all felt as if "she threw him away—as if he were garbage to be incinerated and thrown away. There aren't even any ashes." His children, who loved him, never got to say good-bye to their father. It would have saddened and, I imagine, enraged him, because he loved his children deeply. He left instructions that there would be no fancy funeral or memorials, but I know he couldn't have meant to leave them stranded with no place for their proper feelings of loss.

. . .

I never wanted to write a memoir about being married to a movie star. I don't write in bitterness. How could I, when I lived the merry dance of our lives? Rather, I'm writing to tell his children, and his four grandchildren, Rebecca, Ben, Anna, and Seamus, about the time of his life that I knew and how I got to be there—and what happened next.

I

I CAN'T CLAIM it was love at first sight—not even from my side.

Billy Rose's nightclub, the Diamond Horseshoe, was in the basement of the Edison Hotel in New York, on Forty-seventh Street between Broadway and Eighth Avenue. The lobby, with its coffee shop, newspaper kiosk, shoe shine stand, and a cashiers' cage, was a bit dingy. A busboy showed me the staircase down to the nightclub.

I had been sixteen years old for three weeks. I was all dressed up in a lavender four-gore flared skirt made by my mother, a polka-dot blouse, a hand-me-down fingertip-length gray-squirrel coat, a pillbox hat with violets, and my one pair of high heels.

I had no strategy, no plan for my life beyond this audition and college in the fall. And, of course, I had my dream. Someday I would be a great actress, Eleanora Duse, Katherine Cornell, Helen Hayes. Or would I be a movie star—Ginger Rogers, Margaret Sullavan, Greta Garbo? No, not Garbo—I was from New Jersey.

That day I felt completely sure of myself. After all, I'd had a postcard addressed to me personally from Billy Rose himself, inviting me to this call for dancers. Down the stairs I went into another world.

The Diamond Horseshoe was luxurious. Near the entrance across the whole width of the room was a Gay Nineties–type bar, brass railed and mirrored. The walls were red velvet. There were crystal chandeliers. At the far end was the proscenium stage, with a horseshoe-shaped runway coming out of it. The inside of the horseshoe was lowered between shows to become the dance floor. Tables for about four hundred people surrounded the runway.

There was no one there except a young man. I took him for another bellboy or busboy. He seemed to be repositioning some of the tables and chairs.

"Excuse me. Is this where the call for dancers is?"

"Yes—but I think you'll find it's tomorrow."

"Oh no," I said. "I have a personal card from Mr. Billy Rose."

"Even so," he grinned at me, "it's tomorrow." He's fresh, I thought, as I fished in my pocketbook and took out the card. "Today's the tenth, isn't it?"

"Come back tomorrow. Today's the ninth." He was still grinning.

"Thank you," I said, as if to an underling. "I will."

He called after me, "Are you a dancer?"

I looked back and deigned to say, "Yes."

"Are you a *good* dancer?"

At that I stopped. "Very," I said, turned on my heel and left.

The scene the next day was entirely different. Six hundred girls had had cards from Mr. Rose. We'd *all* been invited personally. The stage manager and four assistants corralled us into groups of twenty. There was a work light on the stage, an upright piano and a trestle table with five chairs, a thermos of coffee, pitchers of water, ashtrays, pads, and pencils. At noon they arrived. The stage manager introduced them: "the director, John Murray Anderson" (white-haired, tough, and sharp-looking); "our designer, Raoul Pene du Bois" (a tall, refined, and delicate man); "Billy Rose himself" (short, with slick black hair, his stubby body encased in a very expensive suit with matching silk polka-dot tie and pocket handkerchief—Rose radiated energy and power, which made him attractive); and then "Gene Kelly, our choreographer." He was wearing an open-necked white shirt, a dark long-sleeved sweater, dark trousers, and moccasins. He seemed to be balanced on the balls of his feet, ready to spring like a cat. The combination of sensitive Irish face and slim muscular body was spectacular enough, but he was also the only one at that table who looked at us as individuals. And he was my "busboy"—the one I had told that I was a very good dancer. I felt the blush begin in the pit of my stomach. When I happened to catch his eye, he grinned at me again.

When my group lined up onstage, I was still blushing. We made a full turn in place as instructed, and then waited to be chosen. It was very quick. Five or six from each group were sent to the dressing room to put on rehearsal clothes. Then another lineup. By one-thirty, we were down to forty girls and I was still there. We broke until two-fifteen—lunch if we wanted it. I wasn't hungry.

Now the real audition began.

We would each step forward and give our name and our credits. The rehearsal pianist sat ready to play the traditional "Bye Bye Blues" forty times. The first eight bars were for the "time-step," then for the rest of the chorus we each did an original routine.

And then we waited.

Gene told me months later how it went.

They were hiring twelve dancers plus an understudy. Seven girls were on all four lists. I was on only two of them—Gene's and Raoul Pene du Bois's. The stage manager nixed me: "She's got no tits—she looks twelve years old." Billy Rose said, "Don't mention ages—yeah, no tits, but she has got the long stems." His chorus line was advertised as "Billy Rose's Long Stemmed American Beauties," so the legs were important to him. Gene fought for me. He said I could dance, and he needed some good dancers. Raoul murmured something about "a small-town Botticelli"—and Billy decided in my favor. He was into Art.

It was thirty-five dollars a week and a contract to be signed. They said, "If anyone is worried about signing, get your father or somebody to sign it for you," which meant, "We don't want to know if you're under eighteen." I was the only sixteen-year-old, but there were two others who were seventeen. We all signed our own contracts.

When I got home and told my mother about it all, she noticed that I mentioned Mr. Kelly a zillion times. "He told us to call him Gene." "He didn't say anything special to me, but he smiled at me once. I think he forgave me for thinking he was a busboy." "He said

Gene when I first met him, 1940

he was going to work us hard." (He actually said "work your butts off," but I couldn't tell my mother that—she'd once washed my mouth out with soap for calling a boy in school a "guy.") "He was so nice and friendly." "He was handsome." "He seemed serious— he plans to do some really good numbers with us—like in a musical on Broadway." Etcetera, etcetera.

Throughout the four weeks of rehearsal, I was walking, floating, dancing on air. I changed my clothes at lunchtime, clean white shorts and cotton top twice a day. My mother washed and ironed them every night. If Gene wanted to try out a step, I was always right there. I guess it was obvious to everyone but Gene and me

that I was besotted. He was too busy working, and I was too innocent. I had no idea why I felt so happy.

Gene had come to New York from his hometown of Pittsburgh
a year and a half earlier. He immediately got a part on Broadway as
a specialty dancer in *Leave It to Me*, a Cole Porter musical starring
Mary Martin and William Gaxton. Then he played the hoofer in
William Saroyan's *The Time of Your Life*. He got wonderful reviews.
The theater world recognized that someone special had appeared.

Those jobs paid the rent for his room with bath and kitchenette
at the Woodward Hotel on Fifty-fifth Street and Broadway. But he
wasn't satisfied; his creative energy and drive were gigantic.

  His friends were other ambitious young actors, writers, and
directors. Their group was intellectual and left-wing. Among them
was our rehearsal pianist, Dick Dwenger. He was a playwright and
Gene's best friend, blond and slight with glasses. He had a quiet
authority and wit about him, and he played the piano.

Because Dick was a hungry young playwright, Gene got him the
gig playing for our rehearsals. They explained to me later that it was
also to keep an eye on Gene. It was Gene's first job as choreographer. Du Bois and Anderson were the big time, very experienced
and brilliant. Gene knew what they could do and wanted to learn
from them. But he also wanted to make his contribution. He was
already aware of what that could be. He wanted to bring guts into
dancing, to relate it to everyday life and bring it to the man and
woman on the street, to people who didn't go to the ballet or the
opera. Dick was to keep him from being dazzled, to remind him, if
necessary, of his goals.

For this show, Gene planned a football number, and a schoolyard scene with identifiable characters: a boy, a girl, a bookworm,
and a bully. (Naturally, we also had the almost obligatory cancan
and South American numbers.) Well, he didn't win the "schoolyard
battle." Billy Rose said, "They don't come to the Diamond Horseshoe to see a fucking ballet."

But the football number was in, and I was chosen by Mr. du Bois
to model his design for it. Each costume was made up for one
dancer first, to try it out for freedom of movement. There was a

gold cloth helmet, a very broad-shouldered, very short—just to cover the nipples—gold leather cape over a flesh-colored net bra, bare midriff, gold latex pants to just below the knee, and gold lace-up boots.

In my general euphoria, I felt pretty good in it. But John Murray Anderson turned it ugly. It wasn't my first exposure to his vicious humor, nor was it to be my last. He'd nicknamed me "Teacher's Pet." I didn't mind that; in fact, I rather liked it. But for some reason, I was his chosen scapegoat. (I've since observed that a great many directors seem to need one.) I tossed my head a bit when I danced, and in the end of the second week of rehearsal, he stopped a number and called me out of the line: "Teacher's Pet, come here. Your head was bobbing like a cork in the ocean again. Kneel down in front of me and apologize." I was terrified and rebellious. But mainly I didn't want to cry. I took a deep breath, stepped forward, and went down on one knee. With a sweeping gesture like a medieval courtier I said, "I'm sorry, Sire." Behind me a couple of the dancers clapped, Gene joined them, and Dick played some chords on the piano. It was over, and I'd won that round.

Now in my golden football costume, Mr. Anderson went for the jugular—actually for my breasts, my tiny young breasts. Was the cape too short, too long, too wide, too narrow? Would I bend over, turn around, raise my arms? Of course, the wardrobe woman had supplied me with "falsies" in my bra, and by spending ten or fifteen minutes fiddling around with the cape, he made me acutely self-conscious and miserable. One to him.

But they were the only two disagreeable moments in that wonderful rehearsal period. I brought my lunch from home and ate it at the bar, usually with a book to read. Dick came back early one day and sat with me. He asked me questions: What was I reading? How old was I really? Did I live at home? What was my philosophy of life? Did I have brothers and sisters?

He was easy to talk to. I answered everything, including the question about my philosophy. There I could only say I didn't think I was old enough to have one except what I'd been told: "Do unto others, etc.," "Brighten the corner where you are," and "If you really

Age fifteen, at the beach in New Jersey,
and ready to conquer New York

Gene and his best friend, Dick Dwenger,
a young, unproduced playwright

want something and are willing to work for it, you will succeed."
But I didn't think all that was much more than Sunday school for
kids. I told him about college, that I'd be going to Sarah Lawrence
next autumn. For the first time that sounded strange to me.

The next day Dick came back early again. I don't know why he
seemed to enjoy talking to me. Perhaps since playing rehearsal
piano didn't exactly tax his brain, he'd had time to notice my
lovesick state before I was aware of it. He was certainly gentle with
me. Maybe he'd taken it on himself to check me out.

Anyway, in a very few days I was being asked to lunch with Gene
and him—not really asked to lunch, more like being allowed to tag
along like a kid sister. And in that role I was comfortable—I *was* a
kid sister. These two "big brothers" were wildly exciting to me.
Gene was twenty-eight, Dick, twenty-nine—they seemed to know

everything. They were interested in politics, and painting and literature. They teased me about how little I'd seen or done, but they were never mean. They announced that they were "taking me in hand." After the show opened they promised they'd give me New York, the Metropolitan, the Museum of Modern Art, Merce Cunningham, Harlem, the Village, Little Italy, the docks, the theater—the whole kit and caboodle.

The last week of rehearsal we worked day and night. I was invited to tag along to supper at their hangout, Louis Bergen's Theater Bar and Restaurant, on West Forty-seventh Street. I met their friends, and they met my father, who came to drive me home at midnight. I think he was reassured because there were two of them and they so obviously treated me like a kid sister. He couldn't guess what was going on in my head and heart.

How could he? I was unaware myself. The wonderful, comical thing about first love is the unconsciousness of it. I was "gone," but I didn't know it. My love flowed through me, but it just felt like natural happiness—like dancing to a dancer, like the sun and rain must feel to a plant.

On opening night, during the cancan finale, I spotted Gene and Dick and a beautiful brunette at the bar watching the show. I'd never seen her before. Somehow I knew she wasn't with Dick. The tears welled up, one or two overflowed. I kept high-kicking and smiling and hoped no one would notice. I couldn't wait to get off-stage. I stayed in the dressing room between shows pretending to read a book. What I was thinking was "silly goose—making up a love story like in the movies. They are just being nice to you. Besides, he's too old and I'm going to college in the fall—I'll meet a million boys from Harvard and Princeton." And then the tears again. "How will I ever see him again when I go to college? I'll never meet anyone in my whole life so wonderful and brilliant." And then the tears stopped; my burgeoning adolescent self thought, "Oh, so this is that famous thing—a broken heart. It's funny how it doesn't seem to hurt much—I don't care—I love him, he doesn't have to love me—I don't care—maybe he will love me someday." And I went upstairs to the coffee shop and had a chocolate soda with vanilla ice cream—and I was ready for the second show.

But as they'd promised, Dick and Gene took me everywhere. I met them in Louis Bergen's every night between shows. There was a big round table at the back. They'd order me a small steak, with french fries, and a glass of milk to be on the table at ten past ten since I had to dance again at midnight. Sometimes, it was just the three of us, but more often it was six or seven people: two lovely and lively actresses, Frances Cheney and Jane White; a very politically minded actor, Lloyd Gough, a tough-sounding, tenderhearted Irishman. He would question me rather sharply, not about my family or my ambitions, but about what I knew and thought. "What about Roosevelt? Okay, and the Spanish Civil War? No? What *did* they teach you in history class at Cliffside High, then?" He started bringing me pamphlets to read, and then he'd check on my understanding. Gene might say, "Take it easy, she's a kid," but I always protested that I wanted to learn it all.

I was coming into New York at noon three times a week now. I'd go to the tap class of Ernest Carlos, a great black dance teacher. His studio was midtown on Broadway over a movie theater. It was one dollar a lesson, and there would always be fifty or sixty dancers there angling to get to the front to be near him and pick up his steps and style. Dick and Gene collected me there.

And my promised education began in earnest. The Museum of Modern Art—Mondrian and Brancusi; the Metropolitan—Greek sculpture and Rembrandt (and Botticelli, so they could tease me). And we'd go to Central Park and the Cloisters, the Battery, the Fulton Fish Market and the docks, Little Italy, Chinatown, the Village—they *were* giving me New York. And much, much more. At about six o'clock we'd go back to Gene's room in the Woodward Hotel. He'd make a pot of tea and some toast in the kitchenette. They had discovered another enormous gap in my knowledge— classical music. I knew all the popular songs back to the twenties, and a bit of opera because my mother liked it, but Mozart and Beethoven were just names to me, and Aaron Copland or Stravinsky not even that. And so they bombarded me with music. I'm afraid I quite often fell asleep in my chair. They forgave me, since I had two shows to do. They never gave up; I was their project. Oh, lucky girl that I was!

They joked that I wouldn't need college.

The Diamond Horseshoe was jam-packed every night for both shows. We had headliners from vaudeville. There was Julian Eltinge, the female impersonator, whose creation was no caricature but an elegant, graceful woman who sang beautifully. There was Pat Rooney, an old Irish charmer who told jokes and sang and danced. And Gilda Grey, an "exotic dancer" who did a kind of arty striptease with two big ostrich-feather fans to maintain her dignity.

But the biggest attraction was the chorus doing Gene's numbers. Walter Winchell wrote that we were the "youngest, prettiest chorus line in New York—and some swell numbers they do. Go see them."

Gene was going away for a month. It hadn't occurred to me that this wonderful time of my life could be brought to a halt in mid-flight. When he told me that he was taking his father to Mexico to show him that beautiful country and drink a few Mexican beers with him along the way, my heart leapt with joy. I guess I'd been afraid of the beautiful brunette. Now I could go on dreaming.

Pop Kelly, as Gene described him, and as I later got to know him, was an alert and quiet man, old before his time, defeated by the 1929 Depression. He lost his job and never worked again. But he was loving and gentle with wit in his blue eyes and the Irish gift of the gab. There were stories of hardship and beauty about cousins and uncles and priests and wild boys back in the old country. He sat in his kitchen, clean-shaven and well dressed, with a constantly renewed pot of tea, for most of the rest of his life. He was like an old wood-burning stove, radiating warmth at the heart of the family.

There were five Kelly kids. Gene was in the middle. He was born in 1912, so in 1930 he was in his freshman year of college. Suddenly there was no money to continue.

Mom Kelly was "black Irish," a tiny, fierce dynamo. She was determined that her two daughters would be schoolteachers and her three sons professional men, doctors or lawyers. Everything could be endured for this goal. Her husband might be sitting in the

Mom and Pop Kelly, 1954

kitchen, she might be exhausted from washing and ironing and patching up clothes. It was all worth it. I think Gene's ambition and a lot more of his character came from her along with his dark eyes and hair. But his charm definitely came from Pop.

Gene and his mother had to take charge of the family. What could they do? Well, Gene could dance. All the Kelly kids had taken dancing lessons. Gene and his younger brother Fred were really good dancers. So they'd start a dancing school. Mom Kelly would run it, make the timetable and keep the books. Gene would be the main teacher. Fred and their sister Louise, though still in high school, would help out.

Somehow they did it. Gene could and did finish college. There was food on the table. The Pittsburgh school was so successful that in a few years they started another in Johnstown on Saturdays.

It was seven years before Gene felt free to leave them and go to New York. By then the schools were making ten thousand dollars a year. In 1937, that was a lot of money. The family was secure.

Gene (center) in The Five Kellys, the family amateur act

It was a good Catholic family. But Gene was no longer a good Catholic—or so he believed. He'd been to Mexico before and been appalled by the extremes of wealth and poverty. He thought if he took his sweet Pop there, and showed him the gold inside the churches and the beautiful dignified people living in clay shacks, Pop would understand his loss of faith. It didn't work. Pop only saw the good the Church does. But they had a great trip and enjoyed the beers.

My sixteenth year was truly thrilling—at the time and looking back. The romantic dreaming part of me was filled by Gene. I had gazed through the windows of my high school across the Hudson River yearning for New York, and here I was, dancing two shows a night and earning money in the big city. And another element was added. Lloyd Gough, the most politically committed of Gene's circle of friends, asked me to join the marxist study group that met in his apartment on Wednesday and Friday from five o'clock to seven.

Of course I said yes. I was flattered to be invited by one of Gene's friends, to be treated as a grown-up worthy of taking part in something serious. And it *was* very serious. Our textbook was *The History of the Communist Party in the Soviet Union*. It was tough going—I have never read a more boringly written book. But that didn't matter. I was completely enthralled by the ideas. And I was eager to learn. I suppose this was my "college" too. There were six of us in the class, with two alternating teachers, "Paul" and "Eddie." That was all I ever knew about them—their first names. I thought they were mysterious and wonderful. They seemed to care more about the welfare of the world than about themselves. I wanted to be like them. The communist slogan, "From each according to his ability; to each according to his need," sounded like a fine prescription for a political program. And the outside reading list was great—John Dos Passos, Upton Sinclair, Steinbeck, Gorky.

But I was not yet like my image of them. I was ambitious. I was thinking about myself a lot. I'd learned that it was much better to be in the chorus of a musical than a nightclub. I was determined to make the leap.

The first show I sneaked off to audition for was *Louisiana Purchase*. The system was that if they wanted sixteen girls in the chorus they started rehearsing with thirty-two. I got that far. At the end of the day for the first three days, they would let five or six girls go. We were separated to left and right stage. At the end of the third day, when I was sent to the left, I didn't wait to be told to leave. I burst into tears and ran down to the dressing room. The choreographer was Robert Alton, the best, most famous on Broadway. As I ran upstairs to escape out of the theater, I met him coming down. "Don't give up," he said. "Take some ballet classes and come to my next call." I thanked him, he smiled and said, "You don't really look much like a sexy Creole maiden, but not every show needs that." So I stopped at the Edison Hotel coffee shop, had my emotional-cure-all chocolate soda with vanilla ice cream, felt better, and went down to the Diamond Horseshoe to dance my head off.

Panama Hattie, produced by Buddy De Sylva, with music by Cole Porter, and starring Ethel Merman was the next big show. In the very first lineup Robert Alton recognized me and said, "If I don't choose you, will you burst into tears?" This gave me hope, and I was right—I got the job. I gave in my notice to leave the Diamond Horseshoe and settled into the two hard weeks of rehearsing all day and doing two shows at night. I didn't mind a bit. Gene and Dick were proud of me. My mother was thrilled. But Billy Rose sent Buddy De Sylva a telegram saying that I couldn't leave the Diamond Horseshoe. I assured Mr. De Sylva that I was leaving. In fact, I'd already quit, I just had to work off my two weeks. Mr. De Sylva said, "Okay—Bob Alton wants you—you're in."

After the first show on my last Saturday night in a nightclub, I went to the cashier to collect my pay. He was a nice old man. "Sorry not to see you again. I'm moving on; I'm in a Broadway musical." I was expecting congratulations and best wishes. What I got was, "Sorry, Betsy, I have no envelope for you tonight. Mr. Rose says you're not leaving." "Is he here?" I asked. "No, he called me from home to give me the instructions about you." "Do you have his telephone number?" There was a long pause. I thought perhaps I shouldn't have asked—my nice old man could get in trouble. Then he smiled and wrote down the number. "Good luck," he said. I went straight to the phone booth in the lobby. An English voice like a butler in the movies answered, "Mr. Rose's residence." I gave my name and asked to speak to him. He was already shouting when he picked up the phone. "Why are you bothering me? You can't leave. You have a run-of-the-show contract. The costumes and boots were specially made for you. Be a good girl—get back to work."

My newly acquired marxist theories flooded my brain. Did he think he owned us? Were we slave labor? I was suddenly part of the exploited class and he was the big bad boss. "Mr. Rose, there's no such thing as a run-of-the-show contract for chorus girls. Besides, you know I'm not old enough to sign anything legally, and the costumes and boots fit the understudy. I'm in *Panama Hattie*." He shouted louder, "You won't be in *Panama Hattie*—I'll fix it. You'll never work on Broadway. I can stop you." My red-haired temper flared up, and I lost my head. "Mr. Rose, keep your thirty-five dollars. You act as if you need it," and I hung up on him.

Frightened and exhilarated, I ran to Louis Bergen's. Everybody was there. Dick immediately noticed my state, "What happened to you?" So I told them the whole conversation. They fell about laughing; it must have gone on for ten minutes. "Calling Billy at home . . ." "Probably in the middle of a fancy dinner party!" "Keep your thirty-five dollars!" And Gene said, "You're some brave kid." I was congratulated and kissed.

The chorus of *Panama Hattie* turned out to be prestigious: June Allyson, Jane Ball, Doris and Constance Dowling, Vera Ellen, and Miriam Franklin, who became a choreographer. After a week of rehearsal June and Jane asked me if I wanted to share a room with them in the Henry Hudson Hotel, home of the American Women's Club. It was the brainchild of Anne Morgan, sister of the millionaire financier J. P. Morgan. She wanted to establish a good home for working girls who couldn't afford the more expensive Barbizon Hotel for Women. The Henry Hudson was on West Fifty-seventh Street, near Eighth Avenue, and eminently respectable. No men were allowed in the rooms—not even in the elevators. It would cost twenty-seven dollars a week for three—nine dollars each. We were making forty-five. I asked them to come home with me on Saturday—I didn't think my mother and father could resist them. Jane was nineteen or twenty, June was twenty-two. They were both tiny and blond. June was exuberant and adorable with her gravelly voice, just as she was in the movies. Jane was beautiful, soft-spoken and delicate. (She had been the Apple Queen of New York State.) Any objections my father might have had to my living in the city melted before their charm, and they reassured my mother that they'd look after me, emphasizing how hard we'd work, and how we'd go to dance class every day.

And so it was agreed. It was a momentous change in my life. Everything was possible. And besides, it was two blocks up and three blocks over from Gene's hotel. I was in heaven.

When we were ready to move in they offered us a better room for the same price. It was for four, and they had a pretty young secretary, Clare Moynihan, to join us. We met her, and we all liked each other. It was done.

With June Allyson and Clare Moynihan in our room at the Henry Hudson Hotel,
when no men were allowed upstairs, 1941

Now my time was my own. I was in the theater from a quarter to
eight till eleven p.m.—I loved every minute of it. In my memory,
the best moment was standing onstage ready for the opening number, waiting for the curtain to go up. When the orchestra launched
into the overture, the excitement, the anticipation, the sheer physical joy is almost impossible to explain. We were very young, very
healthy, we had beautiful costumes and excellent routines, and
Cole Porter's music was great. There were sixteen of us, so you
couldn't even have stage fright. And we all loved to dance.

We always knew when there was a movie star in the audience—
Charles Boyer or Tyrone Power or Clark Gable. June, who was the
smallest of us and therefore at the end of the line dancing off the
stage, would somehow contrive to trip and fall—and get noticed.
She'd leap up in charming confusion and get a hand. Good for you,
I thought.

My daytime education and gallivanting with Gene and Dick continued for a while, and I went back to the marxist class on Fridays. But now that I got to Louis Bergen's at eleven-fifteen or so, and lived in the city, the night became the important part—and it was every night. Sometimes we stayed right there until two or three in the morning. There were arguments, discussions, jokes, gossip. I didn't have much to say; I had so much to learn. They seemed to manage to see everything—plays, movies, musicals, poetry readings, dance recitals, jazz sessions, exhibitions—all that goes on in New York.

One night a college friend of Dick's joined us. He challenged Lloyd about the show trials in Moscow in 1937–38. Lloyd was adamant. He'd gone to bed for six weeks, he said, and read all the way through the transcripts in translation. They were legitimate— he would swear on it. Gene said to me, "It's true—he did disappear for six weeks." Dick's friend said, "And Orwell and Koestler?" "Renegades," said Lloyd. And I, in my ignorance, thought I now understood why they were forbidden to us by our marxist teachers. I made no connection to the fact that the other proscribers of books were Hitler and the Catholic Church.

Some nights the three of us went uptown to the Apollo Theater or the Cotton Club in Harlem. We saw Cab Calloway, Buck and Bubbles, and the Nicholas Brothers. Gene and Dick drank beer, I drank ginger ale. But I was high on love; I think they were high on energy and ambition.

One night we went downtown to the Vanguard, a small club in Greenwich Village, to see The Revuers, Betty Comden, Adolph Green, Judy Holliday, and Alvin Hammer. They combined true originality, sweet and high-spirited wit, and rare musicality. Adolph and Alvin were perfect partners to the ravishing beauty of Betty, dark-haired and elegant, and Judy, blond and voluptuous. They must have worked hard to create their act and their songs, but they performed with such joy that it looked easy and spontaneous. They took New York by storm. Everyone fought to get into the crowded club. We were okay because Gene already knew them; they'd been in a revue together in 1939 in the summer theater at Westport, Connecticut. It was the beginning of the long road leading to *Singin' in the Rain* and to the lifelong friendship of Betty and Adolph.

When Gene would say he was taking me dancing, Dick would drop out. We danced at the Copacabana, at El Morocco, at the Rainbow Room, but our best place was the Polish Folk Hall. We danced the polkas and mazurkas until we were breathless. I don't know how Gene found it. Everyone else there was Polish. We ate pickles and sausages and I drank tea from a glass for the first time.

A ritual developed at the end of each evening. They would escort me to my door and I'd say, "Thank you. Now I'll walk you to your hotel, and you can walk me back. I promise I'll go in and go to bed then." And we usually did just that. But when I was alone with Gene I'd leave out the promise and manage to prolong it to another round trip.

And toward the end of the summer, when it was almost dawn and we'd done the back and forth of the five blocks about six times, Gene said, in front of his hotel, "Okay, I'll lend you a toothbrush," and I said, "And pajamas?" And so I spent my first night with him, sleeping in his arms, in his pajamas.

I don't know what he thought. I don't know when he fell in love with me. I only know what I saw and felt, and how he behaved.

I was sixteen and a half. I was in love. I was eager for life. I never questioned it at all. It seemed inevitable to me. Dick called me and my innocence the "irresistible force."

But Gene was an honorable young man. What remained of his Catholicism manifested itself in his attitude to women. There were "good girls" and "bad girls"—and I was an exaggeratedly good girl. He never made me feel rejected, rather that he was taking care of me. He let me spend the night sometimes, but he didn't make love to me. He'd kiss me gently and explain that I was too young for more than that. I was happy. I felt secure. I just waited with no impatience—or, at least, not much. . . .

Gene was offered the leading role in *Pal Joey*, the new Rodgers and Hart musical based on the stories of John O'Hara and directed by George Abbott. It was a great part for him. He was electric as Joey, the small-time nightclub hoofer looking for the main chance.

Central Park, 1941

There was the rich older woman, the wonderful Vivienne Segal, who sang "Bewitched, Bothered and Bewildered," and a sweet ingenue, Leila Ernst, to whom Gene sang "If They Asked Me I Could Write a Book." June Havoc stopped the show with "I'm a Red Hot Momma." There were a couple of boys in the chorus who we would see a lot of later on—Van Johnson, who had a few specialty spots, and Stanley Donen.

Buddy De Sylva gave me the night off to go to the opening, and I went with Dick. Raoul Pene du Bois had borrowed a beautiful evening dress for me, lavender chiffon with iridescent paillettes on the bodice, narrow straps, and a crushed-velvet cloak. I was transported back to *Of Thee I Sing*, when I was seven, the first time I'd been to a theater, and forward into some kind of paradise. The last lines of Gene's song, "And the world discovers as my book ends / How to make two lovers of friends," were written for me—I was sure of it. Perhaps Lorenz Hart didn't know that, but I did. That was the paradise that was coming.

Pal Joey was a hit. Gene was a smash. By now, I was recognized by his friends as more than a "kid sister," but I think they were puzzled about what I really was. (I didn't know then and never found out what happened to the beautiful brunette.) We did our shows, matinees and evenings. We met in Louis Bergen's. We played baseball in Central Park as part of the "Broadway League," even on opposing teams when *Panama Hattie* lost to *Pal Joey*. We talked and laughed and danced through the streets, in nightclubs, in the Polish Folk Hall. Gene and Dick came home with me to Cliffside quite often on Sundays.

2

I'D POSTPONED college that autumn. I couldn't leave New York and Gene. Everything was too exciting. I convinced my parents that I could wait until September 1941; I'd save more money, and I'd still be only seventeen.

Soon after Christmas, we were joined in our hangout by William Saroyan. Gene's first acting role on Broadway had been in *The Time of Your Life,* Saroyan's Pulitzer Prize–winning play. He was a big, handsome, jovial man about thirty-three with a loud voice and a sharp and sensitive eye. He seemed to bring the Pacific Ocean with him when he entered a room. After about an hour of the usual talk and argument and jokes, he turned to me and said, "Are you an actress?" I wasn't prepared for his question. There was one of those moments of silence, into which I said, "Yes." Everyone looked at me. Someone said, "Betsy, what are you saying?" "I am," I insisted. "I know I'm a dancer, but I speak a line in a Broadway show, so I'm an actress now too." Betty Hutton, one of the stars of *Panama Hattie,* had gone to Hollywood. June Allyson, her understudy, had moved up out of the chorus into her part, and I had inherited June's line in the opening number, the immortal words "Hello, sailor." They all laughed, but Saroyan said, "I want you to be the ingenue in my new play. Where do you live? I'll send it to you tomorrow." When he'd left, Gene and Dick told me gently not to take it too seriously: "He says that kind of thing to every taxi driver."

The next morning I was called from the front desk of the Henry Hudson Hotel. There was a package for me. I dashed down to get it.

It was the manuscript of *The Beautiful People.* There was a note from Saroyan to call him at the Great Northern Hotel after I'd read it.

The Great Northern Hotel was a place I knew. All the dancers and showgirls in New York—as well as strippers and ladies of the night—used its twenty-four-hour beauty parlor. When I wanted to have my hair up in a fancy way to go to an opening at the Copacabana, I was taken there by a very jolly dancer, Amarillo. (She had taken the name of her hometown so "no dude'll get any high-handed ideas—he'll know right off when we meet that my pappy has a gun.") It was unlike any other hairdresser, more a combination of Roman bath and chorus dressing room. There were women, mostly great-looking, wandering around in various degrees of undress, smoking, eating takeout, being attended to in every way; pedicures, manicures, hairdos, hair and eyelash dying, massages, leg and underarm waxing, pubic-hair waxing, pubic-hair dying. The last two took place in open cubicles around the big room as a slight concession to modesty. The atmosphere was exciting—a bit like a harem, I supposed.

And that was where William Saroyan stayed in New York.

I read the play and called him. "Can you do it?" he asked. I answered with the sublime confidence of my just seventeen years: "Yes." "Do you want to?" "Oh yes," I replied. "Okay, I'll see you tonight after the show. I'll bring my producer to meet you."

So that night, Mr. Pat Duggan, looking like a successful businessman, with his suit, tie, snazzy polo coat, and fedora, came to Louis Bergen's. He came, he saw, but he wasn't completely conquered. To Saroyan and Gene (who was being very protective—almost as if he were my agent), he said I was perfectly typecast for the sixteen-year-old St. Agnes of the Mice, but I had a tiny voice. He couldn't agree until he saw—and heard—me onstage in a theater. Gene took the play home and read it that night. The next morning we started working on two scenes.

The four of us met at Louis Bergen's and walked to the Lyceum Theatre on Forty-fifth Street. Gene and I went onstage, as he was reading the scenes with me. Bill Saroyan and Pat Duggan went up to the back row of the balcony. Gene clasped my hand, gave me a serious little smile, and we started. We'd exchanged six or seven lines when Saroyan stood up and started down the aisle, calling out, "Okay, that's enough." Gene leapt to my defense: "Give her a chance, Bill." Saroyan just laughed. "I said okay—I heard every word—she's okay."

Saroyan directed the play himself. There were five wonderful experienced character actors. The two young leads were Eugene Loring and me. We were both dancers—he was a ballet star, I was a chorus girl. We had never acted before. But Saroyan loved us all. He sat up on the back of a seat in the fifth row with his feet on the seat and his hat on the back of his head. We would read through an act and at the end he'd clap and take us all to lunch and tell us stories.

The old actors helped the two novices when we got on our feet—they really blocked out the moves. But after about ten days, I began to feel panicky. I'd been saying to Dick and Gene that it seemed to be going well; now I admitted to them that I was scared. Gene offered to work quietly with me, and with Eugene Loring if he wanted to. He did want to, and Gene saved our bacon.

I began to see the beginning of my professional life, the first step toward making my dream become reality. I had a role in a Broadway play. It was by William Saroyan. It was at the Lyceum Theatre, with its long history. As the rehearsal started each morning, I had no thought of anything else, only the work to be done. There is such joy in the immediacy and the strangely ordinary concentration of rehearsal. Everyone writes and talks about the "smell of the greasepaint," and the excitement of opening night—or, for the movies, the luxury of it all, the first-class travel, the lights, the attention, the premieres. But that's not it at all. There are words on a page that cry out to be explored. Their truth must be discovered and a way found to communicate it, to express it delicately or robustly, humorously or grimly—the choices are infinite. And this very difficulty of choice is the fun of it. Because it's like an ascent on Mount Everest or a polar expedition. The director, the designer, and all the actors are in this search together. They depend on each other, and success or failure comes from their joint effort.

Getting ready for my first play on Broadway, William
Saroyan's *The Beautiful People,* and with Curtis Cooksey
(below), who played my father

With Gene and William Saroyan, 1941

So I think a chorus line is a surprisingly good starting point for an actor. As a dancer, you learn the routines. You practice and practice and get better every day. But it's not about individual vanity, it's about striving to be as good as possible in the group, in the line, in the show.

I can't say that I carried this absence of personal ambition over perfectly. At the end of the second act during the first preview of *The Beautiful People,* I had a quiet moment alone downstage playing on the floor with the flowers the mice had supposedly left for me. Way upstage on a winding path to our arty, unconventional house, an insurance man appears wearing a boring hat and business suit and carrying a briefcase. He was a good and skillful actor, and he got a laugh as he trudged toward me. I was startled and upset and struggled to keep my concentration. At the interval in my dressing room, I burst into tears and said to Bill Saroyan, "He ruined my moment." Bill was gentle with me but firm. "He didn't ruin anything, and it wasn't your moment, sweetie. He is carrying the play forward for the last act. I want him to cut across the whimsical poetry of Agnes and the mice, to counterpoint it. And if the audience laughs, it's all the more touching."

I was too inexperienced to realize this by myself. As we played on night after night, I gradually learned that it was right as long as I kept my concentration.

Saroyan had a revolutionary idea. We didn't go out of town to try out the show. Instead they put ads in all the papers that the first week was free for anyone who had never been to the live theater. Instead of a cool sophisticated opening-night audience, we had the most enthusiastic full houses ever. We gained confidence with each performance. On opening night the two proudest people were my father—and Billy Rose. Billy had sent me long-stemmed American Beauty roses. He claimed to have discovered me—the thirty-five-dollar episode forgotten. And my father seemed to have forgotten Katherine Gibbs and learning shorthand and typing—the future he had seen for me. Now I was making one hundred dollars a week, a fortune in his eyes. My mother took it all in her stride; she had always believed this would happen. She just beamed at me with tenderness and love.

So here we were—Gene and I—both in Broadway shows. He was brilliant, singing, dancing, acting, carrying the whole thing. I was playing my part in a lovely delicate play, working hard and learning, but fortunately for me, the demands of the role were not enormous. I was perfectly typecast. The two leading critics, George Jean Nathan and Richard Watts, both of whom had given the play and me good reviews, had a public debate in their respective newspapers. The question was, "Could Miss Helen Hayes, our leading actress, play St. Agnes of the Mice as well as this newcomer who *is* the young girl?"

Like anyone my age, I had no conception of time, of the shape of a life. I had no scrapbooks; I never cut out and saved anything. It didn't occur to me that someday I might want to look back and read about it all, or that I might have children or grandchildren who would be interested.

When I was last in New York, I looked myself up in the Lincoln

Center Library for the Performing Arts. One journalist wrote that I "looked like she'd just come from playing high-school basketball in her bobby socks and saddle shoes, but she has red hair and the white skin of beautiful women." He finished his article with the sentence, "This is one 'mouse' Kelly better do right by." ("Mouse" was what Pal Joey called women.)

Richard Watts said in his review of *The Beautiful People:* "The gentle sweetly sincere and completely moving gravity and innocence of Miss Blair's utterly right performance is so infinitely more touching and beautiful than any studied portrayal could be, that her contribution to the work is gracefully enchanting."

Now I ask you: If you read all that about yourself, might you not think that you were special, that you were destined for great things?

There were articles and photographs in the newspapers and magazines—all the hoopla. It must have gone to my head. No, it *did* go to my head.

Gene had offers from Hollywood, and I was asked to make screen tests. I have a letter just given to me after fifty years by Clare, our roommate. When I asked her why she had it, she said, "You never saved anything, so I did when I could." It was from the head of talent at Twentieth Century–Fox, hand-delivered to me. "Stage Door, Lyceum Theatre and bring receipt to Mr. Pincus." Mr. Pincus, plump, bespectacled, and benign, had written, "My dear Miss Blair . . . Your agent tells me that you do not wish to make your test tomorrow until you are assured that you will be tested in the scene from *Claudia.*" (I was already doing a scene from *Our Town,* but I knew they had bought *Claudia,* and I was crazy enough to imagine I might get the part in the film—it was crazy because Dorothy McGuire was so perfect on the stage and screen.) "[Y]ou have my assurance that as soon as we find an actor to assist you in the *Claudia* scene and are properly rehearsed, we will make this test also. I also agree to hold up shipment of any of your tests until then. As we have gone to great expense in renting the studio, hiring cameramen, electricians, make-up man, etc., I shall expect you at our studio tomorrow at the appointed time."

I not only had the nerve to impose these conditions, but in the end I foolishly decided not to accept a seven-year contract with Fox. I didn't want to be a "starlet." I was now sure I was destined for great things.

As for the other half of my life, by May or June Gene and I were in love, and we were lovers. The horizon glowed with a golden light.

And then, David Selznick appeared. Since *Gone with the Wind*, he was the most famous producer in Hollywood. He had his own studio. Gene was captivated by his intelligence and enthusiasm, and agreed to make three films for him. They spent long evenings talking about Gene's passionate ambition for the dance in movies—I think David was captivated by him too. But first, Gene had a new show to choreograph, *Best Foot Forward*, with George Abbott directing.

And one moonlit night sitting on the edge of the fountain in front of the Plaza Hotel, Gene asked me to marry him. He said he wanted me to be the mother of his children, and besides, he couldn't leave me alone at the mercy of New York when he went to Hollywood. I said yes yes yes yes yes!

The plan was that in September, when *The Beautiful People* had closed, I would come to Philadelphia, where *Best Foot Forward* was trying out, and we'd be married quietly by a justice of the peace. But it was not to be. I was home in Cliffside one Sunday when Gene telephoned to say it was impossible. I was too young, I had to have my father's permission. So I called my father to the phone. It seems I said, "Daddy, this is a very important moment in your life," as I handed the phone to him. My parents had gotten to know Gene over the past year. I think my father respected him, and I know my mother was crazy about him. And they were happy that I was so happy. Now it was to be a proper wedding—not just proper but in a Catholic church. I was amazed by this and questioned it, but Gene, only half joking, said, "Of course it has to be in church—do you want to kill my mother?" Despite my marxist leanings, I dutifully went to the priest and promised to take instruction to become a Catholic and to bring up our children as Catholics. (My fingers were crossed behind my back, because I was lying.) And so it was that I was allowed to marry Gene at a side altar with both our families present. My mother and I had bought a lovely pale blue silk suit for me, and a little flowered hat with a veil. My father gave us a wonderful wedding breakfast. I was now the ecstatic young Mrs. Gene Kelly, rarin' to go into my new life.

3

IN EUGENE O'NEILL'S *Long Day's Journey into Night,* Mary Tyrone says, "The past is the present, isn't it? It's the future too."

I know the facts of my childhood, and I remember my feelings. Everything seems natural then, inevitable even; everything just happens. I imagine it's the same for all children. You dream, you rebel, you love and hate, you're happy and sad. You think you must have been left by the gypsies; this can't be where you were destined to be. And then you have summer days on your bicycle, or winter days sledding in the snow, days when everything is perfect. And so you grow up.

In my very first memory, I'm sitting on a pale gray velvety carpet. I think I was three years old. I've had a big dish of vanilla ice cream and been given a new coloring book and crayons. Next to me are more presents to take home, for my two brothers.

My mother has taken me to the Waldorf-Astoria on Park Avenue to see my great-aunt Gladys. The two women are drinking tea and talking. It's mainly about "Lois and Scottie." I perk up and listen when I hear "Scottie," but when it becomes clear it's not a puppy, I go back to my crayons.

Standing open, on the other side of me, is a steamer trunk. When we arrived at the hotel I'd been shown its marvels—the heavy brass clasp with a key, the shoe compartment under the wooden hangers, the big and small drawers on the other side. It's twice as tall as I am and covered with brightly colored stickers with pictures of boats and buildings.

I remember feeling happy and sleepy. I lean against the trunk, and there by my shoulder, half falling out of an open drawer, is the loveliest thing I've ever seen. It's soft and shiny and silky, beige or blush pink or ecru—in all the years since I've never been able to find the exact color of my memory—I touch my cheek to it and fall sleep.

Great-aunt Gladys was about fifty years ahead of her time. She married at eighteen, and then her young husband died of pneumonia. She married again at twenty-one. She and Mr. Moran had a baby, Lois, and then, four years later, he was killed in World War I. She became a very rich young widow.

But she didn't stay in Philadelphia—the safe society she had grown up in was not for her. In the lawyer's office, when the will and the trusts were explained to her, she listened politely and said, "Good. I want to take five thousand dollars now. I've always been interested when the men talked about money—I want to play the stock market. And Lois and I are going to live in Paris."

The family legend has it that she was so clever that she never had to touch the other money. She didn't lose in the Crash of '29. She adopted another little girl, and brought her up.

When I was seven, I was invited by myself to a matinee in a Broadway theater. I was dressed in a blue velvet dress and coat with an ermine collar. My mother had made this wondrous outfit from an evening cloak and an ermine muff that Great-aunt Gladys had given her. I'm afraid my mother cut up many a Paris gown—probably couture—to make my dancing school recital costumes. I remember specifically a Nile green chiffon with pearls and paillettes! My parents had been to the opening night and picked up my ticket at the box office. Now the front-of-house manager handed me a little posy tied with blue ribbons and a tiny box of chocolates and escorted me to my seat on the aisle in the fifth row. The show was *Of Thee I Sing,* starring Victor Moore, William Gaxton, and my second or third cousin, once or twice removed, Lois Moran.

In about 1950 I asked George Kaufman, who directed it, about Lois. I didn't care how distant the connection was, I had claimed it in my bones at that matinee. He said she was a miracle: she sang like a bird, was a good dancer, a true beauty, and quietly very intelligent. He remembered her at Sardi's after every matinee eating alone and reading a book. In fact, he couldn't recall ever seeing her without a book. Since I'd chosen her as my secret guardian angel at the age of seven, I was more than happy to hear all this.

That matinee with the music, the lights, the audience laughing and clapping—not to mention the chocolates—coupled with the silky, satiny Parisian camisole hanging over the drawer of the steamer trunk, probably sealed my fate. The seeds were planted and then nurtured by my mother. She was sure I was "special," so I thought so too. She believed I was capable of great things, so I was blithely confident. Somehow I thought I could have—no, I *would* have—a life filled with light and music and applause and maybe even satin underwear.

Years later I learned that "Scottie," far from being a puppy, was F. Scott Fitzgerald. Great-aunt Gladys had decided to come back to America to keep Lois away from him. My mother, in one of her rare moments of wickedness, said, "I think Aunt Gladys liked him herself."

But on that day of ice cream and satin when I was three, we just went straight home to Cliffside, New Jersey.

4

EVERYONE in town knew us, and we—three kids, mother and father—knew everybody. It was a small town, but if my big brother Billy had not been an athlete, a jalopy nut, and drop-dead handsome, we might have missed the two extremes of Cliffside society.

My mother taught school, the "entering class" of five- and six-year-olds. Their young parents were respectful of the "sweet little, pretty little Mrs. Boger." And fifteen or twenty years later, when the children's children filed into her class, they remembered her with love, and felt secure.

My father, an insurance broker, worked in New York City. Every Sunday morning he washed, polished, and vacuumed the car, and cut the grass or raked the leaves. Two or three other men doing the same things, to the same kinds of cars and the same small gardens, would stop to chat and have a lemonade or a cup of coffee.

My middle brother, Fred, tall, shy, redheaded, sang in the choir of the Episcopal church. At ten, he started asking questions about God and Death and Sin. At twelve he announced that he wanted to be a Catholic. He'd been to the church and talked to Father O'Brien. The priest came to see us, and at thirteen my brother was baptized. So Father O'Brien and a nun (one of the four McCarthy girls—the other three taught school with my mother) became friends of ours.

It was through my mother that we knew a cross section of the whole town—children, parents, grandparents, and teachers. My

The three Boger children: left to right, Betsy, Billy, and Fred, 1928

father added the men of the neighborhood; my brother Fred the Catholics.

As for my beautiful big brother Billy, with his perfect teeth and curly black hair, his Bing Crosby–ish voice, and outgoing nature, he brought the Italians into my life. My mother knew them too, of course—their children passed through her class. But she also knew that Cliffside, right on the Palisades across the Hudson River from New York, was where the Mob, the Mafia, stashed their wives and children. On Sunday, we might see them at Bischoff's ice cream parlor, resplendent men in flashy clothes, treating everyone to sodas and sundaes. My mother would nod to the wives, but they wouldn't come to the table. Billy knew them, from playing football with them. Billy would dash out after supper before anyone could ask where he was going. And somehow—perhaps because I was once awake when he came in smelling of garlic and wine—I became his confidante. He would bring me treats—a piece of pizza before we knew what it was, or an Amaretto biscuit. He taught me *arrivederci* and *ciao,* and some ruder words, but they were secret. Books and movies and this Italian connection were the main spurs to my imagination until I got to high school and our poetry-loving English teacher, Mr. Pulver.

There were ordinary hardworking Italians too, of course, the shoemaker, Mr. Costello, and Mr. Fiori, who owned the garage. But a hint of disapproval came from my father even about them. He was a Republican, my mother, a Democrat. At every election he would say, "But you're just canceling out my vote," and she would nod her head in agreement and smile. She was a natural Democrat. Everything she had learned—and she'd graduated Phi Beta Kappa from Adelphi College—combined with her teaching and her sweet nature, gave her a generous appreciation of every living soul. For her, there were no "kikes," or even Jews, no "wops," or even Italians. We were all equal as in the Declaration of Independence. That was her Bible. We attended the Episcopal Church. I loved the drama of it, the tragic deep purple–shrouded Good Friday changing into the glorious gold and white of Easter, and the Christmas tableau and procession. But we were not a religious family—except for Fred, of course.

When I was thirteen, and had my first date to go to a high school basketball game, I chose to go with Joe Costello, the shoemaker's son. I know now that it was the opening salvo in my inevitable war with my father. Then I only thought Joe was good-looking and lots of fun—and besides, he'd asked me. I mentioned the date, ever so casually, at supper—"an Italian boy in my class." There was a silence. Billy had gone off to Northwestern University by then, or he would have saved me. "No," said my father. "You'll go to the game with your brother and me as you always have." I looked at my mother. She smiled her "canceling-out-his-vote" smile and said, "Which Italian boy?" I didn't realize she was worried too. "Joe," I said. As she stood and picked up the empty macaroni and cheese dish, she actually winked at me. I'd never seen anyone wink, except in the movies, but I understood. As she passed behind my father on the way to the kitchen sink, she trailed her hand across the back of his neck. All she said was, "We'll talk about it," and the battle was over. I didn't know if I'd won, but I seemed to be seeing things I'd never seen—or maybe never noticed—the wink and then my mother's hand on my father's neck, just above his collar. And on Friday night when Joe rang our bell, in a shirt and tie, well-shined shoes, and slicked-down hair, I knew Billy was laughing with pleasure way out in Illinois. *"Ciao,"* I said.

The summer before he went to college, Bill bought a jalopy for ten dollars. He worked on it all through June, July, and August. He took it completely to bits, motor and all. He made a deal with the Orchanians, an old couple across the street who had a double garage and one car. In exchange for washing their windows, cleaning their car, and doing any other odd job they needed, he could use half their garage. For him, none of it was too much trouble, but my father thought he was mad—"his tin Lizzie would never work, he was wasting his summer," and so on. But Billy persisted. He wanted to drive to college. He hung around Mr. Fiori's garage, he asked questions, and sometimes they gave him bits and pieces. He also made friends with a McClave son. The McClaves were the richest folk in town. There were about six families like them. Their mansions stood above the Hudson River behind gates and long drives. Their children went to private schools, and on Sundays, they went to Englewood to the cathedral and then the golf club. But Buddy McClave had a motorcycle, so he was in and out of Fiori's garage all that summer. He was sixteen to Bill's eighteen—I was ten. As he worshipped Bill, I worshipped him. When he roared up on his motorcycle, I would swoon. (Though we didn't say "swoon" yet, because Frank Sinatra was still in some high school in Hoboken, and except for my mother, we hadn't read any Brontë or Jane Austen.) Buddy would greet us all. He had naturally perfect manners. He'd tousle my hair. "Hi, kiddo," he'd say. Only Billy called me "kiddo," but I loved it. They'd cross the street to the Orchanians' garage. Buddy often brought some needed piece for the car—the "miracle project Super Speed," as they called it. The day he brought the hood ornament from the Packard his family was trading in was the day I knew he was my *fate*. Most mothers said the reason for clean underwear was the possibility of an accident. My mother said, "You never know when your *fate* is around the corner." Mine was now across the street. I'd meander over, wheeling my bike, hang around a bit, then pedal wildly around the block, then back and forth in our street, up and down curbs, no-hands coasting, until Bill would yell, "Hey, Red—hey, kiddo—get us a cold drink." In a flash I'd be back with an iced tea for Buddy and a Dr. Pepper for Bill. They'd take a five-minute break. I'd be so happy and satisfied that I could then go play with my own friends.

Bill started going on the back of the motorcycle to the McClaves'. There were four McClave children, from seventeen to ten: Anne, Buddy, Jacqueline, and Jean. All the details of the house and the parents and the children would come out at supper. This was for the whole family—not like our secret Italians.

The day the car was ready, dark green paint dry, chrome polished, motor not exactly purring, but sounding sturdy, and the Packard ornament welded to the hood of the roadster, the inaugural drive to the McClaves' was to take place. Luckily I was back from a week at summer camp. Bill and Buddy bowed me into the rumble seat and we drove off, down Anderson Avenue, past the high school, to Buddy's gates. He stood the gates open, and we slowly made the circuit of his drive three times. The gardener waved to us, and the housekeeper or the laundress—I didn't know then that they could be two different people—stopped hanging out the sheets to watch us. And when we stopped in front of the door, Mrs. McClave and Anne greeted us. Anne was pale and slight with

My brother Billy's jalopy: Betsy, Billy, and Fred, 1933

wispy blond baby hair. I thought she was beautiful, and I noticed that Bill did too. (When he graduated from Northwestern, they were married for a short time—but that's another story.) For now, he'd introduced me to the two extremes of Grantwood society, the Mafia families vicariously, and the rich in reality.

And when I went to work as a dancer and decided to change my name, it was the summer of the jalopy, and the memory of my crush on Buddy McClave, that led me to my choice. I'd always liked Betsy, and Buddy went to Blair Academy. So there I was: Betsy Blair.

5

MY MOTHER had a rich uncle—"crazy Uncle Sam," my father called him. He loomed large in our lives. He *was* very large, over two hundred pounds, and in my memory he is always dressed in a white linen suit and a Panama hat. Energetic and agile, he traveled the world between the wars—Venice and Istanbul, Rio and Paris— and every summer he came to Cliffside. Long before I was born, there had been an Aunt Edith for a short while. But in the years I knew him, my mother was the center of his attention.

She had always been his favorite. He sent her presents. Once a lace shawl from Brussels, which was welcome. But then a three-foot-tall bronze statue of Joan of Arc with a removable sword came, and was decidedly *unwelcome.* Not only was there customs duty to be paid, but a place of honor must be found for her. For Joan, the landing halfway up the stairs was a perfect spot. She could be seen from the front door, and we could run up the stairs, grab the sword, twirl around, and replace it before running the rest of the flight. The customs duty was more of a problem. The brown United Parcel delivery van was enormous—not the regular one that came from the department stores in New York and handed over coat-sized boxes and demanded no money, but a monster that needed thirty-five dollars before unloading the crate. Now thirty-five dollars was not just hanging around in our house—or in any other house in our neighborhood. That day, my mother had $14, I had $2.15 (in my secret stash) and the sugar bowl in the kitchen cupboard had $9.50. The sugar bowl money was for extras—sometimes new tap shoes for me—or for emergencies. My father was at his office, my brothers never had any money. I was the squirrel of the family, hoarding my nickels and dimes. My March of Dimes silver cylinder, part of President Roosevelt's campaign to raise money to find a cure for polio, was almost full, but it was inviolate. When it was full—fifty dimes, five dollars worth—my mother and I would go to the bank on Anderson Avenue. The bank manager, Mr. Malone, would ceremoniously empty it into a ten-gallon glass container, give me a certificate, and return the cylinder to be refilled. It was thrilling and sacred to me—inviolate. So Joan of Arc had to wait a week to be delivered. My father, with some grumbling, provided the money.

I think that was the week when I first understood about "inheritance"—that is, death and wills and families. What I gleaned was that Uncle Sam was rich, that he had no children, that my mother was his favorite, so she would be his heir. Because of this, my father would reluctantly pay the customs duty and put up with his visits.

The rest of us adored his visits. He treated Billy man-to-man, Fred was interested in his travels, I just liked having a fat great-uncle with a lap to climb onto and breathe in his smell of bay rum, cigars, and lemony cologne.

And my mother loved him. With a smile, she served up, at breakfast, lunch, and supper, the stewed tomatoes that he'd been told at a clinic in Switzerland would make him lose weight and prevent cancer. And he proclaimed her tomatoes better than those of the great Caesar at the Ritz in Paris.

Uncle Sam was an early riser. By six a.m., he was clean-shaven and immaculately dressed. He would position himself in the hall between Fred's room and mine. (Billy bunked in with Fred when we had a guest.) He'd tap both doors simultaneously and whisper-call, "The first one downstairs gets a dime." But there were rules in this game. You couldn't just tumble downstairs in your pajamas— you must be washed and dressed, teeth cleaned and hair brushed. Probably because my room was just next to the bathroom, I usually won. I had figured out very quickly that the strategy was to lay out my clothes at night—underwear, shorts, a shirt and sandals—grab

My mother's "crazy Uncle Sam"

them, get into the bathroom first, and lock the door. The March of Dimes did well in the summer—I claimed at least ten of the fourteen dimes that Uncle Sam dispensed.

In the late morning, Uncle Sam would establish himself in the side yard facing Columbia Avenue. From under a tree, his jacket neatly draped on the back of the chair, his hat tilted slightly, and a Japanese fan in his hand, he would hail any passerby—the iceman, the doctor, an old lady. "Sit a minute," he'd call. "Have a lemonade." There were glasses and a large pitcher, frosty with ice, on the table beside him. My fastidious father was embarrassed by this behavior, but my romantic mother giggled and saw Columbia Avenue transformed into a street in Paris and our garden furniture—incidentally bought by Uncle Sam—as part of a French café.

I don't know what the grown-ups talked about. I don't know how it was worked out about money, about my father's pride. I do know that the garden furniture, the washing machine, the first and only new bike Fred ever had—he'd always inherited Billy's—my porcelain doll from Paris, and the Tiffany silver sugar bowl and creamer all appeared in September after Uncle Sam had gone.

And then he was gone. He didn't die—he was just gone. I was seven or eight, and for the first time, I was aware of a mystery in the house. My mother would sometimes cry, my father was uncharacteristically placatory, and although my mother had always talked things out with us—she believed in explaining things to children—this time she would only answer my questions with my baby talk: "Come and give me a hug and a tiss."

Uncle Sam did die when I was fourteen.

My mother cried a lot then, and my father was grouchy. There was no inheritance, and the mystery lingered in the air.

As with all family secrets, over the years there were bits that I could have pieced together. But I was too busy with the way my own life was unfolding to remember it all. Besides I turned against anything that made my mother cry: at seven or eight, it was Uncle Sam; at twelve it was my father; now, at fourteen, it was the whole idea of inherited wealth. Two years later, when I was in a marxist study group in New York, I was told that inherited wealth is wrong, even sinful. This fell on fertile ground. Uncle Sam, I wrongly assumed, had done the spadework.

My father died a sudden terrible death when he was only fifty-one. He fell down the subway steps on his way to work one morning and was killed instantly. The night before his funeral, Bill, Fred, and I stayed up late. We sat around the kitchen table and mourned him. We talked and fought and cried and laughed—and Fred and I finally heard the whole story of Uncle Sam.

In the spring of 1932, at one o'clock in the morning, there had been a phone call from Uncle Sam's ultra-respectable brother. He

Uncle Sam on his travels, in St. Mark's Square,
Venice, 1936

was a judge in Philadelphia, and in "society." He would only speak
to my father—what he had to say was "not fit for the ears of a lady."
He instructed my father to go at once to pick up Sam at the Central
Park Hotel in New York. The judge would telegraph three hundred
dollars to the night manager to thank him for his services. My
father must then drive Uncle Sam directly to an address in northern
Pennsylvania. When my father expressed some reluctance, the
judge shouted, "He propositioned a bellboy—the scandal—it's
unforgivable!" So my father went.

The address in Pennsylvania was a private sanatorium. When
they arrived at what looked like a country estate, Uncle Sam, who
was quite drunk and had slept for most of the three-hour drive,
woke up. Energetic as always, he bounced out of the car, put his

arm around my father's shoulders, and marched into the fake chateau. There was a buxom redheaded woman—a doctor, actually—waiting for them. Uncle Sam greeted her gaily: "Are you my little playmate for tonight?"

So "crazy Uncle Sam," who wasn't crazy at all, was committed by his brother and locked in the sanatorium until he died, at the age of sixty-eight.

My father had every right to be grouchy when there was no inheritance. He had done what seemed right in the middle of the night. But Uncle Sam knew who had driven him to the sanatorium—my mother's letters to him came back unopened. In his eyes he'd been betrayed by the brother he hated and the niece he loved.

I only hope he found some playmates—of either sex—to brighten his days. He had sure brightened ours.

Uncle Sam, Great-aunt Gladys, my brother Billy, me—I like to imagine a streak of adventure and curiosity running through my family. Certainly I was eager to learn everything, to go out into the world and embrace whatever came.

6

IT PROBABLY happened sometime around my sixth birthday.

From the age of two, I would stand on the closed toilet seat and share my father's shave. He'd swipe his razor across the strop, run the hot water, take his badger-hair shaving brush and twirl it in the shaving-soap bowl until he had a good lather. He decorated his cheeks and chin and, carefully, the mustache area of his upper lip with the wonderful white foam. Then came the important moment when I screwed up my eyes while my cheeks and chin were daubed. I had to open them again cautiously so I wouldn't miss the skillful scraping of the whiskers and the rinsing of the blade.

Sometimes he sang one of his nonsense songs, "If you like-a me like I like-a you," or the one about monkeys, "Under the Bamboo Tree." But even when he didn't sing, I was patient. The lather might start to tickle. I didn't care. He cleaned and steamed his face with the hot washcloth, and then it was my turn. With the dull side of the blade he "shaved" me. He hotted up the cloth again under the tap and pretended to be an English barber. "Is that all right, sir?" he'd ask, then he'd say, "Smooth as a baby's bottom." We would feel each other's cheeks, and he'd pick me up and give me a hug.

And then almost every day, my family tells me, I'd look straight at him and say, very solemnly, like a promise, "Daddy, when I'm six, I'll be a boy."

It was a promise I couldn't keep. I could run fast, I could roller-skate and bicycle like a demon, I could do back flips in dancing class, I could play baseball and basketball in high school. I could be a tomboy, but not a boy like my big brothers.

By the time I was seven, I had made the adjustment to girlness. My Patsy dolls and all their clothes, my own new outfit every Easter, my dancing school costumes, lace and satin and organdy—they all became an integral part of me. And most importantly, I had my loving mother, with her slender skillful hands, her soft cheeks, and her beautiful, smooth back in the only evening dress I remember her having—black with narrow shoulder straps.

Looking back, I think my acceptance of girlhood was a big event. I somehow felt I could have it all. I *was* a girl. I could keep the freedom of a boy, and celebrate being a girl. I had red hair, I was my daddy's "sweet patootie" and my mommy's angel, everything she'd wanted and prayed for. I didn't give up my brothers' books, *Bomba the Jungle Boy* and *The Hardy Boys*, but my hero became Jo in *Little Women*, or the clever audacious Nancy Drew, "Girl Detective" and, most of all, the aviator, brave, real-life Amelia Earhart.

The red hair was important. When I had a fight with Fred or any disappointment came my way, I'd say to myself, "I don't care, I have red hair." I felt blessed and singled out. The fact that Fred had red hair too didn't come into it. He wasn't a redheaded girl. But I was. And I was the baby. I could stamp my foot, I could proclaim my opinion, I could fight to be the best, at home, at school, at dancing class. After my outbursts my mother would soothe me. "If you're fortunate enough to have such beautiful hair you must learn to control the temperament that goes with it." She instilled in me the idea that my hair was beautiful, my ears were tiny and perfect—and, as my feet got bigger, that it was aristocratic to have long narrow feet. She never said I was pretty—one didn't in those days, the child might get vain. She did say, "You must brighten the corner where you are," as did many a mother. But she added, "Wherever you are, they're darned lucky to have you." No wonder I grew up confident and unafraid.

Fred was the gentle soul in our family, probably the most like my mother, both in spirit and intelligence. We all three had college

My father, Willett Kidd Boger, about 1913

scholarship opportunities—the schoolteacher's children were good at school. Billy had the choice of an academic scholarship to Princeton or a football scholarship to Northwestern. He chose the latter to get away to Chicago and for the glory of playing on a Big Ten team. Fred dutifully went to the Wharton School at the University of Pennsylvania, which, with Harvard, was considered one of the best business schools in the country.

According to my father's plan, both of my brothers were being prepared to join him, and his partner, Mr. Ferguson, in their insurance brokerage firm. I can see now that it was a poky office, one room divided into a tiny foyer for the secretary and two chairs for clients, and the partners' office with a large desk for each and leather armchairs. But at the time I thought it was magnificent. They had a good address, 27 William Street, in the heart of the financial district, with gold lettering on the door: Arthur David Ferguson and Willett Kidd Boger. The business seemed to tick over just about well enough to almost support the two households and pay the secretary. But I know we were never secure. My father, tall, dark-eyed, handsome, well dressed, was never strong. He had pneumonia twice. In those days that meant the hospital, with its cost, then four or five months of recuperation at home. It was my mother's salary, small and steady, that enabled her to keep up appearances. That was extremely important to her. During my early teens, I silently accused her of being hypocritical, always pretending everything was perfect.

My father was not perfect, and probably she wasn't either. His flaws were venial; there were other women in his life. He was vain about his good looks and sarcastic in his wit—even to me. In puberty, for whatever developmental reason, I made quite a lot of noise swallowing. I could take the teasing of my brothers, but my daddy—raising a sardonic eyebrow and saying, "Is there by chance a horse in the pantry?"—would bring my tears.

I didn't know about his women friends. But I could feel that my mother and I were in a kind of struggle to be good enough, to be better than some distant amorphous force. That was odd, because my mother had married "beneath her," as they said in those days. College educated, she came from a family that had a carriage and horses, a large house, stables, meadows, and an orchard. Her father was a judge. My father's parents kept a boarding house and later a small apartment building.

After my mother died I read the small packet of my father's letters tied together with a blue ribbon from the early days of their marriage. They revealed an eager, ambitious young man, uneducated and rather shallow, but loving and sexy. I can guess that my mother was strongly attracted. I'm sure she felt daring and adventurous. She probably believed that her love would mold him into a finer sensibility, to match hers.

But his favorite actress was Alice Faye, blond, zaftig, and acquiescent—the opposite of my mother.

My mother was sweet, intelligent, well mannered, and she loved my father. She was gentle with everyone, but I think now that she unwittingly made my father feel inadequate. Beneath his sardonic, witty manner and his immaculately turned-out man-about-town appearance was the Staten Island boy from the other side of the tracks. He found admiration and solace elsewhere.

And as my mother lost him, so did I.

I thought I was being independent and rebellious. I was in league with my mother. I was safe with her. My brothers coped with all this better than I did. They were older, and so responded differently. Billy refused to go into the Ferguson and Boger office, but Fred, always dutiful, managed to bring new methods and contacts and, therefore, more profit to the small firm. Billy had a successful career with the Prudential, and a wonderfully happy second marriage, with Dorothy Bentley. She had been in high school with me, a lovely girl who grew into one of the loveliest women I've ever known. So my darling big brother had a happy life with Dottie and their three great kids.

Although I wasn't conscious of a big hole in my life, I sure set about filling it quickly. I'm not saying that I saw Gene as fatherly. I never thought in those terms. Besides, he was too vital and sexy to be cast as a father. But I find myself wondering over and over why that twenty-eight-year-old man wanted the child I was at sixteen. It's true he had been forced to take over and be the "man" in his family at an early age. His older brother James was more like Pop Kelly and not inclined toward being in charge of anyone. But Gene was a natural carer and a smart, creative, and benevolent boss type. He didn't want to be the center of attention, he wanted to quietly control the whole thing. I don't think for a moment that he was aware of this. And I don't deny the force of love, attraction, and fun that brought us together. Equally, I can now see that our needs meshed perfectly: my need to be swept away by a man, to be held securely and adored by a man, and his need to find the girl who would be pliable and receptive to his idea of a couple, who wouldn't question his unspoken authority. I don't mean he wanted a mouse—and he knew very well he wasn't getting one. He enjoyed my spirit and smiled with indulgence at my quirks and radical ideas. But it was *his* life that I was becoming part of, not my life nor even our life, but his.

7

SO I HAD CHOSEN to be on my mother's side. My mother, my pretty, tiny, hardworking mother. She was so quick she always seemed to be running. But I was her beloved little girl, so she always had time for me. She used to say she'd have had ten children if the first nine were boys. This was very nice for me. My brothers never told me how it made them feel—perhaps it was one of the things that drove Fred into the welcoming arms of the Catholic Church.

Here's my mother's day: She was up at six, cooked breakfast for us all, sent my brothers off to school with their lunchboxes, and made sure my father had a perfectly ironed shirt. (If it wasn't perfect, in his over-fastidious eyes, he might just rumple it up and throw it in the dirty-clothes basket.) Then she and I would practically run the four blocks to School No. 6. After school, while I played or danced or read, she would tidy the house, and put the dirty clothes into the washing machine in the cellar and then through the big old mangle to wring them out. By then it was time to get supper ready. I was in and out of whichever room she was in. I wanted to help her. But she would only let me set the table, to make it as pretty as I could. Then she'd say, "Sit down, I'll tell you a story." And while she peeled the potatoes or shelled the peas, I heard about the Norse gods, about Odin and Thor, or the story of Mimi in *La Bohème,* or Helen of Troy, or Pierre and Marie Curie. I remember those late afternoons in the golden haze of childhood, as soft and sweet as a toasted marshmallow and as thrilling as a sleigh ride.

My mother, Frederica Ammon, about 1913

After supper, when she'd done the dishes, my mother had lessons to mark. We'd do our homework and my brothers would scamper out as fast as possible to their wild games of ring-a-levio or hide-and-seek on the street. I wanted to be out there with them. After all, I was sure I was like Jo in *Little Women*—if only I were older. But I had to go to bed at eight. At nine, my mother, yawning in her nightgown, would give me a last kiss good night, and set her alarm clock—not for six, but for one in the morning. Then, in the quiet house from one until three or four, she ironed and cooked a stew or baked a pie, she darned the socks and made my dancing school costumes; she did whatever needed to be done. Then she went back to bed until six. It was only when I left home that I learned that not all mothers dragged themselves out of bed for several hours in the middle of the night to be sure their families were well looked after. And she never talked about it.

But I was not taught to cook or iron or sew by my mother. I was to dance and dream and roller-skate and read. Now I understand— I was not to have a life like hers. And as it turned out, she succeeded; I didn't.

My grown-up life, the life I've led, started very early—the year I was nine. Every Thursday night at the movie theater in Fort Lee there was an amateur show. I'm told I was considered the star pupil at the Swift Sisters School of Dance. Helen and Mae Swift had been in vaudeville and still read *Variety*. Helen looked a bit like Ginger Rogers (I thought she was even prettier). Mae was plainer, but a better dancer and a better teacher. I loved them both. They taught "Toe, Tap, and Acrobatic." Tap and Acrobatic were for me. I confess when I finally had the yearned-for, begged-for toe shoes, I could only stand the pain and bloody toes for two weeks. The good Mae comforted me: "Okay, you won't be a ballerina. You'll do 'interpretive dancing.' " And she showed me pictures of Isadora Duncan and Mary Wigman and Martha Graham—all with bare feet.

When the Swift sisters were invited to send "a suitable young person with chaperone to Washington for the weekend, *all* expenses paid, to entertain the President's wife on Saturday afternoon," I was chosen. The senator from New Jersey was giving a garden party for Eleanor Roosevelt, the first lady. Washington, D.C.! My mother was even more excited than I was. She'd never been to the central heart of her democratic beliefs. She made a "suitable" costume for me and bought a guidebook. We set off on Friday from Pennsylvania Station in our best summer clothes (I had a new "Deanna Durbin" cotton dress, with navy polka dots and big white collar). I carried a small suitcase, my schoolbag containing the sheet music of the Moonlight Sonata (we'd been told there would be a pianist to play for me), and the guidebook. The entire train journey

Tap-dancing in a movie theater in 1934
in the amateur show that toured New Jersey

was taken up by my mother's strategic planning of every hour of our stay. There had been a discussion about whether I should curtsy when I met Mrs. Roosevelt. Mae Swift said yes, my mother said no. They reached a compromise; I would shake hands in true American democratic fashion, and curtsy to the first lady as I started to dance.

I barely remember flitting around the lawn and eating cake afterward, but the Lincoln Memorial and Mrs. Roosevelt's smile are vivid still. At supper six months later, when my father made one of his customary insulting cracks about Mrs. Roosevelt's appearance, I

In my "suitable costume" to dance at
a garden party for Mrs. Roosevelt, 1933

gritted my teeth to hold back my tears, managed to say, "She has beautiful eyes," and left the table in full nine-year-old dignity, before dessert—and it was my favorite, applesauce.

That same year in our recital my solo was a Hal Leroy imitation eccentric dance after I sang a chorus of "College Rhythm."

> Snap your fingers, walk around a bit
> Shake your shoulders, go to town a bit
> When its gotcha
> You'll get hotcha
> That's College Rhythm!

My costume was a cinch for my mother—an old shirt and trousers from my brother, borrowed suspenders, and a fedora hat. She only had to shorten the trousers.

I was a smash hit. The consensus—from the Swift sisters and my mother; my father didn't voice an opinion—the consensus was that

At a hairdressers' convention in Atlantic City. My dancing school
had supplied the models. I'm second from the front of the line.

I should have a go at the amateur show. And I loved the idea; it
seemed perfectly natural to me. All my life I'd had nothing but love
and approval, so I wasn't scared. I didn't even know you were supposed to have stage fright.

And I won. The prize was twenty dollars—a lot of money in the
1930s. The hometown girl and "College Rhythm" beat the Irish
tenor and "Danny Boy" on the applause meter. Mr. Henry I. Marshall, Master of Ceremonies, piano accompanist, and—as we soon
learned—manager of the troupe of "amateurs," invited me to join
them. I was to be paid five dollars every Thursday, win or lose. Soon
I was taking a "singing and presentation" lesson from him every
week, so two of my five dollars found their way back to his pocket.
And if I won—which, being so young, I sometimes did even as far
away as Teaneck—fifteen dollars stayed with him. But my mother
and I loved it all. She escaped one night a week, and the "men" had
to get their own supper. We got to see the movies free. When it was
Astaire and Rogers, or Eleanor Powell, or Ruby Keeler, I was rapt

learning the routines. With my feet, my fingers on my knees, my eyes and ears catching every moment, I could memorize an amazing number of steps. My mother was concentrating on the costumes, the ones she considered suitable for me. Ginger Rogers's satin sailor suit, Ruby Keeler's black leotard over an organdy puffed-sleeve blouse, Eleanor Powell's bolero and ruffled skirt—I had them all, made in the wee small hours of the night in our silent house.

Mr. Marshall got a radio show for himself and his troupe. He named us "The Climbers," and wrote a theme song for us.

> We're the Climbers
> Climbing up to Fame.
> The Climbers,
> Building up our name.
> We're the future Cantors,
> Kate Smiths and Vallees too,
> We'd like to grow up to be Penner
> If it's all the same to you.
> The Climbers,
> Someday we hope to be
> In the money
> Then this'll be funny,
> But you just wait and see
> For good old opportunity
> And Mr. Marshall—gosh oh gee!
> We'll climb and climb and climb to the top
> We're the Climbers.

I remember that I worked very hard on the little catch in the throat between "Mr. Marshall" and "gosh oh gee!" and believed every word. Every Sunday morning at eleven on WNEW, in direct competition with NBC "proudly presenting the Horn and Hardart Children's Hour," I imagined the RKO radio waves on their movie logo, carrying my song and tap dance to the world.

Yes, I tap-danced on the radio. We had to invest my first two eight-dollar fees in a "tap board"—a wonderful contraption, two and a half feet square, made of one-inch-wide slats of hard wood on a strong canvas backing. It rolled up neatly and fastened with a carrier strap. I could manage it by myself later, when I made the trip alone on the bus, the Forty-second Street ferry, the trolley car across town, and the bus uptown.

When I was ten, for Mother's Day, my father took me to a fancy department store, Arnold Constable, to have my picture taken professionally as a present for my mother. We didn't know that for the month before Mother's Day, all the children who were photographed were automatically entered in the *New York Daily News* Beautiful Child Contest. This time I didn't win, but I got an Honorable Mention. My picture was published in the paper with the caption, "For charm and character in the face." Everyone was thrilled, even my brothers. But I can't say that I was overwhelmed by "charm and character." In my dreams I was ravishingly beautiful—at least I planned to be when I grew up. How else could I dance with Fred Astaire?

Then a letter arrived from the John Robert Powers model agency inviting us to come and meet Mr. Powers. Maybe "charm and character" were enough for now. My mother turned to Great-aunt Gladys, our only contact in the big wide world. She advised us to go, that it was the best and most reputable agency. She added rather tartly that when I started making some money I should have diction lessons to lose my "New Joisey" accent. My feelings were not hurt; my favorite actor at the time was the very English Ronald Colman, star of *A Tale of Two Cities.* I'd seen the movie twice and cried my eyes out both times. I had already taken on a few affectations: "fah"—as in "fah, fah better thing I do"—and "atall" rather than "at all."

On the first day of the summer holiday, my mother and I went to the elegant busy Powers office on Park Avenue. I was signed on and sent to have photos taken that same afternoon. By the time I was twelve I had a photographic job once or twice a month, for magazines or catalogues or department store brochures. I was in the "back to school" lunchtime fashion shows every year at the store where it had all started, and I'd even been filmed for the monthly news magazine that was shown in movie theaters, *The March of Time,* in an item about that new invention from England, television.

With all this going on, I was suddenly absent from school—for the dentist or a bad cold—too often to be believed. And then a Lux soap ad appeared in *Life* magazine with my name: "Betsy Boger, Schoolgirl." Everyone saw *Life.* My mother had to come clean. She was formidable. She defended my right to do these special things since I had the chance. The principal of the school, her boss, gave her an ultimatum: "A teacher's child cannot be absent from school with false excuses. Either this will all stop or she should be sent elsewhere." My mother appealed to Great-aunt Gladys. I don't know how it was worked out. I assume Great-aunt Gladys paid my tuition for the Professional Children's School in New York, and I was happily launched into a new adventure.

PCS, a school for "pros," soon focused my attention. Most of the students were actors—for radio, Broadway shows, and, at the top of the hierarchy, the circus kids. They were exotic, foreign and skilled. They could stand on their hands on a tilted chair, make clown faces behind the teacher's back, walk on ledges. In November, they left for Florida and winter training, and the Broadway kids moved to the top of the hierarchy. I was impressed and intrigued by them. Every Wednesday, matinee day, they gathered their books together at eleven-thirty in the morning. They clattered noisily down the hall and out into the street to have lunch and go to their theaters.

And I looked at them and I knew then, when I was twelve, that it was all for real. It was all possible. I would be a dancer and an actress. It wasn't just a dream in a movie theater or on the trolley car. I would do it.

But that spring my mother discovered that my beloved PCS was not an accredited high school—I couldn't go on to college from there. So it was back to New Jersey for me. The school board didn't make it easy; they said I'd have to do my freshman year again. My little tigress mother went into battle for me, and they finally agreed that I could take exams for placement. Lo and behold, I

From the John Robert Powers Agency catalogue of models, 1936

Betsy Boger, schoolgirl (second from left). The ad where I was named and quoted: "My mother uses Lux for all our best clothes."

In the uniform of the Cliffside Park High School
Fife and Drum Corps

skipped the sophomore year and became a third-year student.

My junior and senior years of high school passed in the mist of adolescence. I was on the basketball team, I played the fife in the fife and drum corps, I was in the senior play, I went to classes, I played kissing games at parties (strictly mouth closed—no "soul" kissing). Some days I stopped in the coffee shop after school and jitterbugged to the jukebox. Some days the entire boys' basketball team came home with me because we had a Ping-Pong table in the basement.

I was a bit of a whiz at Ping-Pong. My brothers warned me I'd never get asked out if I always beat the boys at Ping-Pong, but I didn't care if I never had a date. I wanted to win. I painted my brown and white saddle shoes in red and black, the school's colors, and created a bit of a fad.

I graduated at fifteen, because I'd started going to school with my mother when I was four since there was no one to take care of me at home, and then I'd skipped a year. I'd qualified for a scholarship to go to college at Sarah Lawrence. It was practically all set. I just had to have my interview.

I'd suddenly grown five inches—I was skinny and gawky. (In fact, the only time I modeled for *Vogue* it said under the picture of me in a gabardine skirt with a bolero jacket, "for your gawky fourteen-year-old.") I wore a bra for no good reason, just because I wanted to. My bobbed red hair was curly, and I was very pale with blue eyes and no makeup, not even Tangee Natural lipstick.

So the confident, gawky child I was at fifteen went to the interview. The result astonished my mother. The head of the Board of Admissions wrote to us that they could not in good conscience accept me that fall. I was not "emotionally or socially mature enough for university life." They would hold my scholarship for next year, and suggested junior college.

For the first time, my mother was slightly daunted. She paused for about a week. My father thought the whole university idea was rather highfalutin for a girl anyway—he said I should go to Katherine Gibbs, learn to type and take shorthand, and get a good steady job. I couldn't say, "Oh, Daddy, I don't want to be a secretary, I want to dance with Fred Astaire." I knew he'd laugh at me. So I went off to my best friend's house by a lake, with nothing decided.

On the train coming home (my mother was meeting me at noon at Pennsylvania Station), I picked up a newspaper somebody had left behind, the *Journal American.* And there it was:

CALL FOR DANCERS
TODAY 2:OO P.M.
INTERNATIONAL CASINO
Broadway and 45th Street

I ran up to my mother waving the folded newspaper, and said, "I don't care what Daddy says—I'm going to this."

She kissed me, reached up and smoothed my hair, took the

paper, and sat on a bench to read the ad. I perched next to her. When she'd read it, she looked at me without a word. I think it was the only objective look she ever gave me. It seemed to go on forever. Then, with a sharp little intake of breath, she opened her handbag, counted the money in her wallet, and said, "Come on, we'll go to Macy's."

She bought me high heels, she loaned me her lipstick, she found a coffee shop around the corner on Forty-fifth Street where she'd wait for me, and she sent me off with a smile. "Don't forget the 'D.E.' " A photographer had once told her that the camera liked me because I had "dancing eyes"—and she'd never forgotten. Nor did she ever let me forget, although I didn't like the idea. I had an image of them jiggling loose.

The entrance hall of the International Casino was like a palace. A great curving marble staircase with brass banisters in Art Nouveau style rose up from the center. A young fellow sitting near the door gestured to each girl coming in to go upstairs, without looking up from his magazine. I ran up clutching the Macy's bag that had held my shoes. Now it had shorts and a top and my sandals, fished out of my suitcase. My mother somehow guessed I might need them.

At the top of the stairs I'd caught up to five or six girls. A couple of them said hi. I smiled and tried to look as if I knew what I was doing. I followed them into a vast, tiered, amphitheater-shaped room.

The International Casino was a thousand-seat very "classy joint," with white tablecloths and gilt chairs. Noble Sissle conducted the twenty-four-piece band. Milton Berle was the headliner, and there were other great acts—Señor Wences and the De Marcos ballroom dance team.

As my group came down through the tables toward the stage, we were directed to fall in line behind the others and walk across the stage. It was an endless line. I didn't know if there were a hundred or five hundred. I just kept following. As we reached the far side of the stage, most of the girls were directed to continue on out—they wouldn't be needed. Some of us were sent to put on rehearsal clothes, they wanted to see our legs. I felt lucky that my mother had foreseen this. I got through both lineups and then we danced, and I was suddenly at home and at ease. I knew how to dance.

I was chosen. Within an hour the six or seven men down there at tables had picked sixteen dancers and eight showgirls. We were to start rehearsing the next day at ten in the morning. The salary was thirty-five dollars a week.

I ran to tell my mother this great news. But for the first time in my life, I hid something from her. This show for which I'd been hired was not for New York but for the sister nightclub in Boston. I was fifteen. I knew they wouldn't let me go to Boston. My mother and I were worried that my father wouldn't even agree to New York. So I put it out of my mind.

There were two shows a night: from eight to ten, then two hours off, and from midnight till two a.m. What would my father say? How would we manage, my mother and I? We were giddy and glee-ful and in cahoots by the time we got home. We'd decided that the only argument we had was that it was temporary—I'd be going to college soon. We were wrong. What persuaded him was the thirty-five dollars a week—more than either of my college-graduate brothers was earning, and I would be able to save for the next year's expenses.

Maybe he secretly liked the idea, because he announced that the only way it could work was for him to pick me up at two a.m. and drive me home.

From Boston? I thought. Obviously I hadn't been able to put the problem out of my mind completely. And then on the third day of rehearsal, the angels smiled on me. The assistant choreographer asked me if I'd like to stay in New York—it looked as if there would be a vacancy. In the International Casino show, there were four specialty dancers, "nightclub ballerinas." One of them was Nora Kaye, who became one of America's greatest classical ballerinas. Now she was leaving to join the newly formed Ballet Theater. One of the "ponies," the chorus girls, was taking her place. By the end of the day—a day in which I worked harder than ever to be good and please everyone—I was offered the job. I was thrilled, and I felt

Above: With one of the showgirls on our way to work
at the Diamond Horseshoe, 1940
Below: The chorus at the International Casino. I'm second from the right;
the captain of the dancers, Billie, far right, and Bunny Waters center back

blessed. I was lucky, and therefore everything would always come out well, I thought. This optimism must have been part of my character already, but this was a a powerful confirmation. I never confessed my deception to my parents.

It was a glorious time for me. It was only three months, but it was packed with years' worth of excitement, learning, growing, and seeing a whole new world.

There was Bunny Waters, the most beautiful of the showgirls, and the most intelligent. She showed me how to do my makeup, including a red dot in the inner corner of each eye, and a white line along the lower lid inside the eyelashes thick with black mascara, and took me to buy it. She also pointed out that if a musician or one of the men in the acts—or, more likely, Milton Berle—tried to back me up against a wall, I didn't have to be polite.

There was June Sitar, with a baby-doll face and the longest legs of the troupe—the showgirls were all six feet tall. She was bubbly and friendly, and after a month she said, "Hey, Red, what do you do with yourself between shows?" I usually went to the Green Room. It was big and comfortable with couches and lamps. I read and slept a bit and read some more. "Come on," she said. "Come out with me—we may go roller-skating." Some nights it was bowling, some nights a Chinese restaurant—learning to eat with chopsticks seemed the height of worldly sophistication. But that first time she took me to Roseland, the dime-a-dance hall. We walked up Broadway a few blocks and came to the brightly lit marquee and the blaring music of Roseland. June greeted the ticket taker; he waved us through, and we went into a little door on the side, up a flight of stairs into a scene from *Guys and Dolls*. It was a smoky room above the dance floor. The thump, thump of the percussion instruments pervaded the air. Through the haze I saw six or seven men in shirtsleeves, ties loosened, playing cards, drinking beer or whisky, or just lazing around. "This is my boyfriend, this is Betsy. The rest of you, hands off—she's a nice kid." She suddenly yelled raucously. "Did you hear me? Hands off!"

And I suddenly made a connection. When we'd been open about two weeks, there was an awkwardly written note for my mother left on the back porch of our house. It was from the father of a girl in her class. It said:

> Dear Mrs. Boger,
>   If anybody bothers Betsy in New York, let me know.
>   Nick the Greek

. . . and nobody ever did bother me.

And there was Billie, the "captain" of the dancers. She was quite ancient, probably twenty-two or twenty-three. I found out later that I got the job because I looked a bit like her as the choreographer remembered her at my age. She sat me down after two weeks of rehearsal. "Do you like Ken?" she asked. He was a tall, skinny chorus boy. "Yes," I said. "He's a good dancer." "No, I mean do you *like* him? Do you have a crush on him?" I was startled. I blushed. "I can see you do—well, don't waste your time, he's not interested in girls." Billie could see that I had no idea what she meant, so she gave me chapter and verse. Now here was something to mull over, something new. I remember that all the way home that day on foot or bus or ferry, I could feel my very soul expanding. The world was so surprising. I knew something for the first time that I hadn't learned from my family or school. I didn't even know if they knew.

And maybe most important of all, I made friends with my father during the ride home and our snack every night in the kitchen. There had been an unacknowledged cloud between us for the past couple of years. It blew in on a night when supper was ready and my father, once again, didn't show up. I think I was twelve. We ate, we did our homework, we went to bed. But I'd seen my mother's face, and from my bed I could hear her crying through the closed door of their bedroom. I couldn't fall asleep, but when I got as far as that closed door, I couldn't knock. I went and sat in the dark on the top step of the staircase.

I must have dozed off. I woke and jumped up as my father switched on the light and started up the stairs. "Hi, darlin'—how's my little sweet patootie?" He was smiling and glad to see me. I was half awake and drowning in the image of my mother's tears. I shouted for the first time in my life, with what felt like righteous anger. "I hate you—I hate you—I'll always hate you." I turned away. My father went past me, and they closed the door. I lay on my bed helpless and frightened, trembling at what I'd felt. Did I hate him—was it possible that I hated my own father?

We didn't talk about it, but things were never the same after that. I never heard "sweet patootie" again. I never got tickled or sat on his lap again. I used to wonder if he missed me as I missed him. There we were in the same house, everything seemed the same on the surface, but it wasn't the same. And yet, I couldn't take it back. I was on my mother's side irrevocably.

Now, in my new world, I could forget all that. On the drive home, it was to my father that I recounted the excitement of each night—the adventures, the mishaps, the stars who'd been in the audience. And on Saturday, when I had my first little brown pay envelope with cash in it, I brought it to him where he waited in the car, as if it were an Olympic gold medal. I wanted his approval and respect, and he cautiously gave it.

On Sunday we decided with my mother that twenty dollars would be put in the bank each week for college, five dollars were for me, and the rest was for my mother to dole out for my fares, my lessons, my clothes. I felt like the queen of Romania—and all for doing something I loved.

New Year's Eve, 1940. I'd had my sixteenth birthday in December. The second show that night started at one in the morning. Backstage was a big party. At midnight we hung out the windows above Times Square. There were thousands of people, and singing and cheering and lights. The Old Year went out, and the New Year danced in on the moving news band at the top of the Times Building. The Green Room, where I'd often been alone in the beginning, was crowded. Ken brought me my first glass of champagne. The bosses and the musicians were there and girlfriends and boyfriends, wives and husbands, and I thought we all loved each other.

Two days later, on Saturday, after the first show, the office where we collected our little brown envelopes was dark. A note on the door told us to gather onstage. There was no money; we couldn't be paid. We were closing that night. There were no bosses in sight. The assistant stage manager had to tell us that they would try to send us that week's salary within the month, and would we please do the last show—there were customers out there.

Of course, we rallied round—the show must go on, and all that. There were only three rebels, one showgirl and two musicians. The musicians packed up and left. Mary Lou, the showgirl, was persuaded to stay.

And it was from her that I heard about unions—unions and the Mafia. Not connected, but rather as direct enemies. If we were only part of Actors' Equity, we would have been protected, according to Mary Lou. Protected from what? I wondered aloud. "The Mob," she explained. "Of course, they're the Mob—we can't stand up to them alone. We'll never see our money." And she was right—we didn't.

More new and amazing facts to absorb and consider. Why weren't we dancers part of Equity? Who was the Mob? How could they disappear and leave this enormous enterprise and all of us stranded?

And what would my father say? What would happen to the fragile budget we were building?

And then two days later, came an all-important postcard:

BILLY ROSE'S DIAMOND HORSESHOW
CALL FOR DANCERS
11:00 A.M.   JANUARY 10TH
HOTEL EDISON
47TH STREET, BETWEEN B'WAY AND 8TH AVE.

I didn't know it at the time, but this was the real beginning of my grown-up life. That little yellowish square of cardboard danced in front of me and led me all the way to Hollywood.

8

THE HOUSE I grew up in was my mother's house. As children we were kept from knowing this. She was too intelligent and too kind to belittle my father in our eyes in any way. And she loved him.

Long before I was a gleam in anyone's eye, my mother, with her two little boys, six and three, had left my father. She never told us why.

She had her college education and her courage. She decided to be a schoolteacher. She had never worked, but now she wanted to be independent. Her parents—the grandparents I never knew—helped her. She moved back into their house on Staten Island and applied to school boards in New York and New Jersey for a post.

And then her father died. She had been a late-in-life baby. Her brother, who was killed in World War I, and her sister were twenty and twenty-two years older than she was.

I don't know the timing of what happened next. My grandmother went to live with her eldest daughter in Seattle, where she died before I was born. My mother was offered a teaching job in Cliffside, New Jersey. Her rich uncle Sam, who had always adored her, bought her a little house in Cliffside on condition that my father never live in it.

And how I came to be, I can only tell you in my mother's words. She said, "Of course, I had to let your father come to see his sons. It was only right for him and for them. And one night before leaving, when the boys were in bed, he put his arms around me. I heard the rustle of the taffeta lining in his sleeves, and I was lost."

I had never really left my mother's house. If I'd gone to college, I would have come home for Thanksgiving, Christmas, and Easter. And gradually over the four years I'd have learned to be on my own. But as a chorus girl, actress, ardent student of Marx, and, finally, lover of Gene, I went home every week for Sunday and Monday like a young girl at school. My mother picked up my laundry every Saturday morning and we had breakfast and did errands together. On Monday morning before she set off for school, my freshly washed and ironed clothes were neatly packed and ready for me to take back. I think I was able to fly away so fast and high because she made me feel that my nest at home was forever safe and warm. There would always be clean clothes and fresh orange juice and her applesauce that I loved.

But now I was actually leaving. The night before I went to Philadelphia for the opening night of *Best Foot Forward* and, more important to me, my wedding four days later, my mother, as she kissed me good night, said, "Men like you to talk to them." And she left my room. As she closed the door, my eyes filled with tears.

She had nurtured me in every way possible for a woman of her generation and background, but we had never talked about intimate things. On my twelfth birthday I was given a book, *Marjorie May's Twelfth Birthday*. It was a discreet and simple explanation of menstruation with a vague promise of motherhood in the future. I spent almost three years waiting—when I happened occasionally to think of it. I realize now that my mother was waiting too, ready to pounce with the sanitary napkin paraphernalia. But it was never mentioned. And now this strange sentence. "Men like you to talk to them." My dear, sweet, hardworking mother—my tears were for her. I think I knew in that moment that she had never been as happy in bed as I already was with Gene. Even as I felt pain for her, I felt blessed. How lucky I was to have found my way when I was only sixteen—not just to Gene, but to a whole world where people were free and passionate about everything, sex and art and politics.

Gene and I (and *Best Foot Forward*) had two weeks in Philadelphia. We were together every minute. I had my first room service breakfast. We walked all over the town, saw the Liberty Bell, and spent most mornings in the museum, looking at the paintings and each other. I sat in the back of the theater when Gene had to restage a number or tighten up the chorus. Stanley Donen was in this chorus too, and June Allyson was one of the leads in the show. Stanley and I had fun. He was only a year older than I was, with a strong southern accent and funny southern words for things like "easy walkers," for sneakers. And June was my old roommate. I felt strangely grown-up around her. Here I was, a married woman, and married to Gene. I remembered the first months in the Henry Hudson Hotel. Jane and Clare and I were virgins, but June was having a love affair with a charming lanky photographer named Tommy. Since Jane danced in the second show at the Copacabana she came home very late. Clare would have gone to sleep early, and when I came in she'd wake up.

And our phone would ring. It was the old upright model with the earpiece hanging from a hook. It would be June saying she'd be out for an hour or two. Clare and I, knowing what this meant, were consumed with excitement. We'd order cream cheese and jelly sandwiches on date-nut bread and cherry Cokes from the drugstore and wait for June to come in. We were wildly curious—and maybe envious. "Come on. Tell us about it, June," was our plea. "What is it like?" Night after night. But she held out. She gloried in her superior sophistication. And finally, perhaps worn down by our persistence, she gave in.

"Well," she said, "it's sort of like sitting on a telephone."

That silenced us. We looked at our phone with wide eyes. I got up off my bed, gathered our Coke containers and sandwich wrappings to throw away, and went and brushed my teeth. Clare didn't say a word. In fact, it was never mentioned again. I'm just glad we all ended up happily married—and without telephone hangups.

We came back to New York for the opening of *Best Foot Forward*. Then Gene and I were setting off for California. We went dancing at the Rainbow Room and looked down at the lights of New York to say good-bye. There was a fairly riotous gathering at Louis Bergen's with love and laughter and a chocolate devil's food wedding cake. And warnings from Lloyd about "going Hollywood." I solemnly promised him that we wouldn't have a swimming pool.

We had to say good-bye to Dick Dwenger. It was hard for all three of us, maybe most of all for me. He'd been so good to me, my first grown-up friend. We'd be back to visit soon, we said, or he'd come to California to see us. We'd be the Three Musketeers again in a new place.

Gene and Dick packed Gene's things into the back of the car, and we all went to Cliffside to spend the last night before our honeymoon trip through Mexico to Los Angeles. In the morning we went off joyfully in a rainstorm. My mother and Dick waved until we were out of sight. We didn't know it was the last time we'd ever see him. When the war came, he joined the navy, and was "lost at sea" in the first months.

I think Gene honored his memory, and commemorated the three of us and our wonderful time together, when he made *Cover Girl*. Phil Silvers, Rita Hayworth, and Gene dance in the streets of New York and meet in the bar and search for "poils" in the "ersters." All the warmth and fun and friendship we had is there in those scenes. Dick would have loved them.

Neither rain in New Jersey, nor sleet in North Carolina, nor hail in the mountains of Kentucky could stop us on our appointed way. We drove into the southern sunshine in Tennessee. We were happy and rich. David Selznick had started paying Gene a thousand dollars a week on our wedding day. This was 1941, when only 5 percent of Americans earned ten thousand dollars a year. We stopped when we wanted to, we ate when we were hungry, we made love wherever we were, we drove through the night if we felt like it. We had ten days to get to New Orleans, where our banana boat from Vera Cruz would be docking, then two months in Mexico, a week in San Francisco, arriving in Los Angeles the first week of December. It was paradise indeed. And it all seemed natural to me. I don't mean that I was blasé; just that I was unsurprised by all this freedom and joy.

On our honeymoon, 1941

En route we stayed in roadside inns or small hotels, some of which Gene knew from his other trips. But in New Orleans, we went to the honeymoon suite in the best hotel. I'd been traveling in a plaid skirt and bobby socks and saddle shoes—not my old painted red and black Cliffside ones, but pristine brown-and-whites. Now it was time for dressing up, stockings and high heels, dinner at Antoine's, the French Quarter and Beale Street and the jazz clubs. There were three days of great French Cajun food and three nights of music and dancing, and then on to the banana boat with our car. We'd been to watch the unloading of thousands of bananas and to see our cabin. There were four: the captain's, ours, and two smaller single cabins. One shipmate was never seen until Vera Cruz. He stayed in his cabin. The other one was a combination of Sydney

Greenstreet and my mother's uncle Sam—Sydney Greenstreet because he was sinister, Uncle Sam for his linen suit and Panama hat. He ate with us—there was only the captain's table—but he never said more than "Good morning" and "Good evening." He paced the decks of the tramp steamer relentlessly from dawn to dusk. We sometimes passed him in surreptitious conversation with the sailors. They were a truly motley crew—South American, Malay, Portuguese, and a gigantic Chinese cook. Our Sydney Greenstreet seemed to speak all their languages. He was the first of the hundreds of strangers Gene and I invented stories about for the next sixteen years. And we played word games endlessly in the car, keeping score over each week. We played Donkey, and Hang the Man in our heads, and a guessing game of associations, "What does it remind you of?" Since we were both such competitive game players, it was a real contest and the result was usually very close.

One early evening after our siesta, while Gene was still asleep, I went on deck to see the sunset. I sat on a pile of rope with just the sea and the sky around me. It was one of those rare moments of stillness. Into the corner of my vision came a creature. I turned my head for a better look. It was a lobster-like shape, I thought, about four inches long. I bent closer. As I stretched my hand toward it, a large meat cleaver swooshed down, splitting it in two and cutting straight through the ropes I was sitting on. The Chinese cook had just saved my life. "No, no, never," he said. "Poison scorpion—death." Forever after, even today, he sometimes appears in my dreams, this huge, dirty, frightening-looking man. But it's not a nightmare; I always know in my dream that he's a good genie and I'm safe.

And I was safe with Gene. When we ran out of gas one night in the middle of nowhere, he settled me on the floor of the car, my head on the seat with a jacket over it, a thermos of tea, our last Oreos, and instructions to keep down until he came back or until daylight. I locked the car door, looked at the stars so bright and close, and fell asleep. I've always been able to sleep anywhere and anytime and even more readily to relieve tension.

For instance, when I was in a play I was always made up and

ready to go onstage at the fifteen-minute call. Then, even on open-ing night—or, rather, *especially* on opening night—I'd lie flat on the floor and go to sleep until the knock on the dressing room door and the call "Five minutes, please."

Now, in the middle of Mexico, I woke up to the sound of hooves and the creak of wooden wheels. I sneaked my head up, to have a look. It was Gene riding on a donkey cart with a farmer in a serape and sombrero. Gene jumped down and turned, holding out his hand with a grand and elegant gesture, the kind he made fun of as D'Artagnan in *The Three Musketeers*. Out of the wagon, from behind her father, a tiny little girl about seven or eight appeared. She had long black braids and enormous black eyes. With a natural elegance equal to Gene's, she took his hand and stepped down. He twirled her around, set her down on the ground, skipped around her, and bowed. She didn't giggle like an American child; she watched him with a grave little smile and curtsied back. Her father handed down the jerrican of gas and refused Gene's offer of money. The little girl climbed up on the cart, and they ambled off into the dawn. A few years later, in *Anchors Aweigh*, Gene re-created this moment in Olvera Street, the Mexican quarter of downtown Los Angeles. He found a little girl with long braids and big black eyes and the same grace and dignity of our little honeymoon girl, and together they danced one of his most charming numbers.

We drove through deserts and green valleys. We climbed Mayan temples and walked dusty streets from another century. We swam on the Atlantic side in the Gulf of Mexico and later, at Acapulco, in the Pacific Ocean. In Mexico City we went to museums and cathe-drals and bars and dance halls. I had two or three baths a day to make up for the ones I'd missed on the road. And then we drove north, across the border, through endless Texas and beautiful New Mexico, up to see the Grand Canyon and on to San Francisco.

For two and a half months we were alone together. I wrote post-cards to my mother, we sometimes spoke to an American stranger in a bar for a few minutes, but those things didn't intrude on our joy at being alone together. I'm sure Gene, at twenty-nine, was

Sitting in the inglenook fireplace of our first home

aware of what was going on. It was the start of what was to be his life, his career—and he'd chosen me to share it. For me, it was just life itself with colored ribbons on it.

San Francisco and the Fairmont Hotel—I could see how easy it is to get used to luxury. I loved it—room service, fluffy white towels, the bed turned down, clothes whisked away to the laundry and dry cleaner, everything taken care of for you. I've never lost my love for hotels.

I'd had instructions from my mother to call Lois Moran, then the wife of a Colonel Young, when we got to San Francisco. I'd seen Lois six or seven times in my life, and she'd written me a sweet note, to "Dear little star . . . ," when *The Beautiful People* opened. I dutifully called her, and Gene and I were invited to dinner. It was in a grand apartment overlooking the Bay and the Golden Gate Bridge. The only other guest was Howard Hughes, Colonel Young's business partner—I think they practically owned PanAm together. Mr. Hughes was well groomed and conventionally well dressed right

Lois Moran—my distant cousin and guardian angel

down to the cuffs of his trousers. Then came scrawny bare ankles and his famous dirty sneakers.

Lois was warm and beautiful, and also good. In 1942, when the human cost of war began to come home, she enlisted me to organize in Los Angeles what she was doing in Frisco. I gathered a group of thirty young women, so there would always be at least twenty available, to visit the Veterans Hospital in Brentwood once a week. We had a tea dance with refreshments, conversation, and records playing for dancing. It was a kind of nonstarry *Stage Door Canteen,* but "our boys" were the disturbed and wounded soldiers.

Frisco was Bill Saroyan's home ground. He took us everywhere, showed us everything, and in Fresno he introduced us to what seemed like two thousand Armenians, all in his family. Now I tasted the food made with the spices I'd smelled and loved in the Orchanians' house across the street in Cliffside, where my brother worked on his jalopy. Saroyan said he'd written a play for us, *Sweeney in the Trees*. It's a lovely play, and sadly, we never played it. But the private nickname "Sweeney" for me, and the response "Geney" for Gene, originated there and stayed with us.

And then we set off for Hollywood and Geney and Sweeney's Big Adventure—two big adventures, really, our daughter, Kerry, and the movies.

9

WE DROVE into Hollywood with the top down, in Gene's little Ford convertible roadster, on Pearl Harbor day, December 7, 1941. We were booked into a suite at the Hollywood-Roosevelt Hotel by David Selznick. We hadn't heard the news.

I stayed with the car while Gene went to get a bellboy for the luggage. We'd been on the road since the middle of September. We'd hardly seen a familiar face in all that time.

Now, as I sat in the open car on Hollywood Boulevard, I suddenly spotted someone I knew walking toward me. My heart leapt with pleasure. "Hello," I called. The big, beautifully dressed man smiled and tipped his hat to the windblown seventeen-year-old. "Good afternoon," he said, and continued on his way. And then it hit me; I realized who he was. Not someone I knew, not a friend or an acquaintance, but Edward Arnold, the splendid character actor whom I'd seen in many films.

I had just had a crash course in fame. I understood in that moment the power of the movies. I saw that I had instinctively responded to the sight of a stranger as if he were a close friend of my father or the principal of my high school. At any rate, as someone I had seen many times and who had therefore seen me. I was making a claim on him when I called "Hello," a claim that had no basis in a shared past. He reacted gracefully, old Edward Arnold, and I thank him for it. It helped me later on when Gene became so famous. I was able to accept the intrusion of his fans, their projected feelings of intimacy, even ownership, not only of him but of

Kerry and me, more easily than I might have without that little exchange on Hollywood Boulevard.

David Selznick was a brilliant, complicated, and generous man who spoiled us both for any future producer. And we were about to embark on the "studio will take care of it" syndrome. Everything was laid on, starting with an invitation to the Selznicks' that night for dinner and a movie screening. Now, with the flowers for me and a basket of oranges for Gene, there was a message to come to dinner, but there would be no screening—we'd be listening to the radio for news. There were arrangements for a visit to a studio to see a film being shot, a tennis club membership (we didn't take it up), real estate agents to show us houses, a bank manager's name, a doctor, a dentist, driving lessons and access to the studio hairdresser for me, and a rehearsal room and an accent coach for Gene (his first assignment, a straight part, was supposed to be *The Keys to the Kingdom,* for which he'd need a Scottish brogue).

Within a week we found a furnished house to rent. It was a perfect little one-bedroom chalet in Laurel Canyon. It cost one hundred dollars a month. Laurel Canyon in those days was mainly wooded hills. The houses were hidden from each other and from the road by tall trees and flowering shrubs and wild lavender. There were butterflies and deer and brightly colored birds. We were on Lookout Mountain Drive. The garage was at street level, then there were ninety-nine stepping stones up to the house.

We moved in and played house. No, *I* played house—Gene was actually there. Gene could cook, Gene could iron his shirts, Gene could sew on a button, Gene could fix the plumbing if need be. But I was lucky; it was like my mother all over again. He didn't want me to cook or iron or sew. When I asked him if I was a disappointment in the housekeeping department, he laughed and said, "What I want is what I have—you—to pick flowers and read by the fireplace and sing around the house—my little white dove with the burnished feathers that wakes up every morning smiling." Well, I was good at all that, especially the smiling—who wouldn't be?

We bought a Ping-Pong table, our first joint possession. It took up the whole downstairs except the inglenook fireplace and the kitchen. We played like demons. I silently thanked the Cliffside basketball team for those after-school sessions where I'd learned to serve aces, to put a little English on it, to lob and slam. We were well matched and equally competitive, and I didn't have to worry about a "date" ever again.

Christmas in California. It was so weird in the warm sunshine for us, the East Coasters, that we decided that after breakfast and presents, we'd drive to the beach at Santa Monica and have a swim. (I think we wanted to tell everyone back home that we were in the Pacific Ocean on Christmas Day. Actually, the water was too cold; we only dipped our toes.)

The week before, when we separated for two hours to go shopping, I slipped into Saks, where we had a charge account—a first for both of us. I bought Gene a cashmere sweater—another first.

It turned out that he'd been busy too. On Christmas morning next to my pile of presents under the tree was a burlap sack. I pretended not to notice it while we did our stockings and had breakfast. Gene pretended not to see the box from Saks. We opened all our books (we'd agreed to start "our library") and kissed each other thank you. I gave him his extra present, and it was perfect. Then he pulled the burlap sack over to me. I played with the moment a bit. "What is it? It's not heavy—it's very squashy—what is it?" He grinned at me, and for the first time I saw a flicker of something like "he wants to please me." "Open it," he said. It was a sackful of beautiful mink skins. "I didn't want to just buy a coat. We'll go down to the shop on Beverly Drive and you can decide on the style." I burst into tears. I hadn't ever thought of wanting a mink coat, but in a sort of clear, perhaps childlike flash, I suddenly saw what it meant to him to be able to give me, his wife, this symbol of success—his success. And I'd be wearing it. Was this the best of all possible worlds?

In 1942 I certainly thought so. The shock of the bombing of Pearl Harbor turned into a great surge of patriotic emotion. Gene would soon go to war. But not yet—MGM wanted him for a film with Judy Garland, *For Me and My Gal*. David Selznick sold half his contract to Metro, who signed him on for seven years. We were invited to Judy's house to dinner—my first chocolate mousse and the toy trains of David Rose, Judy's husband. After coffee we had to go into the garden and ride on the child-sized carriages. Judy, vibrant, funny, and friendly, was absently indulgent during this. Gene and I were polite; we thought some aspects of Hollywood were strange, but we loved Judy. Gene is on record in his gratitude to her for her generosity and help during the shooting of his first film. She made it easy for him, gave him hints about how much the camera sees and how little projection of emotion is necessary, not like in the theater—and she made him laugh. With Judy to steer him, he sort of sailed through the movie.

And in February I was pregnant. I was joyfully ready to sail through my great adventure. The obstetrician said all was well, but he couldn't recommend living with ninety-nine stone steps that might be slippery when wet. We packed our books and clothes and left our little paradise. In a way I was glad. I thought I was ready to stop playing house.

MGM transported the Ping-Pong table to Edie and Yip Harburg's house, at 506 North Alta Drive in Beverly Hills. The studio found it for us to rent, checked the inventory, arranged three housekeepers for us to interview, and altogether made the move as easy as driving to a friend's house for dinner.

I passed my driving test, and on Valentine's Day Gene gave me my first car, a Pontiac convertible, blue and white and beautiful.

Gene started rehearsing. I started reading books on child care. I settled on Gesell and Ilg as my bible. I was so pleased with myself and my body doing this wonderful thing that I decided two things. First, that I didn't want to miss the great moment of birth, so there would be no anesthetic. There was no such thing as "natural childbirth" then, but I somehow felt connected to all the other women in the world who had babies in fields and forests. I don't know, perhaps the idea came from my political feelings. And second, that I would take care of my child myself. There would be no nanny. I think this was my first grown-up, independent, responsible move; I hate to admit it, but it was unique, the only one for quite a few years.

There were new friends: Ethel and Saul Chaplin, Fay and Michael Kanin, Marcia and Norman Panama, Jessica Tandy and Hume Cronyn, Lena Horne and Lennie Hayton, Phil Silvers, Evie and Keenan Wynn. And there were old friends from New York. Lloyd Gough arrived to live in Los Angeles with Karen Morley; Betty Comden, Adolph Green, and Judy Holliday came to do their show at the Trocadero on Sunset Boulevard. Elliot Reid, known as Ted, a young actor, became one of my closest friends. Signed by MGM were Hugh Martin and Ralph Blane, the composers of *Best Foot Forward,* Van Johnson, and Stanley Donen—who practically lived with us.

We started having a kind of open house every Saturday night. The big, black, cheerful Mamie, our housekeeper, cooked up a storm. I'd say what we'd like to eat. Mamie would say what she wanted to cook. She knew much more than I did about entertaining, and since she did the shopping, we always ended up with her splendid menus. The friends who wanted to be in the Ping-Pong tournament arrived about five-thirty. It was deadly serious. If we played doubles, Gene and I won more often than not. Then there was eating and drinking leading up to "the Game." Our version was a racing version of charades. Two opposing captains—usually Gene and me, because the others claimed that if we were on the same team, we were unbeatable—chose up sides. Someone made a list of twenty quotations, sayings, titles of films or books, lyrics, puns, headlines, anything at all. (David Selznick once came with a prepared list of medical terms—he was as fiercely competitive as we were.) The list maker sat in the hall; the teams were in separate rooms. The captains got the first clue together, and raced to act it out for their own team. Whoever guessed it would race back for the next clue. We ran and screamed and shouted, tempers were lost, we occasionally collapsed on the floor laughing.

And then came my favorite thing of all, the only thing I miss from my years in Hollywood other than my friends. Usually Saul Chaplin, or sometimes Hugh Martin or Lennie Hayton, would sit at Yip Harburg's piano and play. For hours. We shared the bench and stood around them belting out Gershwin show tunes or *Porgy and Bess* or Cole Porter or Johnny Mercer or Harold Arlen songs. Sometimes Gene would dance; if Judy was there, she might sing. Ted Reid would give in to requests and become his funny but seriously brilliant Russian director or Mexican peasant or hick American. We'd eat and drink wine and laugh and sing until a glass of milk and Oreos for all at one or two in the morning.

When L. B. Mayer saw the rushes of *For Me and My Gal,* and at the insistence of Arthur Freed (who produced the best musicals at MGM, where the best musicals were made), Metro negotiated with David Selznick to buy out the rest of his contract with Gene. I give the credit to Arthur Freed, because when L. B. Mayer saw Gene in *Pal Joey,* he said, "Too short, too sexy, not sympathetic, not for us." Objectively (or perhaps impertinently), I think he was confusing the role with the personality. (Some talent scout had earlier sent a report about Fred Astaire. He was "balding, not sexy, not for us"— another great star spotter.)

Contrary to L. B. Mayer's opinion, I found my husband very sympathetic. Gene was a wonderful father-to-be, tender, jokey, protective, loving, and interested. David Selznick, who was now a friend rather than a boss, had been present at the birth of his son. Gene and I debated—no, debated is the wrong word—we *discussed* this possibility. I was so euphoric I couldn't debate; I had no arguments; I was agreeable to anything.

As to Mayer's other comments, "sexy"—even "too sexy"—is good, and "short" is debatable. Gene was five foot nine. When I met him, I was five foot five—quite tall for a chorus dancer. But I was still growing. At the doctor's office I discovered that I was now five foot six and a half inches. Add three-inch heels, and I was no longer looking up to Gene. I liked looking up to him, and it was better for photographs. So with the excuse of pregnancy, I sadly put my high heels in the back of the closet. It was flats and sneakers from then on. I think Gene noticed, although it was never mentioned. I know he was glad. He was too independent and serious an artist to consciously want to conform to the conventional image of a male movie star, but I think he liked me to look up to him—

actually and metaphorically. Perhaps it was even a necessary element for us as a couple.

And as a couple we were sailing before the breeze on blue water with no rough seas. I was taking to California life like the proverbial duck.

Beverly Hills was a village then. Rodeo Drive had a grocery store, a bookshop, a dry cleaner, a shoe repair shop, a drugstore, a hairdresser—just like Anderson Avenue in Cliffside. I drove everywhere in bare feet, blue jeans, and one of Gene's shirts. There were no parking meters and only about six policemen. I soon knew them all by being caught not quite stopping at the stop signs. With my red hair and the Irishness of the name Kelly on my license, I was only ever scolded and waved off with a smile. I never got a ticket. Most mornings I drove to the beach at Santa Monica. I'd walk on the sand at the edge of the waves, dabbling my feet, swinging my arms about for exercise. For a couple of hours alone I'd dream about my baby. Occasionally a wisp of thought would stray into my head that someday I'd be an important actress with my own theater doing important plays to change the world. But for the moment I reveled in my expanding body and the grandeur of the Pacific.

My mother came to see us for the Easter holiday. I'd spoken to her on the phone at Christmas, on her birthday and mine, and when I knew I was pregnant, but the long-distance phone call was still rare in those days. She wrote to me, and I scribbled notes back. Now she was there. Her joy shone from her eyes—the house, Mamie, my car, my whole life was what she'd always wanted for me. I was so healthy, Gene was so happy and always so sweet to her. We took her everywhere, the best restaurants, the commissary at MGM for lunch. She met the movie stars. But what she liked best was to be in my nice clean house, to check the linen closet, to give Mamie her recipes for angel food cake and applesauce and to find something that needed to be done. My friends remember her always with busy hands. On this first visit they were knitting baby blankets. It was agreed that she would take a leave of absence from School No. 6 and come back on October 1 and stay through Christmas. Our baby was due in the second week of October. I was delighted with this plan. It's only now that I realize that the two grown-ups in my life—my mother and my husband—made the plan and presented it to me, tentatively, of course. Would I like it? Metro would arrange the train tickets. (Since it was wartime, their influence was useful.) Gene would make sure my mother had enough money. Wouldn't it be easier and fun for me? "Yes," I said. "Great." And it was. She never intruded, she just quietly watched over me and reassured and helped me, as she'd always done.

On October 14, the doctor called to say I would go into the Good Samaritan Hospital the evening of the fifteenth. I was due, and there was a bed free. The hospitals were all full because of the war, but he had managed to get me a room. He'd give me an injection to induce labor on the morning of the sixteenth.

I hugged Mamie and kissed my mother good-bye. She would be coming to the hospital in the morning when Gene went to the studio. Gene and I took my already packed little suitcase and set off on my big adventure. I got into my hospital bed. We played Battleship for about an hour, then we talked, then Gene sang me a couple of songs. The nurse brought us a cup of tea. We said good night and lots of other nice things. I felt wonderful. I think I fell asleep happy before he'd left the room.

October 16—B-DAY—Big, Beautiful Day—Baby Day. Betsy's Best Day. At seven the doctor dropped in, gave me my injection, and said he'd see me later. The nurses prepared me. In those days that meant an enema and the shaving of the pubic hair. I didn't even mind those two horrible things. I was irrepressible. When my mother arrived, I announced that just as Queen Wilhelmina of Holland had declared her hospital room in Montreal part of the Netherlands so her baby would be Dutch, I was declaring my hospital room to be New York. I thought it was a more glamorous place to be born. (Actually, for the first few years in Hollywood I lied, saying *I* was born in New York, not in laughable New Jersey.) I couldn't stay on my bed. I was practically dancing around my mother. A nurse suggested maybe I should rest up, but I couldn't sit still. I was too excited; I felt too good. At noon the waters broke. I'd

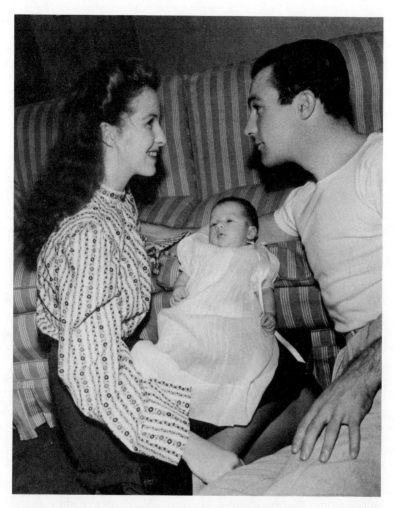

With our baby, Kerry, 1942

read so many books I knew all about it, but the great warm gush was still surprising. Now I was willing to do as I was told. The contractions started. At two o'clock I was transferred to a curtained cubicle by the delivery room with my mother holding my hand. When the doctor came to check my dilation, I whispered urgently, "Get my mother out of here." It wasn't that I wanted to be alone; I just wanted to concentrate on what was happening. Even more, I wanted to feel free to yell or cry when it hurt, and I couldn't in front of her. On his next visit the doctor said I was doing well. He'd call Gene to give him time to get to the hospital and get gowned up. The doctor was not enthusiastic about the father being present at the birth, but Gene was determined.

Soon I was in the delivery room. It all started to go very fast. I was working hard. The great moment came at four o'clock. I saw our precious daughter in the doctor's hands, and I didn't exactly faint—I sort of went absent. I don't know exactly what happened. As I was wheeled into the hall, Gene arrived, running. He'd missed the birth, but he could hear me saying, "I want Gene—I want Gene," over and over as I came back. And then there was our perfect little girl, strong and round. Gene was wild with joy. My mother had a new love in her life, "my daughter's daughter—my baby's baby." I was Queen of the May in their eyes. As for me, I just thought, "I did it, I really did it—I made this miracle and she's real," just exactly like every other mother in the world, I suppose. We named her Kerry.

Now we were three. Gene was fast becoming a movie star. Kerry couldn't come to film premieres or nightclubs, but apart from those rare occasions, we went everywhere together. When Gene was rehearsing or shooting, I'd take Kerry, in her laundry basket padded and gingham-lined by my mother, to the beach or a friend's house or to the studio for lunch. She came to dinner parties with us, to a cabin at Big Bear Lake, to New York in the spring. My mother brought the old crib down from the attic for her so Gene and I could go to the theater and dance around the city again. I couldn't bear not to see her for more than one night, although I knew she was perfectly cared for by my mother. But I remember when she woke up at night and I sat by her crib singing her to sleep, I would solemnly promise my four-month-old infant never to live my life through her, to let her go when she grew up. It was a secret, obliquely critical thought about my mother. Perhaps it was harsh. After all, I had taken and was taking everything she gave me. And she gave me so much. I still treasure the black and white school

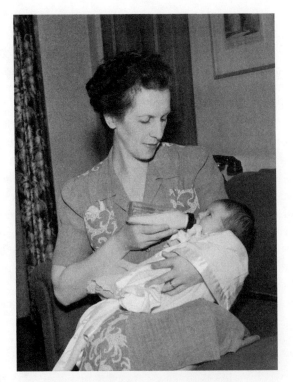

My mother, Frederica, from then on called
"Nana," with my daughter, Kerry

exercise book she lovingly wrote out and filled with household
hints and recipes: how to make furniture polish (you boil linseed
oil); never put anything you've worn *even once* away in mothballs.
And the recipes—Christmas cookies, the best birthday cake,
brownies, lemon snow, and, of course, applesauce. No soups, no
stews, no macaroni and cheese, no roasts or vegetables. Nothing
everyday, only happy frivolous food. Was it how she saw me, or was
it a reflection of what she wanted for me?

And how did Gene see me? He treated me like a little angel, like
his beloved playmate to share his bed and his life—and perhaps like
the eldest daughter in a motherless house. We had charge accounts
everywhere now, the department stores, the bookshop, the grocery

store, the gas station, the drugstore, and the dry cleaners. We had a joint checking account where there was one hundred dollars spending money for me every week. From being a good little squirrel putting half my salary in the bank when I was working in New York, I quickly developed the knack of never thinking about money at all. Gene paid the bills, Gene took care of everything.

There was one occasion when he questioned an account from I. Magnin. I'd been shopping with Jeannie Coyne. Jeannie had been a student at Gene's dancing school in Johnstown, and she came to New York to start her career just in time to replace me in the chorus of *Panama Hattie.* When MGM decided to put some dancers under contract for their musicals, Stanley Donen and Jeannie were among them. These coincidences conspired to make us friends, but the true basis of our friendship was her lovely, straightforward, funny, self-deprecating personality. She was a year older, and we looked a bit alike. She was shorter and rounder and not as pale, but our hair was the same color and we had "Irish kissers"—in her case legitimately.

One day we both fell in love with a gray cashmere turtleneck pullover at I. Magnin. It was too expensive for her, so naturally I bought two, one for each of us. Gene happened to notice and dared to ask "Why two?" I somehow didn't want to be questioned; I blurted out, "What happened to the $1,800 I saved in New York? I suppose it just got mixed in with all the other money." That made him laugh, but as I remember he never again questioned a bill.

So I had no responsibilities except the one I'd chosen—taking care of Kerry. And even that wasn't a responsibility, but a joy. It may have taught me a few things. For instance, it was only for her I was on time. No that's not exactly true—I was always very professional for work. But that was like being a good girl in the school where your mother is a teacher—it was necessary. For the rest, I was carefree and careless. But I loved having a little girl. I know now that it was the most wonderful thing of all, that I was exceptionally lucky. I didn't have to wash the clothes or cook dinner, or even do the grocery shopping. I could play with her, laugh and chat with her, go to the beach or roller-skate with her, take a nap when she did.

But now it's time to give my darling daughter her right to privacy. Her birth may have been mine, but her childhood, with all the stories I could tell, most definitely belongs to her. I'm full of admiration and proud of her for how she coped during her years with us. To have a famous father, to be a little kid and live in the public eye because of his success, is not an easy ride. Many a good child has fallen by the wayside under this pressure. But as Kerry grew up, she managed to keep the gaiety, the knowledge, the advantages she undoubtably had, and yet to make a completely independent life of her own. Her family, the wonderful Dr. Jack Novick and their three children, and her profession—psychoanalysis—must both be accorded privacy.

She was always central to our happiness, and for me she was, and is, a profound joy.

10

CALIFORNIA sunshine and flowers, a great daughter, a happy house overflowing with love and fun and friends, and no worry about money—all this stemmed from Gene's work.

It's a kind of miracle when everything comes together in one person at exactly the right time. From the beginning in New York, Gene had a clear idea of what he wanted to achieve, but I don't think even he realized how far he would go.

You take a young man with big ideas from a working-class neighborhood; then you add his gifts—perfect rhythm, boundless energy in an athletic body, musicality, imagination and humor, and, since we're talking about the movies, sexiness and charm. Then add his character—hardworking and confident. And finally you mix in the unique ingredient, the one that makes all the difference—his unparalled ability to use his own life experience and communicate it to the whole world through dance.

Then, at the right time, you put this particular young man at the right studio, Metro-Goldwyn-Mayer. There, in the 1940s, under Arthur Freed, musicals are flourishing. The best composers are writing great songs. Young, original screenwriters like Comden and Green are enlisted, and directors like Vicente Minnelli and George Sidney are at work.

And then there was Judy Garland. She wanted Gene to play opposite her in *Me and My Gal.*

And when all this happens at once you get a movie star—not just any old star, but the one that was Gene Kelly.

The Revuers: Judy Holliday, Alvin Hammer, Adolph Green,
and Betty Comden, 1940

Many distinguished judges have written discerningly, apprecia-
tively—and critically—of Gene's work: Arlene Croce, Pauline Kael,
John Updike. There will surely be others over the years. But I'm not
one of them. I just thought he was great. Maybe I was like the baby
duck that follows and is fascinated by the first creature it lays eyes
on, whether it be a man or the momma duck. In my case, it was the
man—and the choreographer and the dancer. And obviously, I
wasn't alone. There were millions of people who agreed.

But I was there next to him. I was fortunate enough to share that
time. And what I know, that's perhaps not obvious from seeing him
in the movies, is how serious he was. He managed somehow, with
all the fun and games, to focus fiercely on his work. I think now
that his work was never out of his mind. I have no idea if this is
good or bad (perhaps those words don't apply and shouldn't be used

about a creative person), but I think now—forty years after I left his world—that for Gene his work was the most important part of his life. This is not in any sense a complaint.

In the beginning, under contract to David Selznick, when everything was new to both of us, we were in it together. I don't mean that I went to his dialect coach with him or sat in at meetings with his agent, but we visited cutting rooms and went to watch the shooting of several movies. We read and reread *The Keys to the Kingdom* (supposed to be his first film) and discussed it. Every day we did a "barre," the regular warming-up and stretching routine of ballet dancers in Gene's rehearsal room at the Selznick Studio, and then we horsed around tap-dancing.

I think we saw every movie that came out, sometimes in a screening room at a studio or at some executive's house. But Gene preferred to "go to the flicks." He wanted to sit in the theater in the dark with everyone else and experience the public reaction and his own. He was learning every minute. I'm writing here about our honeymoon phase in the tiny house in Laurel Canyon.

But there were changes acomin'. Gene went to MGM, I was pregnant, we moved to Beverly Hills. We had a housekeeper, and I had my own car. I didn't think of any of this as change. It seemed to me to be the natural progression of our life. I guess it's true of all "firsts"—the first time you're in love, the first job, the first trip, and the first success. There is nothing to compare them to, so they seem natural and inevitable.

And perhaps they were. Given our characters, and the circumstances we found ourselves in, I don't, even now, see any alternative. As with all things, we had to grow and change.

Gene did his growing in his work. His character was already fixed in concrete. I did mine in every direction *except* my work. I never lost my dream of becoming a serious actress, but the time for that was not now. Now was the time for having a baby, for loving Gene, for learning. If I'd been at a university or trekking the ancient Silk Route from China, I don't think I could have learned more. I'd always been a reader. I was the cliche of the flashlight under the covers and books at the top of my Christmas list. Now with

Gene—and my political ideas—to guide me, I was ready to absorb everything.

And there was this new life jam-packed with variety. We were invited by Norma Shearer to a formal dinner at her house. The other guests were all elegant members of the royalty of Hollywood: Claudette Colbert and her husband, Dr. Pressman; Kendall and Lewis Milestone; Mr. and Mrs. Charles Boyer; David Niven and his wife; and us. We were the new kids in town. After dinner Norma Shearer asked me if I wanted "to powder my nose." I said, "No, thank you, I'm fine." "Do come along," she insisted charmingly. "No," I smiled, holding Gene's hand. "I'll stay with Gene." Then I caught on—the ladies were "retiring" while the men had brandy and cigars. I would have given in, but by now Gene gave my hand a squeeze and sat me in a chair. I hadn't meant to be rebellious, I sort of fell into it. But Gene loved it. He never wanted to be anything but what he was. He had no pretensions, no "society" aspirations. And if his child bride voiced bumptious left-wing opinions, wasn't smothered in lipstick and false eyelashes, and made a social gaffe by not retiring with the ladies, that was just fine.

Now, more than fifty years later, it's strange trying to disentangle my memories from my feelings and the idea I then had of myself. When my daughter was sixteen, and later when my granddaughters were sixteen, I would sometimes look at them in amazement. Each one was lovely, and it was clear they would grow up to be fine women. But it was also clear that the growing up was still to be done.

So what were we doing, Gene and I? I guess it's true that he couldn't "leave me at the mercy of New York." He fell in love with me. I think he wanted to protect me, but also, in a way, to "create" me. He wanted to have and keep forever the girl I was, shaped by his care and love. Sure I was pure and idealistic and loving and cheerful, but I was also a snippy kid, rebellious and confident and ambitious. I now think that because of the power of his personality, the love between us and the joy of having Kerry, and because of the dream-made-reality of our life, something happened. Betsy Boger/Blair, the reckless redhead, went into happy quiescence. I

MGM lot, 1940

was delighted to be taken care of, spoiled, adored. I spent my adolescence as a married woman and was completely happy. And the inevitable forces of nature, growth and rebellion, were postponed. But they came later.

For now there was MGM. It was a ten-minute drive, in those happy traffic-less days, from Beverly Hills to Pico Boulevard, past Twentieth Century–Fox to Culver City. And there was Metro—a metropolis of its own. I felt that I was part of it through Gene, and it was thrilling. From the first day, we could drive onto the lot. The uniformed man at the gate waved us down, holding his list. "Mr. Kelly? Welcome to MGM. I'm Jim. Is this Mrs. Kelly? Hi, Mrs. Kelly. Your bungalow is straight ahead, just after Stage 7, across from the makeup department."

The bungalow was like an upmarket motel, living room with a sleeping alcove, kitchenette, bath, and dressing room. It was decorated tastefully but anonymously in desert colors, lots of wood and beige plaid couches. Stage 7 and all the other great soundstages had heavy double doors with red lights to signal "No Entry—Shooting," and inside a labyrinth of cables and arc lights, the gantries way up under the roof, pulleys to "fly" scenery or hoist it around, and a sound booth. The solidity of these structures, the industrial power they seemed to represent, was awesome. We could observe this reality but in truth, we were joyfully dancing around below the surface, let loose in our imaginations to all our childhood memories. Here we were, in the very birthplace of *The Wizard of Oz, Camille, Grand Hotel, Andy Hardy,* and all the way back to *Ben-Hur.*

We explored the vast acres. We drove to the back lot, with its giant cycloramas, its artificial lake, its city streets and country towns and Western saloons. There was a section the size of a city block filled with freestanding staircases leading nowhere except to the sky—it was Daliesque and fantastic.

The "Writers' Building"—a whole building just for writers— was a small office block with a writer or two in every room. At any one time there were about fifty of them working away on original screenplays or on adaptations of books, or plays, or old movies that MGM already owned.

The great hairdresser Sydney Guilaroff, a tall, slim, attractive man, was the uncrowned king of MGM's makeup and hairdressing department. He ruled with gentle charm and intelligence—and, of course, his talent. And all the stars adored him.

Music, costumes, editing, sound, camera equipment, lights, storerooms for furniture, artwork, chandeliers and lamps of all periods—projection theaters, big and small—everything had its own space. There was a reference library, a schoolhouse for child actors, rehearsal rooms, dressing rooms for actors, communal ones for the extras and bungalows for the stars. Tucked away behind the stages were small studios for voice and singing coaches, a diction and dialect teacher, and the still photographers.

The executive dining room served L. B. Mayer's special chicken soup every day and catered his birthday party every year, where each employee—above a certain standing—made a command appearance. (It was at one of these parties that I saw June Allyson, fast becoming a star at MGM, perched on Arthur Freed's knee saying, "Uncle Arthur, do I have to pay income tax?") The commissary was more fun because everyone ate there. I wonder whether there has ever been another restaurant like it, where some diners are in black tie and evening dresses, others in cowboy outfits or Gay Nineties bustled gowns, and still others in tights and sweatshirts and tap shoes.

And all this was to be Gene's playground and workplace for the next fifteen years.

Me and My Gal, Gene's first movie, was a combined show biz and World War I story. The man Gene played had elements of his character in *Pal Joey.* A singer and dancer, devious and ambitious, he crushed his hand with the lid of a trunk to evade going into the army. It was a daring scene, especially in 1942, during the war. The audience gasped, and the wonderful, lush MGM film music swelled. And we, the irreverent New Yorkers, sang to ourselves, "Coward, I love you." Of course, the character saw the light and did his bit for his country and was redeemed in the end. Judy Garland's character could love him again; they could sing and dance into the sunset. It was a lively, charming picture with some light and shadow, and wonderful performances from Judy and Gene. The public really took to this "new face," with its hairline scar across the cheek. Over the years there were many stories about that scar, which had actually come from an ordinary fall in childhood. His fans invented more glamorous causes, and I'm sure the MGM publicity department didn't discourage them.

In the late 1940s and early '50s, the postwar years of growth and optimism, it was the general policy of the Hollywood machine to suffuse the world with a rose-tinted vision of life. With a few exceptions—Garbo, Dietrich, Crawford, who carried the mystery and glamour of the more dramatic 1930s with them—we were all the "boy and girl next door," clean-cut, faithful, hardworking simple folk. Harmless items for the gossip columnists were supplied, interviews for fan magazines were written at the studio, still photographs were churned out and disseminated.

No one questioned all this. It was considered, I think rightly, to be part of the actor's job, his obligation even, to cooperate in creating interest and excitement. Jimmy Stewart was once asked by an English journalist why he was granting him an interview. Mr. Stewart replied, "Well, it's all part of this ball game I'm playing in, son." For the studio that paid you, for your own name, and for the specific film you were in, you went where you were sent—to New York or Chicago for an opening, to interviews at the studio, at home, or even at Louella Parsons's house. (Parsons was one of the two most frightening columnists in Hollywood. The other was Hedda Hopper, who was even more despicable because she was so reactionary.) And you had to be charming to them. In a way, it was fun. Even Gene and I, who would seem in ourselves to be everything the studio wanted, went along with some fakery. For instance, we were photographed in the kitchen, with Kerry on Gene's knee and me at the stove pretending to cook in an apron borrowed from our housekeeper.

And the studio protected its own. We've all now read about the arrests for brawling or drunken driving that were hushed up at the time, and more serious offenses that were "fixed." I can't say that in those days I knew about any of them. Besides I was so innocent that when I heard a bit of scandal about a threesome in bed involving a star I'd had a crush on in high school, I didn't believe it. He was always cast as a fine, well-bred, honorable young man—the kind your mother likes. And when I sat next to him at a dinner party and looked at his lovely face, I *knew* it wasn't true. It seemed too bizarre to be possible—at least to the girl I was. I'd actually sat next to him once before, when I was thirteen, in the coffee shop at Rockefeller Center in New York. He was at the counter reading a script when I came in. I slid onto the stool next to him and ordered what he was eating, a glass of fresh orange juice and a toasted English muffin. He didn't see or hear me, but I didn't care. I wouldn't have been able to speak if he'd noticed me. But here in Hollywood I could speak to any old movie star. After all, my own husband was one of them.

After *For Me and My Gal*, MGM cast Gene in two nonmusical films—sort of B movies. "Program pictures," they were called. In

Judy and Gene rehearsing *For Me and My Gal*

those good old days there was a double bill from Thursday to Sunday and another from Sunday to Wednesday. So each studio had to supply their own chain of movie houses with four films every week. Perhaps the powers that be were biding their time to see how the public reacted to Gene. Perhaps they were trying him out as a straight actor, or maybe they were just getting their money's worth—if he's being paid, he should be working.

Gene took on these assignments wholeheartedly. In the first one, *Pilot #5,* he costarred with Marsha Hunt and Franchot Tone. They were good actors, and intelligent and cultured. Gene was enjoying himself and learning. He began to see why the camera was where it

Jean-Pierre Aumont, Gene, Donald Curtis, and
Jack Lambert in *The Cross of Lorraine*, 1942

was, and he talked to me about his excitement when he understood
how the camera captured what the director wanted the audience to
see at each moment, and how a shot was framed so it would express
atmosphere and emotion. I think it was during this film, when he
wasn't dancing, that he formed the notion that dance should be
shot, almost exclusively, in full figure; that is, the dancers should be
seen from head to toe. He admired Busby Berkeley, but mechanical
images of a hundred legs revolving on platforms making patterns
didn't interest him personally. He had quite other plans.

His next film, *The Cross of Lorraine,* was a French Resistance
story. Directed by old-timer Tay Garnett, it was tight and fast moving. Tay was a gentleman-adventurer filmmaker, a sort of forerunner of John Huston. He stressed the importance of the scenario, the
camera work, and the acting. He put directing in fourth place—but
that may have been a charming pose. He kept his professional eye
and a tight rein on everything. And he cast an outstanding group of
actors. This little movie had, besides Jean-Pierre Aumont and Gene

Gene swashbuckling in *Dubarry Was a Lady* with Lucille Ball

as the leads, a list of great actors: Peter Lorre, Hume Cronyn, Richard Whorf, Sir Cedric Hardwicke, and Joseph Calleia.

Gene was in two more musicals in 1943, *Dubarry Was a Lady* and *As Thousands Cheer.* In the first he got to swashbuckle like his adored Douglas Fairbanks. He swung from elegant draperies and leapt onto balconies while fencing his way out of life-threatening predicaments, either to save a fair maiden or defend his king. But even here, in the French court, beautifully presented by the art department of Metro, he had a trace of the street kid about him. Perhaps that's what the public responds to most, why they create a star. They seem to like to be able to "recognize" the person behind the role. No matter how good the acting—think of Bette Davis in *Jezebel* or *Mrs. Skeffington*—the audience that is carried away by the performance will talk afterward about proud Bette Davis, who defied Henry Fonda and wore a red dress to the virginal white-dress ball, or who, after mistreating Claude Rains, was spared the humiliation of growing old in his eyes, when he went blind. They don't talk about the character, but about Bette.

It seems amazing now, when it takes two to three years to get a movie together, to raise the money, cast it, find a director, and then shoot, edit, score, and market it, that by September 1943, Gene had five movies under his belt.

And with the Metro publicity department's work, Gene was beginning to be popular and recognized wherever we were. It didn't seem to affect us personally, either his ego or my pride. I don't think either of us took it very seriously yet. It was just exciting and fun. Gene Kelly fan clubs started to spring up, with encouragement and a lot of goodies from Metro. If a fan club had ten members, MGM would send them ten portfolios of photos, including one that was "personally" signed by Gene—except that it wasn't. Someone at the studio would do it for him, as they did for all the stars. They'd also send a small poster from a film and ten sample-size records of the songs from *For Me and My Gal,* and potted biographies and newsy little stories that they made up.

At the studios in Hollywood, and in the head offices back in New York, Gene's star was rising. Columbia "borrowed" him from Metro for *Cover Girl,* to costar with the beautiful Rita Hayworth.

The actor—the "property"—that was borrowed and loaned never knew in those days what the deal was. Did extra money, above the star's salary, change hands? Were there trade-offs earlier or later of other stars in other films? Was it a system of favors done and markers called in? Whatever the facts were, *Cover Girl* was an excellent move for Gene. It had songs by Ira Gershwin and Jerome Kern, it was directed by Charles Vidor, and Gene would choreograph his own numbers. And there was Rita Hayworth, with Phil Silvers as their pal.

Rita was sensational and sexy in the movies, but in real life she

Rita Hayworth, Gene, Charles Vidor, the director,
and Phil Silvers on the set of *Cover Girl*

was sweet and gentle, soft-spoken and polite—and very beautiful in both. Her love affair with Orson Welles was at its height; they were married right after the shooting of *Cover Girl*. Gene said she worked like a trouper. She had originally been a dancer and had a very individual and feminine grace and style.

It was on *Cover Girl* that Gene and Stanley Donen first worked together. Stanley had been in the chorus of *Pal Joey*, where Gene was the star, and again in *Best Foot Forward*, where Gene did the choreography. He was a very attractive figure, eager to learn, ambitious and funny. And he had become our close and dear friend, an intimate in our household. Although he had an apartment of his

Michael Kidd, Gene, and Stanley Donen,
during *It's Always Fair Weather,* 1955

own, he practically lived with us, so much so that George Cukor
once asked, "Who is that young man who's always asleep on your
floor?"

Stanley had been among the dancers put under contract by
Metro and brought to California to dance in their musicals. When
the studio tried to use him and some other dancers as extras, he
refused. He was "suspended"—that is, he would not be paid, but
until his contract ran out he belonged to them—he couldn't work
anywhere else. It was an iniquitous system much hated by one and
all. When Warner Brothers tried to add "suspension" time to the
end of Olivia de Haviland's seven-year contract, she took them to
court and won the case for herself and all the other actors.

Now, for *Cover Girl*, Gene asked Stanley to be his assistant choreographer. It wasn't only a friendly gesture. The main reason was that Gene knew and liked him; he considered Stanley bright and talented, and recognized that he would need him behind the camera when he was performing his own dances for the first time onscreen. Of course, Gene was the central creative force in this initial collaboration, but he was always generous about Stanley's contribution. And when it came to the innovative "alter ego" number in *Cover Girl*, where there were two Genes onscreen dancing together and in counterpoint, chasing each other, leaping over each other, illuminating the inner conflict of Gene's character, it would have been impossible to achieve the intricate timing and technical skill to make it all work without Stanley—or at least someone with exactly his qualifications.

After the war Gene and Stanley codirected two of Gene's best films, *On the Town* and *Singin' in the Rain*. Looking at their work together, you can see that they must have been really good collaborators. Stanley went on in his career and made some wonderful films of his own. Unfortunately, and mysteriously for me, Stanley, over the years, has been less than gracious about Gene. As someone who was there during that early period, and as his fellow student at "Kelly University," I find myself surprised and bemused. Ah well—never mind.

II

GENE WAS GOING into the navy—six weeks of boot camp at San Diego, then wherever they sent him. He didn't want to be in the film unit or the entertainment group. His brother Fred was one of the stars of *This Is the Army,* but he'd been drafted and found his way to the show on his talent alone. Gene was afraid Metro would pull strings to protect their property. He didn't want that; he wanted to do his bit like everyone else.

Our housekeeper Mamie was going to work in a munitions factory. As soon as we knew that Gene would be stationed on the East Coast for officer training, Kerry and I were off to New Jersey to my mother to be near him. Suddenly we were back in real life.

And back in real life, and in my old room so near New York, I started to think about acting, about the theater. I can look back now and see that my attitude to the movies was probably defensive. The logic I had constructed was that it was all right for Gene to be under contract to a studio because he was a great artist with a mission that could be fulfilled only on the screen. But I couldn't be a contract player, a "starlet," that belittling word, because I was to be a great actress with my own theater. "Vainglorious" must be the word for Betsy at that time. I'd been in my high school play, I'd said "Hello, sailor" in *Panama Hattie,* and I'd played one role on Broadway for Bill Saroyan. But along with the lists of classic plays we must do that I was forever making up in my head, I also made up a rule: There would be no applause when I made my entrance. It would disturb the play! Vainglorious indeed—and foolish and pretentious. Fortunately, I managed to keep all this inside my head. (I can't think why I'm confessing it now!) There was another part of my brain that knew I had a tremendous amount of work to do just to become a good actress.

And then those angels smiled on me again. I was called to meet Tennessee Williams, Eddie Dowling, and Audrey Wood. Audrey Wood was Tennessee's agent, Eddie Dowling was directing Tennessee's new play, and Tennessee was Tennessee. I was asked to understudy Julie Haydon. The play was *The Glass Menagerie*.

I had seen Tennessee's second play on Broadway, *You Touched Me,* starring Montgomery Clift. I was so thrilled by the play and by Monty that I went backstage to see him. I smiled my way past the stage doorman and knocked on Monty's dressing room door. He never let me forget the first words I said to him: "I'm not a fan. I'm an actress. And I don't have designs on you. I'm married to a movie star—I'm married to Gene Kelly. I just think you're great and I wanted to tell you. Okay?" "Okay," he said solemnly, but his brilliant, intelligent eyes were laughing, and in a minute we were both giggling. He walked me to Forty-second Street, and I took the crosstown trolley to the ferry to go home to Cliffside. Later, when we became friends, he often teased me with, "You're the one who's not a fan, aren't you?" But of course I was a fan of his enormous talent and his unique and delicate nature—I loved him.

Now I was to be involved with the work of our country's greatest playwright. I was ready to say yes immediately. It seemed perfect to me, but I waited to ask Gene what he thought. He agreed. Kerry was safe at my mother's. I had to be at the theater just before eight, and I could leave at nine-thirty, if I didn't have to go on. As it turned out, I never went on. At least six or seven times I was made up and ready at eight-fifteen when Julie Haydon would rush in saying, "George [her boyfriend, the critic George Jean Nathan] says I have to go on," and she always did.

Laurette Taylor was the star of *The Glass Menagerie*. Laurette Taylor! I saw her, I knew her, I watched her, I listened to her, and I tried to understand her style of acting. At her insistence, there was

The great Laurette Taylor, who opened the door
and invited me into the world of serious acting

an understudy rehearsal every week. And it was in these rehearsals
that I started to learn my craft. She was a genius. Talent like hers
can't really be explained; it just leaps out like a flame. But I'll try.
Every moment of her performance was filled with her grace. She
was still but fluttering; she was real but intensely poetic; she was
tragic and comic; dark and light—dark with sadness and light with
gaiety. It was her ability to combine and glory in these contradictory elements that made her unique.

I've seen the actresses I've admired most—Maureen Stapleton,
Uta Hagen, and Kim Stanley—give wonderful performances with
many of these qualities. But the magic of Laurette Taylor lay in the
quicksilver flow of her emotions. She was sublime.

At this time, she was small and round. In life, she looked cozy.
Simone Signoret once said about herself, "I got old, not like an
actress, but like the postmistress." So did Miss Taylor. (I always

called her Miss Taylor, and no matter how friendly she was to me, she never said, "Call me Laurette.") But on rehearsal days she asked me to sit with her in her dressing room while she got ready to inhabit Amanda, her role. I don't think I understood a lot. I didn't know she sometimes drank too much. Watching from the wings I saw her leave in the middle of a scene, come offstage and throw up, and float right back into the play. The enchantment she cast was so strong that I don't think the audience was even aware that it had happened.

She told me stories about her childhood, about Hartley Manners, her playwright husband, and her theatrical adventures. At the height of her young career, the Moscow Art Theater, led by Stanislavsky himself, had come to New York. She was invited to play a benefit performance with them, she in English, the rest of the players in Russian. Stanislavsky rehearsed with her through an interpreter. In her words:

> He was very formal and correct. I was very impressed. I'd been told about his "Method," so I was trying to feel everything, to be truthful. I had a moment sitting at a table alone downstage where I had to pick up a bracelet, hold it up to the light and look at it, then put it down. As I said to Hartley that night, I was trying to convey my motivation, to express the character's feelings, so I was absolutely surprised when Mr. Stanislavsky stopped the rehearsal, came down the aisle to the footlights, and said through his interpreter, "Miss Taylor, pick up the bracelet slowly, hold it to the light and count—one—two—three—four—five—then slowly put it back on the table." Well, I didn't hold with that kind of acting by numbers, and Hartley said I should just do what I wanted to do, whatever I felt like doing. So the next day I did, and he stopped the rehearsal again at the same spot, walked down toward me, lifting his arm: "*Odin—dva—tre—cheteri—piat.*" He lowered his arm and said "That was exactly right, Miss Taylor—one—two—three—four—five." "I just smiled," she said, smiling at the memory.

Gene in uniform with his friend Russ Haydon

Gene was now a lieutenant in the U.S. Navy and very dashing in his uniform. We were together whenever it was possible. Sometimes he came to spend the night in Cliffside, sometimes we stayed in the Algonquin Hotel. The six weeks of boot camp was the longest separation between Kerry and her daddy—we were very lucky. The navy assigned him to the film unit at Anacostia, in Washington, D.C. He had fought against it—but go fight City Hall, or the Navy. They knew where they thought he'd be most useful. Kerry and I were going with him. He could live off the base, and there was a house for us in Georgetown.

I gave in my notice as understudy. It doesn't sound very important, being an understudy, even for a fine role in a great play. But it was a vital turning point for me. Rehearsing with Laurette Taylor and having the right and the freedom to be backstage, to watch, to listen and learn, gave me a proper approach to acting. Gone were the grandiose daydreams about my own theater. In their place was a new modesty and seriousness. For now I would read plays, and when the war was over I would study and work. After all, I knew how to work. I was a dancer, and dancers are of necessity disciplined.

Miss Taylor gave me a farewell and good-luck present, her own silver-handled rabbit's foot for applying rouge. I used it and treasured it for twenty years. Then I passed it on to a very talented young actress that I was close to and cared about. Her life went its own way out of the theater, so the rabbit's foot disappeared. But I remember it well.

12

OUR ELEGANT HOUSE in elegant Georgetown was infested with fleas. The previous tenants had a cat, and with no animal to feast on, the fleas attacked Kerry and me. In two days we were covered in huge red itchy welts from the knees down. The navy sent an exterminator to our rescue—just as MGM would have.

For the six months we were there, I kept house like a new bride. I burned biscuits, and I cried over lumpy gravy, but I managed. Gene got breakfast while I washed and dressed Kerry. Then he was off to work, and I was alone with my little girl. It was bliss. We did the grocery shopping, we went to the park and the swings, she rode her new tricycle, we read books and sang songs. Then we got ready for Gene to come home. I cooked simple meals with advice from my mother and the *Ladies Home Journal.* Gene always dried the dishes. When he invited someone from the base, I made chicken pie, topped with mashed potatoes—my pie crust was still prone to disaster.

Ensign Lois McClelland came into our lives and stayed forever. Tall and strong, with a great figure and a wide smile, Lois is gently spoken, loving, and loyal. She was also a very good secretary. The navy assigned her to Gene, and she quickly became a friend to all three of us.

Gene made several films for the navy. He acted in one, a sort of recruiting film. But he directed the second one, a semidocumentary about returning veterans who were war-shocked and mentally disturbed. He shot it in a naval hospital using the actual young men.

There was only one professional, Jocelyn Brando, Marlon's little sister and a fine actress herself. She played the sweetheart of one of the men. Gene's cameraman was named Arthur Napoleon, and there was many a joke about never giving his name while they were working in the hospital or he might never get out. They had their jokes, but they made a beautiful short movie. I haven't seen it since, but I remember it vividly. It was simple, compassionate, and hopeful. It was another side of Gene, and made us both believe that after the war he should try his hand at serious drama, both acting and directing. Of course, he couldn't give up dancing, nor did he want to. He hoped to do both. As it turned out, MGM had its own agenda—which didn't include drama. In 1945, when Elia Kazan sent Gene *Death of a Salesman* and asked him to play Biff, the oldest son, on Broadway, Gene was thrilled. Kazan was a fine director, the play was great, the role was demanding—what else could an actor ask? MGM knew what else: the "star" part. Their decision was that they would not release him from his contract, even for six months, to play "a secondary role in a new play." I'm afraid I don't believe there were any executives at MGM at that time who read that new play, *Death of a Salesman,* and understood that it would become a classic of the American theater. Gene accepted their decision, albeit with difficulty, because of the big plans being made for him at the Arthur Freed unit. Perhaps MGM was right in some way. Gene did produce some of his most brilliant work in the next ten years. But I think he always remembered, and regretted, that missed challenge.

After VE Day, there was great rejoicing. But now Gene was to get his wish. He was to go to the Pacific battleground to join a fighting unit. We packed up the house in Georgetown, and decided that Kerry and I would go back to Hollywood and wait for his return. I was to find us a house to buy and settle in. Lois left the navy to come with us to be Gene's secretary in peacetime. And for the next forty-five years she was and is still part of the family.

Kerry and I kissed Gene good-bye. He was being flown to San Francisco to await his orders. We took the train to Chicago, then on to Los Angeles. Someone from MGM met us and took us to the Beverly Hills Hotel. "The studio will take care of everything" had started again. In two weeks I found the house at 725 North Rodeo Drive that was to be Gene's home until he died. Johnny Darrow, who had been Gene's agent in New York and was now selling real estate, showed it to me. He was a clever and handsome fellow who didn't waste time on unsuitable houses. We'd only seen three when we walked into the old wooden New England–style farmhouse—it had actually been a farmhouse, and was one of the oldest houses in Beverly Hills. I knew it was for us. I'd been on the phone to Gene reporting everything, and when he heard my description and my enthusiasm, he said, "Go ahead." I wrote and signed the check for $42,500, and it was ours. I felt pretty important and grown-up. I was not yet twenty-two.

I bought sleeping bags, and Lois and Kerry and I moved in. We slept on the floor in the living room and acquired pots and pans and dishes and sheets and towels as we needed them. Johnny helped me find painters and carpenters, plumbers and electricians. Everything started getting done.

Then came August 6, 1945. We bombed Hiroshima, then Nagasaki. The war was over. Gene wasn't being shipped out, he was coming home to us. I burst into tears when I heard this—it was only then that I realized how frightened I had been.

I bought a great big bed and a Ping-Pong table. We'd given the first one away when we went back to the East Coast. I bought the furniture for Kerry's room. I bought a bed and a desk and a typewriter for Lois. Now everything moved brilliantly. Everything had an urgent purpose. I thought it was the best house in the world—and maybe it was, at least for us, since Gene thought so too. We painted the living room white and the front door red. That red front door became rather famous, because it was never locked until we went to bed. It was the outward sign of the inward grace that our years in that house acquired, mysteriously and without effort.

13

GENE WAS FLYING HIGH—up among the "stars." Kerry was healthy, serious, and adorable. I expected to get pregnant again—it never happened. I didn't worry about it, because I had all the time in the world. I was busy and happy.

There was a new housekeeper, Bertha. She was a round, cheerful, energetic woman, a great cook, and she loved Kerry. She and her husband, Irving, who worked in the post office, had a room and bath at the back of the house. Lois had a room and bath and office on the ground floor. Kerry's room, our room, and the guest room were upstairs. Living room, bar, dining room, den, breakfast room, kitchen, and laundry room: and there was the house. It was modest for Beverly Hills. In the garden were two enormous avocado trees, together giving about a hundred avocados, the bounty of California. When Gene broached the subject of a swimming pool, I was adamantly opposed. One avocado tree would have to go, and they wouldn't be able to cross-fertilize each other. The gardens on either side had pools we could surely use once we knew our neighbors, the beach was fifteen minutes away. I had lots of reasons, but the true one was my old promise to Lloyd Gough not to "go Hollywood." I knew Gene wasn't a "capitalist"—there was no "inherited wealth" (an evil thing, as I'd learned in my marxist classes). He earned his money by his labor, and I knew, better than anyone, how hard he worked. Sometimes I'd wake up at two or three in the morning and find his side of the bed empty. I'd go downstairs to see if he was okay, and there he'd be in the den, either sitting in his chair work-

Our farmhouse on Rodeo Drive, set among the fake French chateaux
and Colonial mansions

ing out a routine in his head, or on his feet, marking out a dance.
He had tremendous physical energy and verve, but I don't think I
truly understood then the enormous demands of the creative
process. And I don't think he wanted me to understand. He wanted
me to be joyful—and I was. He wanted me to have fun—and I did.
He wanted me to read books—and apart from Kerry that was my
greatest pleasure. He really always wanted me to be the carefree
sixteen-year-old he fell in love with—growing and learning, of
course, but still sweet, as in "sweet sixteen." I would joke about
going to "Kelly University," but it wasn't a joke, it was the truth.
The other undergraduate was Stanley Donen. We were both eager,
naive kids when he met us. It was Gene who showed us the way. He
gave both of us more, much more than a college education.

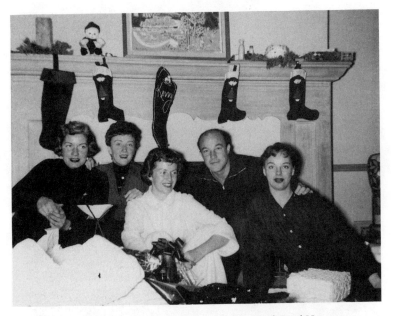

Lois McClelland, Jeannie Coyne, me, Gene, and Carol Haney
the year Kerry got a camera for Christmas, 1950

So I won the dispute about the swimming pool—we never had one. (He built one the year after I left Hollywood.) But I managed to keep my foolish left-wing promise. We had a volleyball court at the far end of the backyard instead.

The volleyball games were a fixture on Sunday at noon. They were serious, as were all the games we played. Saturday night had fallen into its prewar routine—Ping-Pong, drinks, supper, the Game, the piano, and the singing and dancing. There were usually eight or ten of us at the round table with the lazy Susan, and then it was "open house." We'd end up with twenty to twenty-five people. There were the regulars: Lois, Jeannie Coyne, Stanley Donen, Ted Reid, Hugh Martin, Saul and Ethel Chaplin, Lennie Hayton and Lena Horne, Phil Silvers. And there were new friends, Ruth and Richard Conte. He was a beautiful fellow, and Ruthie, who became my very best friend, small and ravishingly pretty with dark curls and wonderful warm, enquiring eyes that never missed a trick. I

My darling Ruth Conte with her husband, Richard, 1950

admired her before I loved her. She had a bohemian background. Her mother was an opera singer, playing small parts and singing at union meetings and bar mitzvahs. And Mischa (not Ruth's father but the man in her mother's life) was a violinist—all very romantic compared to Cliffside, New Jersey. Ruthie was progressive in her politics and very knowledgeable, but always charming and clear-headed in discussion. She was fun and cozy, but extremely sophisticated in my eyes. And she was Jewish. When I first arrived in New York I couldn't understand why *I* wasn't Jewish. This may sound silly, but it's true. There were all these exciting talented people with a history and a culture and a way of looking at the world, at art, and politics, and literature, with passion and humor. Ruthie was—and is—all these things, and I still love her.

Our life became normal. Well, for Hollywood, anyway, it was surprisingly normal—that is, normal rich. When Gene was rehearsing or shooting he was off to MGM in the morning. If not, he slept until noon. Kerry started nursery school. I was up with her, and when I'd dropped her off, I had three hours before collecting her. This was my reading time. Shakespeare, Chekhov, Ibsen, Odets, the Greeks, Molière, Pirandello—I hadn't forgotten the resolution I'd made during *The Glass Menagerie*. I read anything anyone suggested (and there were always lots of literary men ready to advise an eager young woman), Theodore Dreiser, Hemingway, Fitzgerald and Willa Cather, Colette and Tolstoy and Upton Sinclair. I bought *First Love* for the title and so discovered Turgenev by myself. I then ordered everything by him that was available. I was a voracious customer at Frances Hunter, the bookstore in Beverly Hills. I began to be aware of how lucky I was. I could buy any number of books and charge them to the account. I had hours to read, since I really only had to say what we should have for supper, and if I forgot to do it, the food appeared on the table as if by magic anyway. Lois and Bertha saw to that.

On Saturday, Gene and Kerry and I would do something together, the amusement park on Beverly Boulevard, the beach at Santa Monica, a bit of shopping for the house, the playground with swings, a friend's swimming pool, or we just might have a picnic in our own backyard. Gene was truly involved in all this, happy and at ease. I have since heard that he could be difficult and demanding at the studio—even dictatorial. I saw no trace of any of that. What I experienced was a man—the one I loved—who was flourishing and fulfilled. His excitement, his commitment to his work, and his pride in "my two girls," as he called us, were irresistible. Of course, life revolved around him, but somehow, without thought or consciousness, my independent spirit, the thing that made me break away from Cliffside, was stirring, putting down new roots, begin-

A family picnic with Gene and Kerry, 1951

ning to grow. Or maybe it was waking up after being dormant for a
few years.

I think I was staking a claim for my self, as a person apart from
Gene. The only outward manifestation of this was political. All my
left-wing ideas had come from Gene and his friends in New York,
from the marxist classes, from reading, and from the people I found
on the committees of the causes I worked for.

I worked for the Independent Progressive Party to elect Henry
Wallace as president. There were many of us, including other residents of Beverly Hills. But strangely, when I went to vote, I was the
only registered IPP voter on the electoral list in my district.

During the Sleepy Lagoon case, which led to what were called
the "Zoot Suit Riots" of 1942, Orson Welles called on Hollywood
names to support the Mexican community in downtown Los

Angeles. I was only a foot soldier, not a name, so for two weeks I rode the good old trolley from Beverly Hills all the way downtown. There, in a little storefront office, I addressed envelopes and made phone calls to ask for support and donations. I ate tortillas and beans and felt useful and good. One of my friends—a perfectly intelligent young woman—was amazed: "Is the trolley all right?" "Aren't you scared?" "Don't they all carry knives?" She believed what she read in the newspapers, which were completely irresponsible about the fear and hatred they were creating with their screaming headlines about rampaging violence on the streets. There was violence, but it wasn't between the so-called (by the journalists) "pachuco gangs," the young Mexicans in their zoot suits, their sharp Latino clothes. It was American sailors, soldiers, and marines versus the Mexican community. Our servicemen had a few nights out, fueled by beer, tequila, and racism. The original case was the murder of one boy found in a gravel pit, for which twenty-four fifteen- to nineteen-year-olds were arrested and tried. Nine were convicted and sent to prison. Two years later the appeals court overturned the conviction and released them. And the court reprimanded the judge who had presided over the trial for the "prejudice and hostility he had shown towards the defendants from the Barrios." In the riots, four Mexican-American boys were killed, and scores more were stripped naked and beaten up on the streets of LA. There was no investigation by the police or the military establishment into those deaths.

In such a dramatic and clear-cut case, I was forced to face the contrast between my life and what was happening outside it. I had always been aware of the fact that Gene and I, and everyone we knew, lived in a happy, safe, productive enclave. In Beverly Hills and Westwood we were like the British in Hong Kong, protected from the hardship and squalor just beyond our tree-lined streets.

A few years later I decided to join the Communist Party. Gene had never objected to any of my activities; he agreed with most of them, and he wouldn't have stood in my way. But now, fresh out of the navy, he said, "All regimentation is bad," and then, with a fond indulgent smile, "and you'll be the worst Communist in the world." I applied to my old mentor Lloyd Gough, in whose apartment in New York I'd attended the marxist classes. He took me for a drive in the Hollywood hills to break the news: "The Party has decided that it is not a good idea, because you are married to a very important man who is not a member." And he consoled me with, "You can be just as useful outside." I was disappointed, but I may have been slightly relieved. I was a bit nervous about my ability to submit to any kind of control. Perhaps Gene was right—he did know me better than anyone.

But Gene never turned into an anticommunist. He believed in unions, freedom of thought, social justice, and racial equality. He never wavered from his democratic principles. And he acted on his beliefs. He signed petitions after reading them thoroughly. He gave money. At the time of the Hollywood witchhunt, the Un-American Activities Committee, and the blacklist—the "McCarthy years"—he was solid. He went to Washington with the planeload of stars in support of the Hollywood Ten, and he didn't recant as Humphrey Bogart did. For quite a few years afterward Gene helped several of the blacklisted writers, giving money for their families and trying to get them jobs under the table.

In this connection, Jules Dassin, the blacklisted director who settled in Paris and made very good and successful films there, tells a story. Year after year at the Cannes Film Festival when Julie was winning prizes, all the Hollywood people shunned him and avoided having their picture taken with him. If caught by a photographer at the same table, they would hide behind their champagne glasses. Then he saw Gene and expected the same reaction. But Gene came after him, greeted him warmly, took his arm, and walked with him up the center of the big staircase of the Palais du Festival, among all the journalists and paparazzi—"the only one who had the guts," Julie said.

And guts and gusto he had in everything he did. The games—Ping-Pong, charades, volleyball—they were played and fought as full-bloodedly as he danced. And I was the same. I wonder now where my competitive zeal came from. Was it from my childhood with two older brothers, or the amateur shows that I soon wanted

The star-studded delegation of the Committee in Support of the
Hollywood Ten, in Washington, D.C. Also in the group were
Evelyn Keyes, Marsha Hunt, and Richard Conte. On their return to
Hollywood, Humphrey Bogart withdrew his support, saying, "I didn't
know some of them were Communists." Presumably Warner Brothers
threatened him, and his career came first.

to win? Or perhaps the lineup to get into the chorus? I imagine all
these things contributed, but the reason was more profound. These
were areas in which I *could* compete. My unconscious seems to have
a strong realistic streak, and I think it recognized that there was no
contest in the movies or the theater if Gene were the competition.

He would win. So I withdrew from that possible struggle without entering into it—or rather, without even being aware of it. I went quietly about my business of reading plays, and started to study at the Actors' Lab.

On the volleyball court, I decided after months of irritation that "they"—the men—were being unfair. In order to win they would cut in front of and steal the shot from any female teammate—except Lois, who was as tall and strong as any of them. Then they smashed the ball across the net to win the point. Again I withdrew—this time consciously. One of my best moves, as it turned out.

Like many children, I'd had moments of imagining that I didn't belong to my family, that I was a foundling. I was attracted to any foreignness I saw around me. The smell of oriental spices in the Orchanians' house across the street, and the fact that (even in snowy New Jersey) they pulled their curtains closed against the remembered noonday sun of Armenia, intrigued me. The Bottinellis, next door, had a lean-to in their backyard where their grapevine flourished. They made homemade wine, they drank it at suppertime, and then they would sing and dance to an accordion. I used to watch them on summer nights from my bedroom window and think maybe I was really Italian.

In Hollywood there were as many Europeans as even I could wish for. The famous directors—Lubitsch, Wilder, Mamoulian, Fritz Lang, Wyler—who came in the 1930s were making some of the best movies. Then there were the stars: Garbo, Dietrich, Anna Sten, Charles Boyer, Hedy Lamarr, Ingrid Bergman. There was an enormous English colony. At Rodeo Drive we had the French. I don't know how it started, but I certainly encouraged it. The Bernheim brothers, Michel and Alain, were soon regular visitors. Michel had been a director in France before the war. He was taken prisoner by the Germans, escaped from a POW camp, miraculously walked across Europe, and managed to get on a boat for the United States from Portugal. *Life* magazine ran a story about his journey, and Warner Brothers signed him to a contract, sight unseen. All his energy now was devoted to getting his mother out of occupied

France to join him and his kid brother in America. He succeeded somehow, and Madame Bernheim, as we always called her, made a small corner of Paris in her apartment near Doheny. Ruthie Conte, Oona Chaplin, Charlie's wife, and I figured out a way to help. We would take a French lesson once a week. But Madame Bernheim was such an elegant lady that we didn't know how to approach the subject of money. We asked her if we could come to tea for French conversation. Ruthie and Oona had a smattering of French. I bought the Linguaphone course. And we went to tea regularly. It was always beautifully arranged—Madame Bernheim had found a French bakery—but we never found a way to pay her a single sou.

Alain, the kid brother, was small and clever and lively. He soon got a job in the Charles Feldman Agency and quickly made his way to being a top agent and eventually a producer. Michel didn't fare as well. He worked on projects for films for years. None of them happened. There was one for Montgomery Clift and me to be made in Rome in about 1950. It was a love story based on an episode in the life of Thomas Wolfe and Aline Bernstein, the designer. We got as far as a free flight from American Overseas Airline, with a whole plane to ourselves. Michel shot a commercial for them with me as a happy passenger, and there would be a scene in the movie featuring the plane. We had a great flight. We invited a few friends, Gene came, and Monty and Mira Rostova, his companion. We were about eight people. We felt as if we were on *Air Force One.* Our excitement was short-lived. In Paris we found that the Italian money for the film was gone, so the French producer was desperate. After ten days, Monty went back to New York. Gene and I went to Klosters for a week of skiing, then home to Kerry and Rodeo Drive. I believe Michel was a very talented man. Perhaps his finest hour was during the war, and perhaps the saga of his escape used up his luck. He was dearly loved and is still missed. Alain married the intelligent and lovely Marjorie and brought her into our lives. They also brought Charles Boyer and Louis Jourdan and Jean Gabin—and Salka Viertel. The most important to me was Salka Viertel.

Salka was not French. She was Polish-Jewish-Viennese-English-Californian and had had a classical European education. She was

Arriving in Paris to start shooting the ill-fated, untitled, abruptly
canceled film about a romantic interlude between Thomas Wolfe
(Montgomery Clift) and the designer Aline Bernstein (me).
Gene came along for the ride.

taught Latin and Greek from the age of six, French and English at
eight. She already spoke Polish and German at home. With all that
she became an actress. She went to Vienna and worked in the theater of Max Reinhardt, playing leading roles. She met and married
the poet and director Berthold Viertel (the half-disguised hero of
Christopher Isherwood's novel *Prater Violet*), and they had three
sons. When Hitler came to power, they fled to England, where their

lives went their separate ways. Salka and her three boys came to Los Angeles. She had a contract with MGM. At that time, the major studios shot some films in several languages simultaneously. For instance, in *Anna Christie,* starring Greta Garbo and Marie Dressler, Salka played the Marie Dressler role in the German version. Her friendship and collaboration with Garbo started there, and she went on to write the screenplays for *Queen Christina,* and *Conquest,* and *Anna Karenina.*

I don't know how old Salka was when I met her. She was probably a beautiful forty-five or fifty. Not beautiful in any conventional way, but alive with her intelligence, her humor, her vitality. Her hair had gone white early, and she dyed it red. When I met her she was letting it "grow out," four inches of pure white hair and then four inches of bright red hair. It looked perfect on her. Her head was like that of some splendid striped animal with bright blue eyes and high wide cheekbones. May my mother forgive me, but the thought that skittered across my brain after that first evening was, "She should have been my mother—she's my spiritual mother."

As a friend, Salka was incomparable. She sometimes looked at me with a wry, amused expression, probably when I was being particularly naive and American, but she treated me with warmth and affection. She welcomed me with open arms.

And she welcomed every European refugee. Her house on Mabery Road in Santa Monica was a very well-known haven, a haven with polished floors and airy rooms with white curtains, and the smell of flowers and baking—she made great cakes and breads. Whatever was needed was found at Mabery Road. Salka never talked about it, but it was known. Her guest house, her extra rooms, her dinner table gave nurture and solace to a never-ending stream of friends or acquaintances or friends of friends. They arrived by many routes. We heard stories of human courage and ingenuity. The writer Leon Feuchtwanger was carried across the Pyrenees into Spain by his admittedly rather Amazonian wife. He was dressed as a woman and claimed to be her grandmother!

Beyond food and shelter, time to recover, and civilized conversation, Salka found jobs for the refugees where she could. She

The wise and wonderful Salka Viertel, 1945

charmed and bullied and shamed heads of studios into giving out contracts. I think she used all her money, her savings and her salary, to help these old friends without hesitation.

There were refugees at her house who didn't need that kind of help—Thomas Mann, the Feuchtwangers, and Arnold Schoenberg, the composer. Although there is a story that Salka had gotten someone to convince L. B. Mayer that Schoenberg was a genius. It would be a great coup if Metro could get him to write the music for a film. An offer was made. Schoenberg expressed interest. He was given a VIP tour of the studio, especially to see the wonderful facilities of the music department. After lunch with some executives and some stars, including Judy Garland, he was ushered into Mr. Mayer's office. There, to the dismay of the head of music, who was proudly escorting him, he set out his understanding of how it would be possible for him to score a film. He must read the scenario, work with the writer, and have final say over the director and the casting of the players. End of meeting—and job.

Living long term in Salka's house was a German couple. My first impression was of a downtrodden, unhappy wife, small, wiry, and always dressed in shabby black, her hair pulled back in a bun. She didn't speak much, but smiled apologetically and rushed to help clear the table or make the coffee. The husband, on the other hand, was a bit of a popinjay, vain though not handsome, dressed unsuitably for California but with a sort of arty Apache-dancer style. He talked incessantly with great conviction. I asked Salka about them. "Helene Weigel and Bertolt Brecht." I waited. "He is a great poet and playwright. She is the greatest actress in Europe or perhaps the world." So much for my powers of discernment. I must look again I thought, and pay more attention.

Salka entertained on Sunday. There would be lunch, a walk on the beach, then an English afternoon tea. We had been invited but could never go. But now that I'd made my move and withdrawn from the volleyball game, I was free to jump in my car and spend the afternoon in what I was sure was the most fascinating place in the world. Sometimes Kerry came with me, but mostly she chose the fun of the backyard.

One Sunday, Christopher Isherwood was there, and the French writer Vladimir Pozner with his beautiful wife, Ida. I arrived as they were finishing lunch, and we all set off for the promenade on the beach. I was wearing sneakers, and I stopped to take them off so I could walk barefoot on the sand. Brecht came back and waited. He fell into step with me. He casually took my arm and asked, "So— tell me—what is socialism?" I had my sneakers in one hand, he was holding the other arm—I was trapped. So I told him. I told him about the shoemakers' children who had no shoes. I explained how the workers should own the means of production. I told him about collective farms and higher crop yields. I quoted percentages. I talked about the redistribution of wealth. Later I asked Salka how I could have been so silly—how could I have spelled out the most basic elements of marxism to a man who obviously could have taught them to me? I blushed for having been so childish and naive. Salka said, "Betsy, Betsy, don't worry. He was flirting with you. It was his Germanic idea of an excellent opening gambit for a young

American. He surely expected you to say, 'Oh, I don't know, do please tell me about it, Mr. Brecht.' Served him right. Sometimes naïveté is a good thing—he had to listen, for a change. It will do him good."

And my refusal to collude in the behavior on the volleyball court did me good. It got me to Salka's and prepared me for my lifelong love affair with Europe.

14

THE HOLLYWOOD FABLE is of a land of glamour and wealth. But actually it's a company town for people who work in the movies. In the first half of the twentieth century, real riches belonged to the old established land and oil families, the nearest thing to "society" on the West Coast.

They never crossed our path; they never entered our minds. Our life was so much more luxurious than we'd ever dreamed it could be. We had a house, two cars, a live-in housekeeper, and a Japanese gardener, and Gene had a secretary. We knew there were movie people—Charlie Chaplin, L. B. Mayer, or David Selznick—who had three or four or even five servants, but we didn't envy them. But I guess I was impressed, and I know I was pleased to be able to report to my mother all the things I knew would make her happy. I have a little packet of letters she saved. In 1942, I wrote,

> We are in the most amazing place in the whole world—Myron Selznick's lodge at Lake Arrowhead. David brought us up. I really can't describe it to you. All I can say is if you could see us here you would probably cry for joy—silver plates and goblets—servants till you can't see—a swimming pool—tennis court—altitude 6300 feet—70 acres—pine trees—about twelve bedrooms in the house besides the guest house—it's really unbelievable—all knotty pine and redwood and stuff like that. We have a bedroom, dressing room and bath—wonderful, wonderful.

When I say it was like a company town, I mean that everything revolved around the filmmaking. Social life was dictated by shooting schedules. Europeans were startled to be invited to dinner at six for six-thirty. But since actresses had to be in makeup and hairdressing at six in the morning, it was only natural and sensible to eat early and be home in bed by ten.

The atmosphere in the makeup rooms was cozy and comforting, with fresh orange juice, coffee, and tea on hand, breakfast to be ordered from the commissary if you wanted. The makeup people were marvels of tact and consideration. If you were in the mood for chat and gossip, they supplied it; if you preferred silence, they did their excellent work without a word. And if you happened to be late, they'd cover for you and rush you through so you were on the set on time. Of course, they couldn't really cover for you, because every move was monitored. The man at the gate wrote down the exact minute you drove through, and the time you arrived at the makeup building was noted. And if you were a repeat offender, you were visited by the studio manager, who spoke about consideration for all the other workers, not to mention the cost if you were late on the set.

The studio system was marvelously productive. The studio "took care of everything" for their stars. But the studio executives did consider them as properties to be used for as long as they were popular.

They may have loved the actors for their talent and success, but they also hated them for their talent and success. The actors had more fun, they were almost invariably younger, handsomer, and more charming than the bosses. With the exception of a few who actively fought for quality and artistry—David Selznick, Arthur Freed, perhaps Darryl Zanuck, and, before our time, Irving Thalberg—they thought of the stars as a necessary evil, as children to be controlled. And the whole system was geared to keep them childish. If an actor wasn't as tough and intelligent as Gene, he was likely to believe his own publicity and lose track of himself.

And I guess I was some kind of oddball; I don't know why, I just never bought the Hollywood system. I didn't want a swimming

The Chevrolet. My nephew Will and his sister Debby and
brother Bentley enjoyed it for twenty years until the salt
air of the East Coast rusted it away.

pool, I didn't want a fancy car. After two winter trips to New York,
where I enjoyed the warmth of my mink coat, I didn't even want it.
I traded it in for a nutria jacket for my mother, a white mink shoulder wrap for premieres and a dark green rabbit-fur coat for me. I
guess I was my mother's child—a democrat. I didn't want to look
like a rich lady.

I kept my Chevrolet for ages. Justifying this, I could point to
Katharine Hepburn, who never had a Mercedes or a Lincoln Con-
tinental. I had evening clothes for premieres and parties, but mostly
I wandered around in blue jeans or a cotton skirt and shirt, often
Gene's (the shirt, that is). Once, when Kerry and Jeannie and I had
been to the beach and were driving back with wet hair and bare
feet, I remembered I had to buy a present. As I pulled in to
Magnin's parking lot, Jeannie said, "We can't go in like this." I said,

"Of course we can—we have natural elegance." What we really had was youth and lots of money to spend, at least I did. And of course they welcomed us in the shop.

About the money—I did use it: I gave to my causes, I paid for the special school that was needed for the child of one of the Hollywood Ten. I helped friends. But I seem to have buried the contradiction between the ease of my life and the ideas I believed in and worked for politically. I don't remember feeling guilty. I managed not to think about money, to pay no attention to it at all. I do recall once when I found the perfect table for the entrance hall. It cost one hundred dollars. I hesitated and then came to the conclusion that if I didn't think a hundred dollars was too expensive for a coat, then it must be okay for an almost two-hundred-year-old Colonial American table. I bought it. That childish equation worked for me. I definitely colluded in maintaining my status as the adolescent in the house—sunny and dreamy and completely indulged. In other words, a spoiled child—albeit a well-behaved one.

As I look back and try to find clues to the girl I was, and evidence of the woman I became, I only see the little wife, loving mother, aspiring actress, and political innocent. But where am I? Where is that hidden self, the one we each carry within us? Of course it was there, the one that knows the truth, that sees everything and has its own opinion.

Saturday was the only night of the week when people stayed up late. As for the Saturday nights at our house, they just happened. They seem to have acquired something of a reputation. Joan Collins, Kenneth Tynan, Leslie Caron, and Saul Chaplin have all written about them. Betty Comden surprised me recently when she said, "Of course, the atmosphere in the house was you—it came from you." I've been wondering about this ever since. If I try to see objectively, to envisage one of those evenings, I put Gene in place as the dominant figure, as he was the dominant figure in our lives. But as I picture him now, he is slightly removed—not aloof, exactly, always pleasant and amused and attending to the drinks, but not entirely there. He must have wanted this way of life, this house full of friends every weekend, or it wouldn't have happened. He enjoyed the games, he didn't sing and shout around the piano. Of course he was older than a few of us, but as I look back he seems older than everyone. He was the patriarch.

But no matter who contributed what to all those evenings, some of the Saturday nights at our house on Rodeo Drive *were* special.

But as we laughed and sang and loved through those sixteen years, there was a silent presence among us—the FBI and its informers.

In October 1998 I received my FBI file—or most of it, "87 pages out of 92 reviewed." I had practically forgotten that I'd asked for it almost two years earlier, under the Freedom of Information Act. The thick brown envelope from the Federal Bureau of Investigation, Washington, D.C., office startled me, excited me, horrified me in turn. And for a moment there was a strange exhilaration— was what I did of some significance?

It was a fleeting moment. As I read through the pages, I could only conclude that neither I nor the contents of my file were of any importance at all. "They" must have taken them seriously, since they sent copies of these trivial and confused reports to their offices in Los Angeles, New York, London, Paris, Rome, and Madrid.

Confused? There are eight pages in which they have not yet confirmed that "Betsy Blair, Betsy Kelly and Mrs. Gene Kelly (Elizabeth Winifred Kelly) who is married to Eugene Curran Kelly, better known as the movie star Gene Kelly," are one and the same person. They could have checked us out in *Photoplay,* the *Hollywood Reporter, Life, Look, Picture Post,* or *Paris Match,* through my Social Security number, or simply by calling my agent.

And trivial? Well, about 40 percent of the eighty-seven pages is blacked out "to protect their sources and foreign agencies," as one of the stamps on each page tells us. Other stamps are CONFIDENTIAL and SUBV. CONTROL and SECURITY MATTER C. About 30 percent is made up of interoffice communications, checklists of dates, number of copies sent and to which offices, and a reprimand or two when they were delayed. As for the rest—the hard information—it is pathetic.

They list the organizations they considered communist fronts: the Joint Anti-Fascist Refugee Committee, the Congress of American Women, the Sleepy Lagoon Committee, the National Council of the Arts, Sciences and Professions, and the Civil Rights Congress, among many others. It's true, I was associated with them all. They were broadly based liberal left-wing organizations and surely had communist members. I never asked; I never even speculated on the subject. The FBI somehow found out and listed the contributions, or some of them, that I made in 1947, '49, and '50. Modest contributions they were, too: the Civil Rights Congress, $40, $25, and $25; the Hollywood Ten Defense Committee—more generously—$250, $200, another $250, and, in August 1950, $10. And several contributions of $10 to the Russian-American Club in 1944, when the Soviet Union was our ally and "Uncle Joe" Stalin was popular even in the Hearst press.

One page, titled "Residence and Employment" October 24, 1956, states:

An agent of the F.B.I. determined through a suitable pretext on October 12th, that Elizabeth Kelly returned to the U.S. from Europe about September 10th, and is currently residing at 725 N. Rodeo Drive, Beverly Hills, California [where we had lived for twelve years, since 1945]. Information was also developed through this pretext interview that she is currently unemployed, and is considering several motion picture offers at the present time.

So a fake newspaper man who unearthed our address that was on every map of movie stars' homes; someone at the airport in London, probably watching Paul Robeson but catching me in the net by chance as I met him there; reports from Madrid, where I was in a film directed by Juan Antonio Bardem; a spy with access to the accounts of leftist organizations or to my bank account on which were drawn the checks I openly made out to various causes—there were informers everywhere.

Of course, I am angry at the violation of my privacy for almost nineteen years. The earliest reference is to the marxist classes in 1940, when I was sixteen and in love with the world. Finally, on September 29, 1958, they close with "In view of the above review of files no further investigation is contemplated by the L.A. Office at this time."

By 1958 the world and I had changed. I was living in Paris. The Soviet Union had sent their tanks into the streets of Budapest. At the Twentieth Congress of the Supreme Soviet, Krushchev had revealed the evil of Uncle Joe and Stalinism. I was older and maybe a bit wiser. But my ideals had always been American, not Russian. They were rooted in the American Constitution and learned at my mother's knee—liberty, equality, justice for all. So my battles and contribution—small as it may have been—were against racism, for strong unions, for the rights of women; to put it simply, for democracy. I was young and naive, and I can see now that there may have been some vanity in my passion (I'm not accusing every left-wing person—I only speak for myself). I liked being someone rebellious and righteous, one of the enlightened fighting for the "masses." I accepted the marxist view that the struggle was between communism and capitalism. Many, like Gene and Paddy Cheyevsky in my own circle, and other serious thinkers outside it, saw that it was really between communism and democracy, and that the fight for social justice is at home in the United States. As Churchill said, ✿ "Democracy is not perfect, but it's the best we have."

But I *was* fighting while living my lovely life. From a letter to my mother in May 1944:

> We have been in such a social whirl—I swear we've been to a party or out to dinner or to a meeting every night since we got back. The primaries are next Tuesday and I've been working for Patterson's campaign every day. When they're over, there will be a slight let up—for which thank goodness. . . . Kerry is the absolute end . . . gets cuter every day. She's 31 inches long—weighs 24 lbs. 6 oz.—She throws us kisses now. Gene loves her so much he doesn't know what to do—just beams— I took her in Danny Kaye's pool the other day and she loved

it—Dickie Whorf brought over Chrissie's old sandbox and I bought some blue and white paint today—I'll paint it tomorrow for her . . . Gene is working very hard every day with Astaire on their number for the Follies—I'm so happy about "Cover Girl." Having been away it was much more noticeable how people like him in it. They all rave.

Preparing the campaigns, the committee meetings, the fundraising parties, there were endless theoretical discussions in which I took an enthusiastic part, but there was concrete work done too. In the January 1999 issue of *Screen Actor,* the magazine of my union, the Screen Actors Guild, there is a six-page article on the guild's history of affirmative action. They began to collect articles from black newspapers for a file called "The Negro Question," in 1938. In 1944, Lena Horne and Rex Ingram were elected to the board. Then two years later—I quote from the article—

Betsy Blair, wife of Board member, Gene Kelly, proposed a resolution that was passed by the membership in the fall of 1946 by the margin of 992 in favor and 34 opposed. The resolution read as follows:

> WHEREAS, Negro actors have a long and honorable history in American theatre and in the motion picture industry and played an important part in the formation of our Guild, and
>
> WHEREAS, unemployment among our Negro Guild members has reached a point more alarming than at any time in Guild history, and
>
> WHEREAS Negro parts are being omitted from a great many screenplays and are, in many cases, actually being cut out of books and plays when adapted to the screen, and
>
> WHEREAS, in several instances producers have even gone to the length of using white actors in Negro roles,
>
> NOW, THEREFORE, BE IT RESOLVED that the

Screen Actors Guild use all of its power to oppose discrimination against Negroes in the motion picture industry, and

BE IT FURTHER RESOLVED that a special committee be set up at once to implement this policy and to meet with representatives of the Screen Writers' Guild and the Screen Directors Guild and the Motion Picture Producers Association in order to establish in the industry a policy of presenting Negro characters on the screen in the true relation they bear to American life.

As a result of this resolution, an Anti-Discrimination Committee was appointed in November of 1946. The Committee which was never able to get together, was dissolved at a Board meeting on March 10th, 1947, the same meeting which saw Ronald Reagan elected as S.A.G. President. . . . The dissolution of the Anti-Discrimination Committee was immediately protested by many of S.A.G.'s African-American members and at the very next meeting on March 24th of that year, it was revived and called into session. The Chair was Warner Anderson and the Committee members included Betsy Blair, John Hodiak, Marsha Hunt, Boris Karloff, Clarence Muse.

The article brought it back to me. I'd forgotten that specific meeting. It was among the things I was busy doing when I was twenty-two.

But there was something else I never forgot. One of the showgirls who had befriended me at the International Casino called. She was visiting LA with "mah new filthy rich Texan husband," she giggled—she was a Southerner herself. I invited them on Sunday at cocktail time. They arrived. There were greetings and oohs and aahs and thrilled to meet Gene and all that. The husband looked nice in a blazer and flannels and an ascot. Our housekeeper was off on Sunday, so Lena Horne and I went into the kitchen for more glasses, ice cubes, and a pitcher of lemonade. My showgirl followed us. We chatted about nothing. Then I asked, "The tall glasses are in the cupboard right behind you—would you get out six for this tray?" She drifted languidly across the kitchen, looked pointedly at Lena, and said, "Why doesn't she get them?" I dropped the ice cube trays, took her arm, led her forcibly back to the living room, and said to Gene, "They are leaving—*now!*" Everything stopped. I glimpsed Lena, with a tolerant quizzical smile, shrug at Gene. He jumped in and escorted the husband rather politely as I was pushing my high-heeled six-foot former friend into the hall. And then they were gone. There was a curious lack of comment—I think Stanley Donen, a completely different kind of Southerner, made a joke about "Miss New Jersey's hospitality." After drinks, supper, a 16mm movie, some piano playing, and milk and cookies, that Sunday evening ended just as usual. At the door, as Lena and Lennie Hayton were leaving, Lena took both my hands in hers, looked at me softly, straight out of those big eyes in probably the most beautiful face ever, and said, "Betsy, if you're really going to be a friend of mine, you must treat me exactly—and I mean exactly—like any other friend. But thank you." I think she meant she could fight her own battles. I never asked, but I never forgot.

The weekly Ping-Pong tournament started about four on Saturday afternoon. One day the handsome, skinny, gentle Hugh Martin, half of the songwriting team Hugh Martin and Ralph Blane, appeared. Now, Hugh was no Ping-Pong player, no game player at all, more an aesthetic appreciator of life and art. He called me into the house, took my hand, and led me to the piano. He sat down and played and sang "The Boy Next Door," the lovely song for Judy Garland in *Meet Me in St. Louis*. I was moved and thrilled by it, and moved and thrilled by Hugh's friendship, which gave me the honor of being the first one to hear the song. For that day the Ping-Pong could go jump in the lake, as we said in New Jersey. I had just heard a great song—newborn. Later that evening, with Ralph there too, they presented the whole score to all of us, including "Have Yourself a Merry Little Christmas" and the classic "Trolley Song."

I can't remember if it was for Gene's birthday or mine that another new song made its debut on a Saturday night. It was given

Lena Horne and Lennie Hayton, 1950

to us as a present by Phil Silvers. Jimmy Van Heusen had written a tune for his wife. Phil put new words to it. With Saul Chaplin at the piano, Phil sang "Betsy with the Laughing Face." Gene and I held hands and laughed and cried. Later, when Frankie recorded it as "Nancy with the Laughing Face," I was still proud—I had the memory of that night. Even today I sing the lyric as "Who wouldn't miss that Irish kisser?"—which couldn't have been about Nancy.

Noël Coward once famously said, "It's extraordinary how potent cheap music is." If he meant popular songs, they were a vital part of our lives at Rodeo Drive. We were fortunate to have exceptional musicians among us, Saul Chaplin, Hugh Martin, and Lennie Hayton. Each one brought his own special qualities.

Hugh Martin and Ralph Blane had been successful singers and arrangers on Broadway. Their work has a particular poetic quality. It grew out of small-town America. They celebrated football games and school anthems, the tradition of Christmas, the trolley car and young love. They had the gift of lyricising everydayness.

Lennie Hayton came from a different world. Russian, Jewish,

John and Robbie Garfield, 1946

intellectual, he had played in many great jazz combos, even with the legendary Charlie Parker. He was a mysterious and charming fellow. "Cool" and "hip" could have been invented for him. In the late 1940s I was in a play, *Deep Are the Roots,* in LA, which toured to San Francisco for two weeks. I couldn't wait to tell Lennie what I had discovered there—Jerry Mulligan and Chet Baker. I was wild about their new sound—new to me, that is. When I raved to Lennie, he listened silently with a smile. I finally caught on. "You know them?" I asked. He nodded yes. "Why didn't you tell me to go hear them?" "Betsy," he said, "there are things in this world that only have real value if you find them yourself—and you did." He made me feel dead cool.

Saul Chaplin and his wife, Ethel, a musician herself and a very bright, witty woman, had their own open house. It centered around music and family. Ethel's mother, father, and sister lived with them and their pretty, talented daughter, Judy. It was a home of exceptional warmth and friendship. Saul was a marvelously inventive and knowledgeable pianist. He was fun on the piano; he could play any song in any style. He made musical jokes in a way I've never heard since. He was the most important element of our musical life. When we first knew him, he worked at Columbia in the music department as composer, arranger, and conductor, and even once, in my case, as vocal coach. I played a nightclub singer in a film at Columbia, *The Guilt of Janet Ames,* starring Rosalind Russell. We rehearsed my number, recorded it, and then the scene was shot. My rendition was acceptable it seems, since it was a cheap club and my character was not supposed to be a singer who would become a star. But then Rosalind Russell fought with the director; a new one was brought in. He decided my song must be redubbed. Saul told me he had a hard time matching my voice. I think he ended up with a young boy singer. And so ended my only approach to movie musical comedy.

But on Saturday nights we continued to sing our hearts out around the piano.

I don't remember who brought Noël Coward, but there he was. He charmed us all, and everyone was eager to entertain him. Betty Comden and Adolph Green performed some of their old Revuers routines brilliantly. Gene and the fantastic dancer Carol Haney improvised a dance. Judy sang. And then Coward was persuaded to the piano. He took his time, he doodled a bit, then, with amazing brio and precision, he sang some of his own songs, "Don't Put Your Daughter on the Stage, Mrs. Worthington," and "Mad Dogs and Englishmen." He modulated into "Mad about the Boy," and finally knocked us out with "If Love Were All." The lyrics say, "I believe that since my life began, the most I've had is just, a talent to amuse. Heigh-ho if love were all, I should be lonely." Certainly, he had a talent to amuse but also to illuminate and to touch deeply.

We had a party for the NAACP. On an occasion like this, we would invite a hundred people. The object was to raise as much money as possible, so there would be outsiders and, therefore, a chance for the FBI—or their informers—to get in. In a way, I'm glad the "sources" in my file are blacked out. My retrospective suspicion has no object. There are no revelations as there were when the Stasi files in East Germany were opened, no discoveries of best friends, or teachers, or lovers, or neighbors as the rats who informed. I can understand the FBI—most of the reports on me were during the cold war. It's whoever was our guest and informed on us that I loathe the most.

On this evening Paul Robeson was the guest of honor. He sang for us. Or, rather, he sang for the NAACP—we were the lucky ones who were there. The program was that he would sing and speak, then Gene would ask for the contributions. Ruthie Conte and I collected the checks and pledges. Saul Chaplin was at the piano.

It was a solemn moment as Robeson started his most famous song, "Ole Man River." And I felt the stirring of that most horrendous nightmare for an actor, to "break up," to laugh inappropriately during a scene. I looked at Phil Silvers, he looked at Stanley Donen, Betty Comden and Adolph Green looked down, John Garfield took out his handkerchief. I didn't dare glance at Gene.

We were stricken because long ago Phil and Saul Chaplin had improvised a sketch about Paul Robeson and Jerome Kern. It was irreverent, definitely not politically correct, and very funny. The setting was the first time Robeson heard the score of *Showboat*. Saul, who was at the piano now playing for Robeson, had been at the piano as Jerome Kern, with Phil singing. Phil held some sheet music as Saul played the opening. Then Phil, as Robeson, the Princeton graduate, started to sing "Ole man—what's this next word—R-I-B-A-H—what's that? Oh—river." He started again with a British accent: "Old man river." When he got to "Don' plant taters," he stopped. "Is that potatoes—I see. Let's start again. *I* don't plant *po*-tatoes." By the time Phil, as Robeson, got to the end of the chorus he was in full voice and belting out the song.

Fortunately, that night our giggles were quelled immediately by the authority of Paul Robeson, and the power and warmth of his voice.

After he sang, he spoke, "Must I tell my children to tell their children to tell their children to tell their children that someday things will be better? We will not wait any longer. We cannot wait

The young Leonard Bernstein, 1946

any longer." His words burned into the hearts of everyone in the room. We raised a lot of money.

Adolph Green brought his friend Leonard Bernstein to meet us. The beautiful, the brilliant, the funny and charming Lenny Bernstein. From then on, whenever he was in Los Angeles, he turned up on Saturday night, sometimes for supper, sometimes after a concert. And he took his turn at the piano.

Our piano, a baby grand, was a gift from my mother. It was her proudest possession. It came from her mother's house. When Kerry was born she said she wanted us to have it as soon as we had our own home. It was duly shipped from New Jersey, and installed and tuned at Rodeo Drive. It served us well. No one ever complained. Neither of us could play it. Both my brothers had piano lessons, but when I came along my father said he wasn't throwing good money after bad; my dancing school was enough.

Then one day Lenny Bernstein said to Gene, "You have to get a better piano—come on—you're a movie star. We need a better piano." We didn't know what to do. We couldn't hurt my mother's feelings. We finally concocted a story about MGM giving Gene a present—a grand piano, of all things. Lenny went with us to choose the new one.

He played every piano in the warehouse, to the delight of all the salesmen and tuners. After about ten minutes the owner and his wife and children dashed in—someone had telephoned them, and Lenny gave them a show. He played seriously, he played delicately, he played flamboyantly. He even gave them a bit of jazz and many bows and flourishes. When he had chosen, Gene wrote a check, and we had bought a new piano. We shipped the beloved one back to Cliffside, where it lived happily ever after.

Bertha, our housekeeper, kept talking to me at every opportunity about a special dinner. She knew about it from several of her friends. A salesman of some exceptional pots and pans, "waterless cookers," came to your clean and empty kitchen at four in the afternoon and prepared the food he brought with him for a dinner party of eighteen to twenty people. The household only provided drinks, dessert, and coffee. He recommended fresh fruit salad. When I finally agreed to it, the wise Bertha made a few pies just in case. I warned everyone that we didn't know what was on the menu—it was an actual case of "pot luck."

The salesman-cook came to meet us the week before, at Gene's suggestion. It turned out that he had served in the navy too. It was also clear that he never went to the movies. He not only didn't seem to recognize Gene, but on the night it was obvious that he didn't know any actors. Hedy Lamarr was there on a first date with a friend of ours, Ruthie and Richard Conte of course, Robbie and John Garfield, and Lena Horne.

The invitation was seven o'clock, for seven-fifteen. The guests no sooner had a drink in their hands when our master of ceremonies for the evening, the salesman, appeared. He clapped his hands to call our attention and asked us to proceed to the kitchen for a few moments before dinner. As we filed in, the doorbell rang. I didn't expect anyone else. I ran to open the door. There was George Cukor. He said, "I knew you wouldn't mind us dropping in. I've brought along a friend." It was Greta Garbo. We'd been in Hollywood for about six years. We knew lots of movie stars—there were five of them in the kitchen right now—but Garbo was something else. And tonight of all nights. Between the front door and the breakfast room I gave a hurried and apologetic explanation. Garbo was perfect. When we arrived in the kitchen, we found our salesman with a large colored chart depicting vitamins and their fruits, and minerals and their vegetables. Garbo gave a general smile of greeting, slipped into a space, and hoisted herself up onto the counter next to the sink. Every one of our friends was dazzled. But not our man with the portfolio; he calmly started his lecture on nutrition. He was interrupted several times by our two irrepressible "bad boys," Conte and Garfield, asking straight-faced dumb questions: "How can you boil carrots without water? Won't they turn black?" And then, near the end of his talk, when he described how this system of cooking with the pots and pans he was selling would make life easier for women, Garbo spoke. She said in that miraculous voice, "Are you married?" He said yes, he was, and now we could go back to the living room. He would serve the hors d'oeuvre.

I don't like to remember what we ate. Suffice it to say that the vegetables and the main dish, a giant rice pancake with nuts and mushrooms, were all unsalted, oversteamed, and tasteless. People who didn't drink decided to have wine. The food had to be washed down somehow.

As everyone fell on the fruit salad and Bertha's pies, the salesman invited anyone who was interested to come into the breakfast room to see him. And first off the mark was Garbo. She bought the whole set of pots and pans for waterless cooking. I think they cost $150, probably equivalent to $4,000 today. Next was Hedy Lamarr, who bought half of them. Nobody else could be persuaded, so Gene, out of embarrassment, took a whole set. So the Garbo kitchen and the Kelly kitchen had the same pots and pans.

When the salesman left, there was an outburst of yelling, with each person trying to top the others with his particular reaction. This brought on one of Gene's lectures—they were quite well known and regarded with tolerant amusement by our friends. We shouldn't be laughing, he said, at a fellow trying to earn an honest buck. He was a navy man, a man who had served his country during the war. Of course, Gene was right—he usually was. (Actually, there was a characteristic gesture he had—sort of a family joke. When there was an argument about a date in history or the meaning of a word, we would look it up. When the correct answer— more often than not—was found to be his, he would leap to his feet, throw his arms into the air, grin, and twirl around, crowing, "Right again.")

The rest of the evening revolved around the presence of Garbo. At some point during supper I slipped away and called Betty and Adolph, who were at a different party. I knew they would want to meet her, but even more, I knew that George Cukor would have described our Saturday nights to Garbo, and this one wouldn't live up to his description without Betty and Adolph's performance. I hadn't invited Michel and Alain Bernheim. They were French. I didn't think I could subject them to the unknown quality of this particular meal. Now I called them. I knew they'd never forgive me if they missed Garbo. They arrived in time for coffee, dressed, as never before, in suits and ties. I'm sure everyone there remembers exactly what she said to them, however mundane. Alain told me fifty years later that when he was introduced, Garbo said, "Ah— French—you must make good coffee." Alain, who had prepared a glowing sophisticated tribute, could only grin and mumble, "I suppose so." "Yes, yes," repeated Garbo. "The French all make good coffee." To me, she talked about the hummingbirds and butterflies in her garden, and I was mesmerized.

There were some memorable Sunday nights too. After volleyball and supper, we always ran a 16mm film on a portable screen set up in front of the piano. A very young and intense Stanley Kubrick brought the film he'd made on a shoestring in New York, *Killer's Kiss*. That was a great evening. His talent was clearly evident even then.

Gene had a letter from San Francisco, from another young film-maker, Kenneth Anger. He was invited to supper and to bring his film on a particular Sunday. He arrived in an overcoat with the reels under his arm, straight from the ten-hour bus ride to LA. He was small and thin with a sensitive face and a kind of forest-animal shy-ness. You felt he might jump if you touched him. After coffee we settled down to watch *Fireworks*.

I don't know how he happened to write to Gene. I do know that none of us had any idea what we were about to see. *Fireworks* is now a famous film, but then it was an amazing shock. Instead of our usual Lillian Gish or Carole Lombard movie, we watched in stunned silence this fascinating surreal homoerotic essay on film. Occasionally there was an audible gasp, but at the end there was an awkward moment of silence. Gene leapt to the rescue, put his arm around Kenneth Anger's shoulders, and took him into the study, where he congratulated and thanked him. Stanley put the film back in its cans, and when they came out we had all collected ourselves enough to be polite. Kenneth Anger took his film, shook Gene's hand, and left. As soon as the door closed behind him, there was shrieking and hysterical giggling at the memory of the cascades of candle sparks erupting from the sailor's crotch. It was actually rather callous and childish behavior, but we were in a state of aston-ishment. And then, there in the hallway within earshot and with a clear view of us, was Kenneth Anger. He had come back for his for-gotten overcoat. He knocked, but no one heard above the din, and the door was unlocked as always. He made a dignified exit with a gallant little backward wave of his hand. We were chastened. We didn't need a lecture from Gene this time.

I've always wondered how Kenneth Anger would describe that evening.

One thing I do know: he was definitely not one of the rats who were there on other evenings informing for the FBI.

15

EUROPE was our destination. We never took a beach holiday—
we were out for culture and history. We weren't corny enough to say
it out loud, but that's what we were doing. We had the excitement
and adventure of seeing the great sights, the theater in London and
Stratford, Paris and the Jeux de Paumes in the Louvre, Venice and
Chartres and Rome.

The first time, in 1950, Gene and I went alone. My mother came
to stay with Kerry. We sailed from New York on the *Queen Mary*,
bound for Southampton.

It was a far cry from our banana boat. We were in the most luxurious cabin, we had consommé served in our deck chairs at eleven
each morning, we dressed up for dinner and danced in the ballroom every night.

We were serious American tourists, and like most we had only
two weeks! We'd studied the guidebooks, and we tried to see everything. We stayed in a glorious River Suite at the Savoy, and learned
to pronounce it accenting the last syllable. This meant our theme
music for the five days in London was "*Sa*-voy, da dum, da dum
daa dum," as in Benny Goodman, but now we sang, "S'*voy*, da
dum, da dum daa dum."

We visited the bombed-out East End of London. There was still
rationing in Great Britain. We came with open eyes and hearts,
and left for Paris filled with admiration for English theater and
people.

Paris is Paris. It is now, has been, and always will be the most beautiful, romantic place in the world. We were both entranced. We knew we'd come back often.

Then on to Rome, where we had a rendevous with the pope!

There had been a lunch arranged for Gene in New York with Monsignor Sheehan. I believe it was organized by Metro, and its purpose was to set up our audience at the Vatican.

For me, good little marxist that I was, Monsignor Sheehan, Cardinal Spellman, and the pope himself (all three very reactionary Catholics) represented the enemy. Gene's argument was that his mother would never forgive him if he went to Rome and didn't see the pope. He wanted to get a medal for her blessed by His Holiness.

Naturally I hadn't been invited to the lunch in New York. If I had been, I wasn't sure I'd have gone. But Rome and all its glory? I couldn't decide what to do.

My friend Sono Osato, the beautiful dancer and actress who had starred in *On the Town* on Broadway, often had an interesting angle on things, and she helped me decide. She looked glamorous, but she was practical and smart. She understood my hesitation, but suggested I go and think of it as research. Study the whole thing. She wanted a full report on what the pope wore. Given a task, an excuse, I became quite enthusiastic. And I was confident I'd keep my cool.

So here we were, in the Hassler Hotel at the top of the Spanish Steps, getting ready. The pope was not at the Vatican; he was in his summer residence at Castel Gondolfo. We had a car and a chauffeur waiting. I put on the hat I'd bought for the occasion.

We drove through the lovely Italian countryside and came to the little village leading to the castle. It reminded me of pictures of the slums in India, small hovels lining the unpaved road, and barefoot raggedy children. And then, in contrast, the castle itself, its enormous gates opening onto a courtyard paved in black and white marble, accented by the Swiss Guards in their flamboyant uniforms. We were met by a red-robed cardinal and ushered into the first of four reception rooms, each more ornate than the preceding one, with more tapestries on the walls, larger and more intricately carved crucifixes and furniture. And every room had a throne—perhaps in case the pope dropped in. In the final room before the audience we joined a Spanish family, three generations and all the women, down to a six-year-old in black with beautiful lace mantillas. There were two French priests, and I noticed a little human moment when the older one gestured surreptitiously to the other that the sleeve of his undershirt was showing at the wrist. He must push it back.

The cardinals and some lesser functionaries rushed back and forth, speaking in hushed tones like extras in a Shakespeare play. I thought it was all a great production, a wonderful pageant perfectly staged to create awe. At the same time I was afraid it might be working; I felt something.

Finally, we were in the most grandiose room of all, and there the pope and his entourage made an entrance that would have been the envy of a great actor. He was in white and cream and gold, an embroidered silk cassock, a linen sort of jerkin—an alb—trimmed in ermine, and fine white leather slippers. He spoke to the Spanish family first. They knelt and kissed his ring and received his blessing.

Then the group swept toward us. Our cardinal moved to stand slightly behind the pope—to prompt him, as it turned out. He made the sign of the cross in the air in front of us and spoke in English. "My blessings on you. My son, I understand you are an actor and dancer and you bring happiness to people in your work. For that heaven awaits you."

"Thank you, Your Holiness," said Gene.

His Holiness turned to me.

"My child, do you have children?"

To my horror, I heard myself being terribly eager to please.

"Yes, oh yes, I do. I have a little girl."

A papal secretary came forward with a small box containing a silver medal. The pope blessed it and gave it to me.

"For your daughter."

All I could think was, If I'm wrong about everything, at least Kerry will be okay. There was a momentary silence, and Gene rushed in to fill it.

"I think a friend of mine came to see you last year?" No response. He tried again. "Frank Sinatra?"

There was a bit of whispered prompting in the pope's ear from our cardinal. He must have said, "He's a singer," because the pope responded to Gene.

"Yes, yes, my son. I love the opera."

Then he blessed the air in front of us again and moved on to the French priests.

Before leaving the palace Gene bought a medal for Mom Kelly. He pretended it was the one that was blessed when we got back to the States, and gave it to her. I wasn't about to give up Kerry's.

In 1951, Gene's accountant told him about a new income tax ruling. The IRS was allowing any American who stayed out of the United States for eighteen months to pay no tax at all on money earned during that period. The logic behind it was to provide an incentive so the best people would be willing to live abroad and expand international businesses, like Standard Oil. Why shouldn't movie folk take advantage of the opportunity?

Gene had been planning an all-dance film—no plot, no dialogue or songs, just dance. It could be done in Europe just as well as Hollywood. He was enthusiastic. I was enthusiastic too, and thought it would be good for Kerry. And it was a fine joke on the IRS. The artists could sneak in under the cover of the international cartels. (The commonly held view of the Left was that as long as capitalism was there, we should get as much as we could out of it.)

MGM was sounded out. They wanted Gene to be happy, and they jumped at the chance to use their funds frozen by European currency laws, so they agreed that *Invitation to the Dance* would be shot in London. While it was being prepared, they would find one or two small films for Gene to do in Europe.

Now "the studio will take care of it" swung into action, and this time it was more than welcome. There had been other occasions, notably one weekend when Gene had a frightful flu and sinus infection, when the studio—represented by the studio doctor—

was not welcome. Gene stayed in bed on Saturday; on Sunday our doctor came and again on Monday morning. He said with a fever of 103, he couldn't allow Gene to go to work. I had called the first assistant on the film to warn him on Sunday afternoon. I called again to report the doctor's decision. Kerry went off to school with Lois, and I gave Gene an alcohol rub (the dancer's remedy for everything) to bring down his temperature. When he was a bit cooler and more comfortable I started downstairs. Halfway down I spotted the MGM doctor getting out of his car. I knew Gene felt that he was completely useless—he wouldn't go to him with a broken fingernail. I sprinted back up the stairs and told him. He said, "Ah, they're spying. Lock the door and tell Bertha not to answer it." We didn't answer. We giggled in the hall as the poor man rang and knocked and rang and rang. When he finally gave up, I peeked out and watched him go to his car. He began to put his bag in the trunk, then turned and started up our driveway toward the back of the house. I pushed Bertha aside and dashed through the kitchen to lock the back door. It had windows in the top half, so I had to crouch on the floor. I didn't have time to escape without being seen, so I stayed there until Bertha came to tell me the coast was clear, he'd driven away. I ran up to tell Gene. He smiled weakly, said, "Good work," and fell asleep. He was better the next day.

Originally there were five of us going to Europe for the eighteen months: Gene, Kerry and me, Gene's secretary Lois, and Carol Haney. Carol was an extraordinary dancer from the Jack Cole company. She was a pixie-faced, humorous girl and Gene's assistant choreographer and partner in staging the dances. She became a star on Broadway a few years later in *Pajama Game.*

And then we were suddenly six. Jeannie Coyne and Stanley Donen had a brief, not very happy, marriage. When it ended, Jeannie couldn't eat. Her doctor prescribed ginger ale and cream, half and half. She could swallow that but not very often. She went down to eighty-three pounds. I was frightened for her. I asked Gene if she could come with us. Now Jeannie had established herself at Metro, not just as a dancer, which is what her contract said, but in a position that hadn't existed before. She created it. Because she was so

Going to Europe with Kerry on the *Queen Mary,* 1949

charming, good-natured, straightforward, and energetic, all the actresses were happy to have her around. Cyd Charisse, Leslie Caron, Debbie Reynolds, Kathryn Grayson, and Judy Garland wanted her to rehearse with them, to go to costume fittings with them, to be sure everything ran smoothly for them. She was a personal assistant for almost every female star in an MGM musical. And the studio appreciated this special talent, the ability to circumvent displays of temperament that might cost money. So Gene had to convince Metro that he needed her in Europe.

I made lists, endless lists. Clothing for all seasons and all occasions, and Kerry would be growing. I packed three snowsuits for her, sizes eight, nine, and ten years old. Gene needed T-shirts to rehearse in, he wore moccasins; Kerry and I wore blue jeans and sneakers. I wasn't completely mad! I knew you could buy clothes in

Carol Haney and Gene rehearsing, with Jeannie Coyne standing by, 1949

Europe, but there was still rationing in England. American sports gear had not yet taken over the world; we had to carry it with us— at least we thought we did.

MGM made hotel reservations in New York and Paris, and bought tickets for trains, planes, and the French liner the *Ile de France*. They sent our suitcases directly to the ship, had cars waiting for us and people to meet us everywhere. I never noticed how much they did until I'd left that world. I appreciated it later whenever I hung onto a telephone to make a plane reservation or stood in line for a taxi at a station or airport. They spoiled us something rotten. I'm glad I survived.

Gene flew to Paris at the end of February. The five women—his "two girls," his secretary, his assistant choreographer, and his assistant—sailed on March 5 for Le Havre, with all the luggage. The voyage across the Atlantic on a ship was the most wonderful way to approach Europe. It was fun onboard, especially this trip with

Kerry there. She knew her way around the whole ship in a few hours. Six days with the sea air and the sky, the limitless horizon, and the motor chugging away through the night gave you time to feel, to appreciate the distance, the movement into another place entirely. You cross the meridians and change your watches an hour at a time, and the anticipation of arrival grows. You're at one with the world and have time to experience the reality of the excitement you felt when you spun the globe on the teacher's desk as a child.

At Le Havre, Gene was waiting with three cars—one for us, one for Lois, Jeannie, and Carol, and a van for our bags. We drove in caravan to Paris to the Lancaster, the chicest hotel in those years. It was small, furnished with antiques, and wonderfully efficient. We had a suite with two bedrooms and a balcony where Kerry and I leaned on the railing to watch as the luggage was disgorged onto the sidewalk. The concierge and the bellboys lined up the suitcases to count them. We counted along with them—yes, there were forty-seven pieces, just as I'd told them to expect. The manager suggested an adjoining room to accommodate them. We took it. Fifteen or twenty of these bags were professional—makeup cases, dancing shoes, rehearsal clothes, and typewriter and files that Lois would need. Then there were ski boots and ski clothes. And I must confess that there were three large navy duffle bags containing toilet paper and Kleenex. We'd experienced those small slippery squares that covered hygiene in Europe in those days, even in the best hotel. I'm afraid we were Yanks after all, no matter how crazy we were about Paris. Through friends I found a small progressive school for Kerry where they spoke practically no English; the lessons were in French. She was amazingly quick to pick up the language, while Gene and I were still struggling with it.

We had quite a few friends in Paris. There were the international ones; Anatole Litvak, the director; Robert Capa, the photographer; and Alexandre Trauner, the great film art director. He had designed all those wonderful French movies, *Hotel du Nord, Quai des brumes, Les Enfants du paradis,* and a dozen others. I had met Trau, as he was called, in 1949 or '50.

One day the phone rang while we were having lunch at Rodeo

Drive. I answered it. Orson Welles was calling from Paris for me. Would I come to Rome to play Desdemona in his film of *Othello*? Would I? Of course I would. I was out of my mind with excitement. While he was telling me the details of dates, and tickets and agents, I was seeing the first time I'd met him. After a matinee of *Panama Hattie,* Rags Raglund, one of the comedy trio in the show, came to the chorus dressing room. He knocked and hollered, "I'm coming in." He pointed to two of us, Doris Dowling and me, and said, "Get dressed quickly. I'm taking you to supper at Sardi's with Orson Welles." Now, I was from New Jersey. When Orson did his famous broadcast of *War of the Worlds,* he set it in New Jersey. There was true panic in Cliffside, and my mother, being a schoolteacher, was a source of knowledge or comfort for many people, who probably couldn't get through to the police station. Our phone rang for at least three hours. I was twelve and told to answer it and say to everyone to stay calm and wait for more information. Neighbors came to our house. Parents of children in my mother's class brought them to her. My mother did stay calm, but she told my brothers to take water and blankets and the flashlight to the cellar. I had also sneaked in at the first interval to see Orson's Mercury Theatre production of *Julius Caesar.* All in all I was very impressed to be going to meet him. I told Rags I had to take my makeup off. He said they wouldn't wait, he'd take someone else. So I went to Sardi's in full stage makeup fairly desperate that Orson wouldn't see that I was going to be a serious actress—he'd only see a chorus girl.

And now Desdemona.

Everything was arranged. I was studying the play and the role from the moment I hung up. A year or so earlier I had attended gatherings at Charles Laughton's house, where he worked with American actors on Shakespeare. His theory was that we shouldn't worry about the accent; American English was closer to Elizabethan English than present-day Received Pronunciation. What we should concentrate on was the rhythm of the poetry. We read to a metronome. I think this gave us confidence, but the real inspiration came from hearing him read Shakespeare.

I flew to Rome, my first trip to Europe by myself. Later, we were to go to North Africa, where the exteriors would be shot. My feelings were completely contradictory. I was proud and humble. I was confident and scared to death. I was earnest and exhilarated, even gleeful. Orson took me to dinner the first night with Trauner. Orson was big, energetic, and brimming with enthusiasm. He was the best talker I ever met. And he talked a lot. Trau, small, sturdy, shy, and observant, didn't say much. He listened, his eyes twinkled. He was a reassuring presence, and I felt as if he were an unknown uncle who could design a movie or build a bridge or drive me safely through a desert sandstorm. With Orson, it was more like jumping off a plane with only one parachute. You had to believe he wouldn't let you fall. And you did believe. He could have charmed the Sphinx if he had wanted to, and he could convince businessmen to give him money to make films time and time again, despite their conservative instincts.

We talked about Desdemona. His conception was of a modern young woman, a rebel against Venetian society. I'd had a glimmer of this idea myself, so I was thrilled to be on the right track.

I learned that I was the second Desdemona. Orson had started shooting several months earlier with the beautiful Valentina Cortese, a fine Italian actress. He ran out of money, and they had to stop shooting. At the same time his romance with Valentina ended. She was quoted later as saying she would rather sell flowers on the Via Veneto than work with him again. I knew nothing of that, and I don't think I would have cared if I had known.

Orson told me how and why he cast me. He was in Paris looking for the last bit of the financing, and for an actress. Anatole Litvak was editing his new film, *The Snakepit*. How he managed to be doing this in Paris, I have no idea, since it was a Twentieth Century–Fox film, shot on the lot in Los Angeles. I had a small but very noticeable part in it. Litvak suggested that Orson look at a couple of reels, and that was it. I got the wonderful phone call.

Trau was flying back in the morning to Casablanca, where the locations were to be shot. The cast and crew were following in four days. Our destination was Mogador, a fishing village with a French

With Olivia de Haviland in *The Snake Pit*, 1948

hotel, a Casbah, and ancient ramparts overlooking the Mediterranean.

Now in Rome, I was taken over by the Italian makeup people,
hairdressers, and costume designers. I think there's a bit of an artist
in every Italian. Perhaps it's because they're born into all that beauty,
natural and manmade. Orson wanted Desdemona to be blond.
Although my hair was a kind of light Titian in life, it photographed
as dark in black and white. Wigs were tried and rejected. Finally, my
hair was bleached and a fall made to lengthen it. I'd always believed
that my best look was natural and windblown. I guess I knew I
couldn't compete in the glamorous sexy stakes. But I adored being
transformed into a smooth, pampered, blond Venetian.

I had a wonderful time in Mogador. We were there for three
weeks. Every night Orson regaled us with his visions of this film
and other projects to come, among them a musical version of *The
Tempest* with Louis Armstrong as Caliban. He apologized to me

As Desdemona (the second of three), with Orson Welles
and Alexandre Trauner, 1952

because I had to hang around. I only shot for two days on the ramparts, to welcome My Lord Othello to Cyprus. Orson assured me
of how wonderful it would be when we got back to the studio in
Rome, Cinecitta, and started the real work.

I wrote postcards and letters to Gene and Kerry and my mother.
I commandeered a bicycle from the production manager and delivered the mail to the set every morning. I went to Marrakech with
the caterer when he needed supplies and fell in love with the bazaar,
the souk. The souk is a big, crowded square. Everything is traded
there: carpets, perfumes, food, electrical goods, books, clothing, oil
lamps, silks, spices, antiques, and camels. And there are acrobats
and dancers, fire-eaters and sword swallowers. A dentist worked in
the open air, storytellers gathered large crowds, scribes wrote letters
and explained official documents. The air smelled of incense and

coffee, camel dung and cinnamon. I drank fresh mint tea full of sugar—the best drink in the world. We had been strongly advised against eating raw fruit or salad or drinking unbottled water. The production couldn't afford sick actors. But I had my forbidden fruit, the prickly pear. In the souk, an agile young man in Turkish trousers with bare torso and a turban tossed the cactus fruit into the air, caught it on the tip of his knife, and peeled it in about three seconds. He then offered it from the knife. I didn't resist. I thought, If it's peeled it must be okay, and luckily it was—and it was also delicious.

The people of Mogador came to watch the filming. The women were veiled. One morning when I arrived on the bicycle with the mail someone said from under her yashmak, "Hello, Betsy." A film and a film crew, especially on location, becomes the world. A voice from outside doesn't seem real. But it was real. It was Helen, a friend from New York, the sister-in-law of Sono Osato. Sono was, and is, married to the handsome Victor Elmaleh, businessman and painter and Moroccan. Whenever the women of the family went to see their grandmother in Mogador, they conformed to the customs and dress of the village. I was invited to the family home. I would get to see a bit of normal life in the Casbah.

The house was white with a small blue door onto the street. Inside was a courtyard full of flowers and a tiled fountain. There were covered porches and beautiful rugs and brass tables. It was cool and spotlessly clean. We had mint tea in tiny glasses, constantly refilled, and sweet cakes. There were about ten women and girls; I saw no men. Helen was translating my questions and the answers, and we were giggling and comfortable very quickly. A group of women alone seems able to transcend nationality and language.

Then Orson trapped me. The pasha of Marrakech had invited Orson to his palace for dinner. Orson didn't want to go—he didn't have time—but he didn't want to give offense. So he sent me.

A large black Daimler with a British chauffeur came to collect me. He told me proudly that it was the same model the king of England had. The pasha's palace was beautiful from the outside,

On location in North Africa
for *Othello,* 1952

rose colored with bougainvillea in bloom covering the walls. Perhaps it was because of the bright sunlight, but the tiled courtyard and the rooms I was escorted through seemed garish and overdressed with carpets and ottomans and cushions and wall hangings. There was a European room with French furniture, tapestries, and too many gilt mirrors. But the pasha and his entourage looked wonderful in simple white djellabas—I think it's the most elegant garment that exists for man or woman. I had already noticed how comfortable and easy the Arab men at the London airport seemed during a hot summer when the rest, the French, Germans, and Americans, were constricted in shirts and jackets and hot leather belts.

A servant beckoned me to an alcove and gave me a cool scented towel and a glass of ice water with a rose petal and a mint leaf floating in it. I'd decided to eat and drink everything I was offered. I would be adventurous—after all, this was an adventure.

One of the sons of the pasha waited for me and led me to a large veranda. Here it was cooler, and young boys waved palm fronds over us as we ate. There were three low round tables for ten with cushions on the floor. Twenty-nine men and me. I was seated next to the pasha, and the feast began. A parade of black-robed and veiled women brought large brass platters of wonderful breads, bright vegetables and fruits, hummus, and couscous. There were bottles of Perrier and Coca-Cola in champagne buckets full of ice. There must have been thirty different hors d'oeuvres. Orson had warned me to take only a smidgen of everything even if I liked one dish particularly—that this was only the beginning. Our dishes were whisked away, more beautiful Limoges appeared. The birds were next—from turkeys to chickens, down to tiny ones I didn't recognize. Then piles of delicate, light meatballs in pastry with candied lemon peel. We paused for sorbet before the main course, a whole roasted sheep.

I did a lot of smiling and charade acting, because the pasha's English was at the same level as my French, almost nonexistent. Finally the youngest son, who was about fifteen, was summoned from the second table. He spoke French, English, and Arabic, so now we could talk. The sheep the pasha was carving seemed to be staring at me, its head right next to my elbow. I asked with assumed innocence why the women didn't eat with us. There were fifteen or twenty of them, richly dressed and veiled, in a far corner at their own tables. Our half-emptied platters were taken to them when we finished each course. My sisterly anger had been bubbling up behind my smiles. I didn't fool the pasha for a second. As his nostrils flared and his eyes flashed, I saw an ancient sheik on his horse, scimitar in hand, racing to war, spreading devastation. But the pasha was a sophisticated man. He smiled a hard smile and answered, through his son, that the women preferred to eat alone. And then he offered me the pièce de résistance—or was it the coup de grâce?—the sheep's eye on the flat of his knife. We were engaged in a battle. I could not back down. I took it between my thumb and forefinger and swallowed it whole. After that I drank glasses and glasses of mint tea to drown the thought of what I'd swallowed.

The pasha and his sons took me to see a room full of cuckoo clocks. There were over a hundred of them, looking bizarre and out of place. And then we went to a vast shed with thirty gleaming cars and forty motorcycles. There my Daimler was waiting for me. My hand was kissed. I was salaamed. I was liberated and at the same time dismissed. I couldn't have been happier to be on my way back to the movie, where I belonged.

Trauner and his assistant, Capellier—Trau and Cap—were my stalwart best friends on the film. Little groups always form on location. They're based on where you choose to sit when you come down to breakfast and who catches your eye during a crisis and who laughs at the same things. And also on respect. I had respected Trau from that dinner the night I arrived in Rome. It was an instinctive feeling, and everything I saw and learned about him and what he had done in the cinema only increased my admiration. He was always an artist, aiming at the best. He could deliver for the money men, the producer, the studio, but his heart was with the project and the director—in this case, Orson.

About ten days into our stay in Mogador there was a crisis. I was in the production office in the hotel one late afternoon when Orson and Trau came in to telephone Rome. Some of the costumes, mine included, had come with us, but the majority had not yet arrived. There was a big scene to be shot in two days' time. The actors, the senators of Venice, must be splendidly dressed, and they had no costumes. Orson pleaded on the phone to Rome; he shouted and threatened and appealed in the name of Art, civilized values, and future work. It was to no avail. If there was no cash on the table, no costumes would be on the plane. And there was no cash.

Orson roared into the dining room and ordered two meals for himself. He inveighed against Fate, Hollywood, the Italians, and his production manager. The rest of us sat in silence. Trau was sketching. When Orson had finished his dinners, and helped himself from everyone else's plate, Trau slipped his drawing pad in front of him. "What is this?" said Orson. And Trau replied in his Hungarian English: "It could be the senators are in old Turkish bath near to the ramparts. They wear towels or maybe not. We make steam."

Now Orson roared with joy. He threw his arms around Trau, picked him up, and danced from table to table. Everyone relaxed, laughing with relief. And so the scene was shot in a Turkish bath and looked great. That crisis was over.

Then one day there was suddenly no filming. There was a schedule, the "call sheet," scenes to be shot, but no Orson. We were due to leave for Rome in three days. No one told us anything. Trau wasn't around much either. I hung out with Capellier, his chief builder in case Trau surfaced. Cap was a big, blond, cheerful fellow, solid and brilliant at his job, but he didn't know what was going on.

The next morning I had a note in my room. I was to pack without telling anyone. The production manager and a car would be waiting for me at eleven o'clock. I was going to see Orson. I was taken to a small hotel in Casablanca and up to his room. He was not well, I was told. He received me from his enormous bed in white silk pyjamas. The film was shutting down; there was no money. But Orson was perfect. Any disappointment I might have felt was dissolved in sympathy for him. He said he knew I'd want to get back to Gene and Kerry and not hang around Rome while he scrabbled for finance. As soon as it was in place, he'd summon me back. It would all be wonderful. He was very excited about our "characterization." He'd keep me posted at all times so the dates would work out. Oh, and by the way, could I buy my own ticket back to LA? It would be reimbursed, of course.

I flew home with joy. I would wait with great hope and complete faith. Alas, I never saw My Lord Othello again. I was the second Desdemona, but, alack, there were three. (There is a fleeting glimpse of me on the ramparts—they didn't get back to shoot in Morocco.)

I did see Orson again. Jeannie Coyne and I were sightseeing in Rome for the weekend almost two years later. On the Via Veneto at the news kiosk there were magazines with a beautiful photograph of Suzanne Cloutier as Desdemona on the cover. The loyal Jeannie commented, "She has cold eyes," and a voice boomed over our shoulders, "Hello, Betsy." I turned; it was Orson eavesdropping. His magnetism is so powerful I was glad to see him. I introduced Jeannie. Orson said, "Are you suing me?" I laughed and said no, I hadn't thought of that. "Good," he said. "I'm taking you both to dinner."

I may have paid for my ticket—actually, I did, and it was of course never reimbursed—but I gained infinitely more. Trau was a friend for life.

Trau knew every interesting hidden corner of Paris, and all the best restaurants. Not the famous expensive ones, but neighborhood, family-run bistros where Monsieur was the chef and Madame the waitress and the cashier. Trau made every meal into a celebration. He was extraordinarily generous with his time and his knowledge. He showed me the artisans of France, the leather workers in one arrondissement, the cabinet makers carving furniture by hand in the suburbs, the goldsmiths in tiny stalls in a glass-roofed arcade making jewelry to be sold at Cartier. He made me love Paris—not just its boulevards and monuments, but the living, working heart of the city. He introduced me to Simone Signoret and Yves Montand, and Jacques Prévert, his closest friend. I was so thrilled to meet the great poet that I stammered out the silly question, "Do you speak English?" With his Gauloise hanging from his lip, he looked down at me and said, *"Jamais."* (It wasn't true—he'd spent six months in New York when he was young, and if he wanted to, he understood.) As for Simone, she became "My-friend-Simone." Back in Beverly Hills, I was teased a lot. It seems in any discussion of Europe, the first words of my contribution were, "My friend Simone says . . ." I didn't mind. I *was* proud to know her. She was beautiful, of course, warm and witty and keen on gossip. I think everyone who loved her, man or woman, was proud to be her friend.

Paris was the refuge for many of Hollywood's blacklisted directors and writers with their loyal wives and uprooted children. John Berry, Jules Dassin, Adrian Scott, Michael Wilson, Paul Jarrico, and Ben and Norma Barzman were the ones I knew best. It was

Jules Dassin on the set of *Rififi*, the first of the many successful films
he directed in Europe

during this time in Paris that I became aware of the odd division in
my life. Gene knew and liked all these people, but his social life,
and therefore mine, was with Capa and Litvak, both of whom had
beautiful French models as girlfriends, with the Klosters crowd,
and with American friends and colleagues passing through the city.
We had a great time; the restaurants were good and the nightclubs
of the 1950s were wonderful. They were like "raves" but without the
drugs. Come to think of it, we were incredibly wholesome. Gene
smoked, at home he drank mostly beer, here he had wine with dinner. I didn't drink or smoke. (Well, that's not completely true.
When Lennie Hayton mixed up a Brandy Alexander I'd have one
because it tasted like a milkshake. And in Paris, at the Russian
restaurant Dominique—where the young unknown Yul Brynner
was playing the balalaika and singing—I would silently toast the
Soviet Union while linking arms and saying *"Brudershaft,"* and

John Berry and Haya Harareet, Cannes, 1960

tossing back an icy vodka. But those were rare occasions.) We went out mainly for the dancing. Remember, those were the days when people still danced with each other. I have to say that we were a pretty flashy couple on the dance floor. I never did get to dance with Fred Astaire, despite my childhood dreams, but I became a bit of a connoisseur of dancing partners. The producer Sam Speigel was a good ballroom dancer and fun, Danny Kaye was marvelous, but Gene was supreme. Jitterbug, waltz, rumba, polka, whatever the music we usually cleared the floor. I think it was not only Gene's fame or skill that people responded to, but also our pleasure in dancing together. But I am being immodest—they never stood back and watched at the Polish Folk Hall in New York before Gene was in the movies.

Lois had an office at MGM Paris. Carol and Gene had a rehearsal room and a pianist. Jeannie helped everyone. Kerry was in school until four o'clock. And I remember a brand-new feeling—

no, I'd had it once before, when I was eleven. My first day of high school, a brisk, sunny September day, and I had a new outfit, red plaid skirt and a yellow twinset. "Red and yellow—catch a fellow," said my brother Fred, teasing me, at breakfast. My father was dropping me off on his way to work. As I hopped out of the car and joined the stream of kids from twelve to eighteen, I had a great surge of excitement and vague visions of dates and proms. I turned back to my father and sang out, "What a field."

Now in Paris I had that feeling again, a feeling of possibility, of opportunity, of the world in front of me. It was dangerous, but I didn't yet know it. What I knew was that I was energetically alive. I could dine and dance with Gene until midnight, walk back to the hotel along the quais, past the Louvre and up the Champs-Élysées, and sleep a few hours. In the morning I'd take Kerry to school and then the day was mine. I devised a plan to get to know Paris on my own. With a map of the Metro, I would ride to the end of a line and walk back, following the stations. I soon discovered that this was overambitious. I never could make it all the way back in time to pick up Kerry—so I'd have to jump into a taxi. But I developed a feeling for the city. I began to understand its layout, and I had a myriad of those tiny encounters that liven up everyday life.

One lunchtime I realized I was lost. I found myself in a street that was deserted except for a man sweeping. The Parisians were all paying proper attention to their midday meal I suppose, as they do. As I approached the old street cleaner, I noticed his broom. I'd never seen anything like it. The handle was a stripped pole of yellowish wood, patinaed from use. The brush itself was a bunch of twigs, fanned out and woven together with raffia. It was beautiful and obviously very effective.

Thinking if I can get to the river, I'll see Notre-Dame and know where I am, I asked him, in my stumbling French, "Excuse me,— *Ou—est—la—Seine? La*," pointing in one direction, *"ou la?"* pointing in the other. He leaned on his broom handle, peered at me intently, and asked me slowly and gravely, *"Tu vas te suicider?"* I picked up the sound of suicide and read his gestures. *This* old man, his gestures said, doesn't want to help this young woman drown herself in the river. It was said so precisely and brilliantly mimed that I would have had him on my charades team any time. "*Non—oh, no!*" I said. Slowly he replied, *"Alors—Bon!"* And with a smile in his eyes he pointed me toward the river.

When I wasn't out exploring, I was meeting my American friends, the blacklisted exiles. Most of them were struggling to find work, to adjust to a new country, and to support a family. At the same time, they were full of enthusiasm for this new chapter in their lives. It's hard to remember just how serious their predicament was, how strange it felt for Americans, newly expelled from the "land of the free," to be among Europeans, with their quite different sense of political life. After all, France was a country where the Communist Party was open and flourishing. In some ways it was liberating for the Americans to be welcomed into this atmosphere.

A large cartoon in *L'Humanite,* the Communist newspaper, showed a wall with the graffiti "U.S. GO HOME," and underneath it said, *"PAS TOI CHARLOT"* ("Not you Charlot"—the French name for Charlie Chaplin). We all felt that *"CHARLOT"* included us. I was not a refugee, and still I felt it too. I was certainly emotionally and socially aligned with them, although I was not yet one of the "un-Americans" who came to Paris to live.

I had a sense of the unity and comradeship that existed among the members of this group, but I didn't realize how far it went. I didn't know they had formed themselves into a collective where "From each according to his ability, to each according to his need" was put into practice. Whatever jobs they found and money they earned was shared out. They were smart and talented and energetic, with good track records, and they managed somehow. Julie Dassin got a European film to direct; John Berry, who had been an actor before becoming a director, started dubbing for Jean Gabin in the English versions of his movies. The writers wrote French and English film and television scripts under assumed names. Of course, they were paid less than their market value, even by friendly producers, but it was enough to take care of their families.

After school and sometimes on Saturday I took Kerry to play with the Dassin girls. But by late afternoon I was unconsciously

gearing up for the other side of my life. By day I was an independent person involved in the struggle of my friends, and then by
night I was a good little wife and mother. None of it was secret. I
always said where I'd been, whom I'd seen, or told the story of the
man who didn't want me to drown myself. I felt no guilt in either
direction. I don't think any of my left-wing friends resented the
Tour d'Argent or the Lancaster Hotel. Kerry and Trau were part of
both sides of my life. And Gene seemed happy that I was busy and
amused by my adventures.

Actually, Gene was altogether happy. He'd been making movies
for ten years. He knew what he was doing. He was looking forward
to his all-dance film to be shot in London. But he loved Paris and
France as much as I did. And he basked in the respect and recognition that Europe accords artists. Away from Culver City and Beverly Hills, from the routine power of the studio, under which he
flourished but against which he chafed, I think he realized his own
power and position. He was a self-reliant and intelligent fellow, and
he was enjoying every aspect of life.

Gene went straight into the first "small film" using up MGM-
blocked funds, *The Devil Makes Three*. This was directed by
Andrew Marton, starring Gene and the delicate young Pier Angeli.
It was a story of international love and smuggling in postwar
Europe. It was shot in France and Germany. I took Kerry out of
school for two weeks so we could go to Munich with Gene. We
stayed in the lovely Bayerisher Hof Hotel. I say lovely now, because
I've been back there since. But the truth is that I didn't notice at the
time, I'd become so used to the extreme luxury of our life. We traveled first class, we ate at the best restaurants, one four-star hotel
suite was like every other. The only one I remember is the River
Suite at the Savoy on our first trip to London, partly because of the
view of the Thames and partly because it gave me my first experience of the glorious bathrooms of great old European hotels, all
white marble and gleaming heated chrome towel rails.

Munich in October 1952 was not my cup of tea. The Oktober-
fest, with its singing and beer swigging in cellars, was all too sug-
gestive of the 1930s and the rise of Hitler. There were bombed-out

ruins to sympathize with, but somehow they didn't move me as they had in London.

Gene went off to the studio or the location early each morning. Kerry and I explored. We walked in the park. We ate frankfurters. We found the Deutsches Museum, a children's science museum. It was the first time we'd ever seen a museum with working models that children could operate themselves. It was a revelation. We spent three happy days there.

But after four days I decided Kerry and I should go back to Paris. She had friends there, and I was finding myself more and more intolerant of the Germans. I didn't like my feelings. I thought of myself as someone who cared about history, who understood the economic causes of war, but I couldn't seem to relate to anyone in a natural way. I saw them all as the Fascist enemy. We left.

The cast and crew came back to Paris to finish shooting. They had a good time, but when the movie came out, it was practically unnoticed—the first time this had happened to Gene.

We went en masse to Klosters for Christmas, a storybook kind of Christmas with snow and sleigh bells. From there we were moving to London for *Invitation to the Dance*. We met an interesting couple in Klosters—at least, the woman was interesting. The husband never made much of an impression on me or anyone else. They were from Egypt and very rich. The wife, whom Capa nicknamed "Pash-Pash," was very pretty. She had two sons, and she and I fell into a routine. After we delivered Kerry and the boys to the ski school, we stopped for a hot chocolate before joining our skiing groups. I was astonished by the parallels and the differences in our lives. We had both been brides at seventeen, but hers was an arranged marriage. She had never met her husband-to-be when she was sent directly from her convent school in Persia to Cairo for her wedding. Her family paid a large dowry, but gained business and financial advantages by selling their beautiful virgin daughter. "Selling" is my word; she didn't think the arrangement unnatural, it was traditional. She had her first son after thirteen months of marriage, just as I had Kerry. This was her first trip to Europe, and she fell in love with it, just as I had. The difference between us was that this

With Jeannie Coyne in Klosters on our way
to ski school, 1953

was her first taste of freedom and feeling of independence, whereas I had never given mine up and never been asked to.

One day at lunch up on the mountain, Pash-Pash got carried away with enthusiasm—she invited all ten of us at the table to Cairo for as long as we wanted. Jeannie and I were the only ones who went.

When we were all settled in a beautiful old house in London, just off Hyde Park Corner, my mother was a couple of weeks into her visit, and Kerry was going to school at the French Lycee, Jeannie and I took off for a week in Egypt. We flew to Cairo, where Pash-Pash met us at the airport. She had persuaded the minister of culture to come with her to meet us and to take us the next day on a tour of the Museum of Antiquity. It was very lucky she did. My passport said "actress," so I was just okay, but Jeannie's said

With Jeannie and Pash-Pash in Egypt

"dancer." Under King Farouk, a pretty young woman "dancer" was assumed to be a whore, and Jeannie was refused entry. I went through immigration to enlist Pash-Pash's assistance. The minister intervened, and we were giggling with relief, when I noticed another American group in trouble. It was Richard Avedon and three models. If "dancer" was bad in their eyes, "model" was beyond the pale. I moved toward them, and Avedon saw me. "Betsy," he called, "do you know anyone? They won't let us in." And I was able to answer, "Just a minute—I have the minister of culture there just behind the customs booth with our friend." I went back up to the gateway, beckoned them over again, and explained, "This is America's most famous photographer and his models. They're here to do a fashion shoot at the pyramids for *Vogue,* our most important fashion magazine. It would be a terrible insult to turn them away." It worked. The Minister looked a bit annoyed, but he did it, and the *Vogue* shoot went ahead.

Jeannie and I had no idea what "rich" meant in a country like Egypt. We couldn't "dress for dinner"; we hadn't packed the right clothes. Two seamstresses who lived in the house somewhere appeared as if by magic. They would alter whatever we chose from a closet full of evening dresses. Mine was a bit short, Jeannie's a bit tight, but when we'd been decked with jewels belonging to Pash-Pash, we could pass muster. All this took place in the atmosphere of a school dormitory. We lounged on beds, we ate chocolates and drank Coca-Cola and mint tea, we giggled, we had our hair done by the resident hairdresser. I had the impression that Pash-Pash was having more fun than she'd had since she left the convent.

I suddenly thought of a harem. Could it be that the ancient, horrific old custom would have been better for Pash-Pash? I say horrific because obviously, to me, an American left-winger, the harem represented slavery, the brutal power of men, and the exploitation of women. But if you're living a lonely, circumscribed life, to be trotted out as an adornment in your Paris gowns, if you've been "bought" at seventeen by a cold, pompous, insensitive man, if your sons are being brought up by any number of nursemaids and later tutors, then perhaps the company of other young woman in intimate daily routine would go a little way toward easing the pain. I don't know.

It's possible the fun she had that week had to do with our being so foreign. Jeannie and I gave her a glimpse of a whole other way of life. We behaved well at the dinner parties, but afterward alone with Pash-Pash, we were completely irreverent about the stodgy businessmen we'd been polite to during the evening. Pash-Pash was shocked but she was also delighted.

I had to be quite strict about the sightseeing, but the principles had been well instilled by Gene. When you're in Egypt you must see the pyramids, the Sphinx, the museums, and as much of the life as possible. Of course, Pash-Pash arranged all this beautifully when asked. We were transported in luxurious cars, had knowledgeable guides, our pictures were taken on camels in front of the pyramids—not, I might add, of Avedon quality, but still nice to take home.

The basis of our host's fortune was cotton, and the day before we left, there was an excursion to the "farm." We'd been driven to Alexandria the night before and set off very early in a station wagon. We passed through a gate, and then we were on the family land. We drove and drove. After an hour I finally asked, "How big is the farm? How many people work on it?" It was not a question Pash-Pash had ever considered. She asked the driver. The answer was that twenty thousand people worked on it. Twenty thousand! It was true that Jeannie and I had no idea what "rich" meant. And it confused me. I couldn't blame Pash-Pash. She was a sweet young woman, kind to everyone. And we had accepted all the privileges and luxury of our visit without thinking. But our pleasures were obviously based on a feudal system. How did the twenty thousand fellaheen live? Should I try in our last twelve hours to talk to Pash-Pash about hygiene and nutrition and child welfare? But how dare I, from my privileged position, confuse her by imposing my values on her? And perhaps I would put her at some risk in her world. I didn't do or say anything. I felt I had somehow failed my mother.

Back in London all was well with Kerry, Gene, Lois, and my mother. The school board in Cliffside was by now eating out of my mother's hand—I should say, out of Gene Kelly's mother-in-law's hand. She had a wonderful record as a teacher, but I don't think they would have allowed her to have three months off every few years but for his fame. Kerry was happy at the Lycee. We had a couple looking after us and our food delivered from Harrods. The house was full and busy.

And Gene was at his best. He was deep into preparation for *Invitation to the Dance.* An all-dance film was a truly revolutionary idea, and he loved London and all his collaborators—the great cameramen English Freddie Young, and the Russian American

Joseph Ruttenberg, and the art directors Alfred Junge, Cedric Gibbons, and Randall Duell.

There were three episodes: a "circus" ballet; an animated Scheherazade story; and "Ring Around the Rosy," loosely based on the Schnitzler play *La Ronde*, where the characters are linked by a bracelet that passed from one to another. He was recruiting the best possible dancers from all over the world for it: Tamara Toumenova and Igor Youskevitch, from New York; Claire Sombert and Claude Bessy, ballerinas from the Paris Opera (where, on Eddie Constantine's suggestion, Gene had found Leslie Caron for *An American in Paris*); and Tommy Rall, from LA. The cartoon sequence was to be done by Hanna and Barbera, who had animated the mouse dance in *Anchors Aweigh*. Carol Haney was dancing the lead for this section. When I saw a run-through rehearsal, she was so wittily expressive that I felt enormous regret that she couldn't be photographed and appear as her brilliant self, but was to be interpreted as a cartoon.

Gene was thirty-eight, with the strength of a man, the energy of a boy, and the enthusiasm of an artist sure of his gifts. *Invitation to the Dance* was an MGM film, but everything was different away from the home lot. At Culver City, each department—sets, costumes, music, camera, and editing—was wonderfully staffed and geared up to supply whatever was needed. Here, in London, Gene worried and fumed a bit because he felt responsible for every detail. This film was his baby, and he tackled the problems with determination—even joy.

I think he was aware of the challenge he faced. As a dancer his aim was to popularize, to reach the big audience. He knew that making a movie in a plotless balletic form might be overstepping the mark, but he did it from serious artistic ambition, not from any pretension.

Anatole Litvak passed through London, and we had dinner. He asked Gene—not me—if Kerry and Gene could spare me for two or three weeks. He needed me, he said, to coach the young French leading lady of the Kirk Douglas film he was making in Paris. He wanted an actress to work with her on her English because he

Sydney Chaplin in California, 1949

believed that language teachers didn't understand dialogue and acting. He had Sydney Chaplin coming to do the same for the French
actor playing the second male lead.

Sydney Chaplin, son of Charlie and Lita Grey, was gorgeous—
tall, handsome, sweet, and wildly funny. He was a good friend of
ours in London, New York, Paris, and at home. He loved our
house, and he loved Kerry. He joked with her that he was waiting
for her to grow up—she was his "fiancée." Gene and I were very
fond of him.

But I don't know why Gene was agreeable to the idea. Perhaps it
was the presence of Sydney, perhaps it was Litvak's white hair, perhaps he was so busy he wouldn't notice my absence. The house was
running perfectly around him as always, my mother was there for
Kerry, Lois was there for my mother. Or maybe he was thinking of

me. It's true that in London I was a bit at a loose end. There were McCarthy refugees here too—Carl Foreman, Stanley Kramer, Joe Losey—but they weren't my chums. All the work took place in the studio. Gene asked me to come along when he was running screen tests, or to see a set and have lunch, but I wasn't part of the action in the way I always felt I was in Beverly Hills. At home, Betty Comden and Adolph Green, Stanley Donen, Saul Chaplin, Lennie Hayton, Carol Haney, Roger Edens and Connie Salinger from the Metro music department, the composers Hugh Martin and Ralph Blane were all friends. They were in and out of our house having dinner, playing games, several times a week. When they were in preparation for a film, Betty and Adolph and Stanley and Gene would be working in the study most afternoons and many evenings; the musical scores would be played in the living room on our piano. Of course, I had no part in their meetings, but Kerry and I would be called to hear the songs, and we never felt shut out. The study had no door, and both it and the living room opened onto the path to the kitchen. They were secure in their work, in those good old days of the studio system. They knew it would come to fruition, that the movie would be made. There was no tension or air of reverence around it. It was just a joyful part of our daily life.

I went back to Paris alone. I stayed in a small cheap hotel on the Left Bank and loved it. I was part of the crew, and I loved that too. I think I was playing at being someone else—or maybe just me if I hadn't gone to Hollywood with Gene.

Sydney and I worked hard. He had taken one look at the French ingenue and convinced me to swap our charges. He coached the actress, I coached the actor. It worked out well. I collected my two hundred dollars' worth of French francs and flew back to London. Strangely enough, I never changed them into pounds or dollars. I just kept them in my passport case for years. I never asked myself why, or thought about what they meant to me, I just kept them.

What can I say about *Invitation to the Dance*? We loved it. Gene was proud of it. MGM was scared of it and couldn't decide how to market it. Pauline Kael wrote later "this picture bollixed the career of Gene Kelly, who directed and choreographed it. . . ." I don't think that's strictly true. But her next phrase—". . . and probably broke his heart as well: practically nobody saw it"—*is* true.

Gene fought for it at MGM. Andre Previn wrote a new score for one section. Looking back, the whole movie may have been a failed dream. An all-dance film with music by Jacques Ibert, Andre Previn, and Rimsky-Korsakov was perhaps too ambitious, and the ambition was misdirected.

Considering the dances in all Gene's films, it's clear that he succeeded in his aims. The revolutionary alter-ego number in *Cover Girl*, the artistry of the ballet in *An American in Paris*, the sexiness of the "Apache" dance with Cyd Charisse (and her fabulous legs), the tenderness of his work with children, the Mexican girl in *Anchors Aweigh* and *I Got Rhythm* with a bunch of French kids, the humor and joie de vivre with Donald O'Connor and again with the Nicolas Brothers, all his numbers with Judy Garland, and, of course, the sublime *Singin' in the Rain*, were accepted and embraced by the public. A sailor suit or his white socks and loafers, or the T-shirts on his muscular torso, gave everyone the feeling that he was a regular guy, and perhaps they too could express love and joy by dancing in the street and stomping through puddles. He was, for all his talent and intelligence, a man of the people. He never lost sight of his vision or succumbed to film-star vanity. He fulfilled his youthful wish. He democratized the dance in movies.

16

IN 1980 I WENT to LA for the marriage of the son of my dearest friend, Ruth Conte. It was a lovely wedding on a hillside in La Jolla. A sort of limo-bus with a butler and champagne was provided by Lee Gershwin, wife of Ira, to transport the guests. I had never known Lee well, although Gene and I had been to parties at the Gershwins' sensational house filled with Impressionist paintings, flower arrangements, and quiet servants. Ira would be wandering around in a dark suit like an amiable teenager—he must have been about fifty at the time—who belonged to his house, but didn't belong at the party. By contrast, Lee, with her slim figure, elegant clothes, and New York nasal drawl, was a kind of grande dame or elder stateswoman of Hollywood. She knew all the dirt, probably more than Hedda Hopper and Louella Parsons combined. But I wasn't in her crowd of shopping, lunching, and high-stakes poker games—nor did I want to be. I always felt that she saw me as a sweet little thing from a small town.

Now, in the limo-bus, she brought me a glass of champagne, sat next to me, and said, "I always knew all about you, darling." Naturally I asked, "What do you mean?"

"Oh well," she replied, sipping her champagne, "whenever you'd been out of town, to Europe or New York or wherever, I knew that there were several offices in the Writers' Building at MGM where your return was eagerly awaited—not just eagerly but with special excitement." No longer the sweet little thing, if ever I had been, I

Lee Gershwin with Oscar Levant, Ira (Lee's husband), and Arthur Freed

just raised my glass to her and smiled. But inwardly I was strangely pleased. Lee Gershwin thought I had been some kind of femme fatale.

I was staying with Ruthie. Very late that same night, after we'd discussed every aspect of the wedding, how beautiful Anne and Mark looked, how lovely the service they'd written themselves was, giggled a bit bitchily about some of the guests, and shed a few tears about Mark as a child, we got onto the subject of a man who had been important in Ruthie's life.

Jay Richard Kennedy was a communist. He was also a con man, a charlatan, and maybe a double agent. I didn't know most of this for sure in 1980. I didn't know any of it in the 1940s and '50s. A communist yes, but not the rest. Jay was a "business manager." Several Hollywood folk got badly burned when they used him to invest their money. (Not Gene, however. He gave Jay $10,000 to invest, with the proviso that after a year he would have it back without profit if he didn't want to continue. And although Jay claimed to have done well for him, showed him figures and lists of stocks and shares, Gene quietly took his $10,000 back, saying he'd been a poor boy, he liked to have his money in the bank where he could see it. He just didn't trust Jay.)

But Jay was plausible and successful enough for my beautiful, intelligent Ruthie to be taken in. It was not a love affair. He had a beautiful intelligent wife of his own who was also fooled—in her case, by love. With Ruthie, the blinkers were political. Had Jay fought in the Spanish Civil War with the International Brigade? Had he been to the Lenin Institute outside Moscow, where they trained spies? Had he worked for the U.S. Treasury Department? Had he absconded with money from the Communist Party in New York, as Arthur Laurents warned us? Or was that a cover story the Party made up so he could work underground, as Ruthie told me? I didn't know the answers then. I don't know them now; I'll probably never know them.

That night, over our cups of tea, Ruthie told me that in the late 1940s or early 1950s, Jay had said to her that he didn't know if I was a member of the Party. The Party was organized in small groups—the famous "cells"—as it had been everywhere from the beginning, so its individual members would have little information to reveal if tortured by the czarist police. Here in the United States, I think this aura of conspiratorial secrecy made the Party more attractive to the free and easy Americans. It made the struggle more real, more immediate. So Jay had said to Ruthie that if I were a member, if I were in his cell, I would make a perfect courier for the Party. I traveled so much, I had a great cover—not just Gene, who would draw attention from me, but my schoolteacher's-daughter manner, my clean, Yankee look, and my youth.

Thirty years later, I was momentarily carried away by these images of myself at twenty-five or so. Lee Gershwin had seen me as "loose." Jay Kennedy had imagined me as a courier for the Communist Party. I heard all this in one day.

I sometimes have a bright shaft of memory. It's like the light that comes from heaven in paintings of saints. We felt such joy believing in the better world that communism would bring, feeling part of the great brotherhood of man. I guess it was a kind of religious ecstasy that we thought would embrace the most deprived and persecuted. Sadly the dawn we awaited proved false, the dream failed. It was a dream based on the lies about the Soviet Union that we accepted so enthusiastically. But it was joy while it lasted!

Of course, I thought I had learned it all, that I understood the concept of dialectical materialism and its theory of the decline of capitalism, which carries "the seeds of its own destruction," etcetera, etcetera. I treasured the little yellow pamphlet with the bold red letters "THE COMMUNIST MANIFESTO." I think I still have it somewhere.

So in the 1940s and early '50s, however minor my role, I was part of what was happening in Hollywood. J. Parnell Thomas, Joseph McCarthy, and the U.S. House of Representatives Un-American Activities Committee attacked the "Reds" in Hollywood. Our own Motion Picture Producers Association caved in. They agreed to never knowingly employ a communist or communist sympathizer. There was a secret blacklist.

Our town split in two.

In the beginning, it wasn't noticeable. The sun was still shining. The making of movies, the dinner parties, the premieres went on as usual. Gene and I were as one about the indecency of this denial of the Constitution and the Bill of Rights, as were all our friends. If you drew a line down the middle of Hollywood, we were on the good side, the left side, the truly American side, defending the freedoms of speech, of association, and of the secret ballot.

The atmosphere darkened, and then the storm broke. Subpoenas were issued. The rumors began. Who had received one? Everyone was wondering what so-and-so would do. What would one do in their place? In hundreds of homes, luxurious or modest, there were fears, tears, battles. Lawyers, business managers, agents, studio executives were consulted desperately. As far as I know, only three studio heads were sympathetic—Dore Schary, David Selznick, and Darryl Zanuck. They advised actors, writers, directors, and producers to lay low, take a holiday, try to work in England. These contacts were private and secret, of course. Publicly these executives went along with the blacklist.

Suitcases were packed for emergency flight. People began to avoid everyone except close friends. Most of us had never socialized or spent time with the right wing, the people who now became the enemy. Robert Taylor, Adolphe Menjou, John Wayne—they'd always lived in a different Hollywood anyway.

Then, in the glare of publicity that McCarthy so desperately craved, the hearings began in Washington, D.C. And the real tragedies started. A branch of the U.S. Government was destroying hundreds of its citizens, and the destruction was there on television for the whole country to see. Kerry remembers coming home from school to find me glued to the little black-and-white set. The accusations, the confessions, the lists of names given to the committee screamed in the headlines of every newspaper. Men and women who had been caring, involved, idealistic became cowards as a result of threats and intimidation—and sometimes out of selfish ambition—denouncing their friends to save themselves. Some, like Elia Kazan, tried to justify their disloyalty by claiming that they had changed their minds, they now believed that communism was a threat to the American way of life. But Kazan must have known that the Communist Party in America was never strong enough to pose a danger to democracy.

But as we all now know—me included—the cold war was real. There were spies and stolen atomic secrets and "Moscow Gold," as the Hearst newspapers claimed to a chorus of our derision.

And yet in the 1940s and '50s in New York and Hollywood, we—that is, the liberals, the left-wingers, and, yes, the communists—were working for basic democratic and human rights, for universal suffrage and education, racial equality, the unions, and social justice right here in the United States. Perhaps we were "useful idiots," as Stalin so disdainfully labeled the Left outside the Soviet Union. But I believe we were a force for good, that what we were fighting for still needs to be fought for today.

As for the House Committee on Un-American Activities, it was a charade. McCarthy's fatal attraction to publicity led him to show business, but the FBI and the committee knew all the "names." There was no need for this American version of a "show trial." Hollywood was not Los Alamos. No one had done anything illegal.

What the writers and directors in the movie business were trying to do (with occasional success) was reflect the true fabric of American life in all its diversity. Today, African-American, Hispanic, and Asian actors are on the screen as heroes, villains, the love interest, the comic relief, doctors, taxi drivers, bums, and millionaires. So progress has been made. But according to the statistics of the Screen Actors Guild, there is still work to be done in films and television to reach a real equality of representation.

The committee hearings on Hollywood had villains—those who betrayed their former colleagues. It also had heroes—the Hollywood Ten. They redeemed us in the eyes of the world, thanks to their refusal to give in and to their faith in the American Constitution. They went to jail for a year for contempt of Congress, but they survived as whole men—at least, nine of them did. One, Edward Dmytryk, recanted, got out of jail early, and immediately signed a contract to make a film.

Hundreds of others, some famous and some not, refused to name names and lost their careers and futures. Marriages were destroyed, friendships betrayed and broken. There were heart attacks—John Garfield died of his—and suicides. McCarthyism is a dark moment in American history. As a country we survive such things, but the personal tragedies are irrevocable and hard to forgive.

There were those who managed to work under pseudonyms or with the cooperation of a friendly ghostwriter, a stand-in who would go to the story conferences, deliver the script and the rewrites, and have his name on the screen. Joseph Losey directed films in London as Joseph Walton. Michael Wilson, uncredited, won an Oscar for the screenplay of *The Bridge on the River Kwai*. (Pierre Boulle, the author of the book, accepted it.)

It took thirty or forty years for the Screen Actors Guild, the Directors Guild, the Producers Association, and the Academy to apologize, to acknowledge screen credits that had been denied, and finally to honor the blacklisted.

All the gaiety had left town. The blithe confidence went missing, perhaps forever. The optimism that had been Hollywood in the 1930s and '40s, the sometimes naive but appealingly popular and cheerful quality of the movies—think of the Andy Hardy films, Deanna Durbin, Astaire-Rogers, and Gene—all this came to an end, never to reemerge.

I don't think this is just my impression. My life at home was the same. Kerry was a great child, busy and bright, loved and loving. Gene was wildly successful and at the height of his creative life. And I was flourishing. Until I was blacklisted, I was working more and more. I was in plays in LA and San Francisco, summer theaters in Santa Fe, Taos, and Westport, and six or seven movies, small parts but each one bigger than the last. I was having fun acting, and my reputation was growing. Lee Strasberg asked me to be in *My Fiddle Has Three Strings,* a play by Arnold Shulman. We opened in Westport, Connecticut, with a fantastic cast: Joseph Bromberg, Fritzie Scheff, Maureen Stapleton, Steven Hill, and Alfred Ryder. It was to move to Broadway. Alas, it didn't make it. We closed in Philadelphia. I was disappointed but not discouraged. I always felt that everything would somehow be all right, that "it," whatever it was—success or artistic fulfillment—was still to come.

One day in particular sometimes comes back to me. Nothing extraordinary happened. I walked Kerry to school on Roxbury Drive. I came back just as Betty Comden, Adolph Green, Stanley Donen, and Roger Edens were arriving to work with Gene. Bertha, the housekeeper, provided orange juice and coffee and tea. Adolph, as always, was irrepressible. There were jokes and laughter. They went into the study to work, and I went upstairs to put on a skirt. I was going downtown. I'm not sure what movie they were working on, maybe *On the Town.* As I left they were all in the living room, with Roger at the piano. I closed the red front door as they played the introduction to a song. I walked to Santa Monica Boulevard, where the old trolley line ran to downtown LA.

As I waited in the sun I had a moment of that special bliss. I'd just left a perfect place, where talented people that I loved were doing great work, and it was my place. But because I was going to do something serious, I had a feeling of belonging to the world too. I was going downtown to address envelopes and make begging phone calls for three or four hours for the Sleepy Lagoon Committee. I was doing a worthwhile thing, not better than theirs—the idea of comparison never entered my mind—but my own thing. Then I'd take the trolley back, walk three blocks, pick up Kerry, who would tell me about school, and we'd all have supper. It *was* blissful.

17

I WAS A MEMBER of the Actors' Lab. We had classes, warm-up exercises, scenes to do, plays to put on. There were excellent teachers—Bobby Lewis, Georges Shdanoff, Daniel Mann. It was a hive of artistic and political activity. I hadn't come here as a little girl or as Gene's bride. I was on my own. I was whatever I wanted to be—no, I was what I was—an actress, the equal of everybody, the same as everybody.

Across the street was the Black Watch Delicatessen, the hangout, a bit of Broadway, a corner of New York in the middle of the desert that LA was built on. It had the usual crummy brown leatherette seats in booths, the salt and pepper shakers, the paper-napkin holder, mustard and ketchup bottles, glass ashtrays, as if it had flown in whole from New York. We were there for "a glass tea" in the morning, maybe for a quick lunch, certainly after rehearsals or a show. All the left-wing intellectuals and artists passed through or sat for hours: Clifford Odets, Arnie Manoff, Jack Berry, Lloyd Gough and Karen Morley, Dalton Trumbo, Albert Maltz, Abe Polonsky, Paul and Sylvia Jarrico, Harold Clurman. They discussed, they debated, they argued, they shouted and insulted each other. They laughed and embraced. They were true buddies—comrades.

I loved them in a different way. I didn't realize exactly where the difference lay. I respected their political passion. I also respected the passion of Gene and everyone he worked with in their artistic endeavors. But the Black Watch Delicatessen was the place where I found what it was like to be a normal twenty- to twenty-five-year-old, not somebody's wife or somebody's mother, just a young woman.

And as a young woman—and, I'm afraid, a flirt—I had admirers. I say as a flirt, but I think all serious young actresses appear to be flirts. We're sensitive to others, we pay attention, we put our best foot forward. Okay, so we want to be loved and chosen—in other words, to get the part. Added to this, I desperately needed to be taken seriously. At the Black Watch Delicatessen, funny as it sounds, I was taken seriously. I didn't sit and listen as I had at Louis Bergen's in New York. I questioned. I discussed. I had arguments and opinions. I was normal, in fact. And I was by myself.

At home I must have vaguely, even unconsciously, wanted everyone to fall in love with me. At the deli it was different. I never thought of the friends I was making as admirers. They were my mentors, and my comrades. I can't think of a better word. (There isn't a better word, whatever its associations.)

I began to be asked on to committees, such as the Screen Actors Guild study group for the "Negro Question," or the Joint Anti-Fascist Refugee Committee. I see now that most of the work I did was about raising money and getting famous names to sign letters or ads, and to appear at benefits. The aim of these ads and benefits was to help refugees from fascism in Europe, to build a new theater for the Actors' Lab, to campaign for Henry Wallace for president, to defend the Hollywood Ten. We worked to make alliances with other sections of the community, the academics, the scientists, to strengthen our forces for all these causes.

When I started to speak at public meetings I turned to my mentors for help. They were almost all writers, and some of them worked at MGM. When I'd written a draft of what I wanted to say, I'd drive to the studio, visit Gene in the rehearsal room or on the set, and then drop in to the Writers Building. It was all perfectly open. I might read the speech to Ben Barzman; he'd say, "Let's show it to Al." We'd go to Al Leavit's office. Adrian Scott might look in. They made suggestions; we'd fix the speech.

So my routine visits to the studio at that time encompassed the two strands of my life. And for me, the exciting part of those excursions was not the glamorous set or the fun rehearsal room but the drab Writers Building and my contact and collaboration with those men and their minds.

Years later in Paris, I was with Jack Berry and Adrian Scott when we heard the shocking news that Jigee Viertel had died. She was a beautiful, smart, sassy woman who had been married to Budd Schulberg and Peter Viertel, and admired by Ernest Hemingway and many others. I had tried, without success, to become a friend of hers. Along with the sadness we all felt, I mentioned this. Adrian smiled his gentle smile and said, "Betsy, she couldn't have liked you. She was the golden girl of the Left, and then you came along—the new kid on the block."

I never felt like a "golden girl," and certainly never was Lee Gershwin's "femme fatale," but I think I was unwittingly laying down paving stones so I could walk away safely. I can see now that I was taking my first tentative steps to a different life.

18

AT NINE-THIRTY one Saturday night in 1950, a journalist from a small Hollywood newspaper, the *Citizen News,* called me. "Could I see you tomorrow?" he asked. I said, "Listen, tomorrow's Sunday. I'll be happy to give you an interview anytime, but not on Sunday." "I have to see you tomorrow. It's not an interview. It's really to help you." Something in his voice convinced me. I agreed to ten o'clock and went back to the all-singing, all-dancing, all-piano-playing fun and laughter that was Saturday night in our house.

When he arrived—I wish I knew his name, I'd like to thank him now—I was waiting. I opened the door before he could ring the bell. When Gene wasn't shooting, there was nary a sound in the Kelly household; everyone went about on tiptoe until he woke up. I suggested that we walk on the bridle path that ran up the middle of Rodeo Drive then. There was never anyone on it, with horse or without.

He told me that the next day in the *Hollywood Reporter* the front-page editorial was about the ground-breaking ceremony for the new Actors' Lab Theatre. The Actors' Lab has been described as the West Coast forerunner of the Actors Studio. The founders were Kazan, Odets, Strasberg, and Bobby Lewis, some of the great talents from the Group Theatre who had been lured to Hollywood by the clever men who ran the major studios then. The members and students were those of us who hankered after what we thought of as the "real theater" and "real acting," or maybe we just missed New York, and needed to practice our craft.

My anonymous friend said the editorial would denounce the whole project, and the speakers at the ceremony, Gale Sondegaard, Lloyd Gough, and me, as a "nest of Reds."

Gale and Lloyd were particularly fine actors and seriously committed people. I was more than proud to be associated with them in either or both categories. So I just laughed and said, "Thank you— don't worry about it."

But he said, "On the back page of the *Hollywood Reporter* there's a small item saying you are being replaced in *Kind Lady* [the film I was about to start] by an English actress as yet unnamed."

That was how the blacklist first lifted its ugly head and leered directly at me.

The Hollywood blacklist was the unacknowledged creation of the House Un-American Activities Committee under J. Parnell Thomas. They were doing what their name implies—investigating un-American activities. The American Nazi Party didn't interest them. For them, "un-American" meant the work of the National Association for the Advancement of Colored People, the American Civil Liberties Union, and any group committed to fighting for unions or against intolerance. When Senator Joseph McCarthy decided they needed a higher profile, either to attract attention or to boost their own careers, or both, they turned to Hollywood. They managed to force Hollywood's own Motion Picture Producers Association to cooperate. Many famous actors and directors— Adolphe Menjou, Cecil B. DeMille, John Wayne, and Robert Taylor, among others—were happy to go along with them. They used *Red Channels,* a magazine put out by a group of extreme right-wing industrialists and manufacturers. This pamphlet threatened a boycott of any film or television program that had in its credits an actor, writer, director, or producer who was on their own list of communists, fellow-travelers, pinkos, or bleeding-heart liberals. That meant no advertising revenue for CBS or NBC, and picketing and bad publicity that would seriously affect the box office for movies. The studios and television stations were running scared. They made their own blacklist.

At the beginning of this part of my story—the blacklist and

me—I have to say that though I'm proud to have been part of the "good guys," I was always aware that I was not as vulnerable as most. I didn't suffer economically—Gene's career ensured that my day-to-day life didn't change. I never felt helpless or frightened. There was never a moment when I debated what to do. Giving so much as an inch to "them" was out of the question.

That Sunday I was defiant. I would not accept that I could be thrown off the movie. I called my agent. I said I would fight publicly. I'd read for the part and been cast in it. I'd been working on my English accent for six weeks with the brilliant Gertrude Fogler, MGM's own voice and diction teacher. She had pronounced me ready to play an English girl. My costumes were made; my portrait had been painted by Miriam Schary, to appear in the film. They had no legitimate cause to "replace" me.

This was a viable tactic for battle, because the studios were denying the existence of the blacklist. I was prepared, even eager, to show up their lie.

Monday morning came, and there it all was. I did have a flutter of fear when I read it, because the printed word is so powerful. (Maybe that's why bad reviews hurt so much.)

And then my agent called. I must have scared or impressed him, because he'd arranged "a friendly talk" with Mr. Mayer—old L.B. himself—for Tuesday at two. *Kind Lady* was an MGM film. And Gene was one of their biggest stars.

L. B. Mayer was the head of MGM, at that time the most successful studio in Hollywood. He was a powerful showman and an equally powerful businessman. His feeling for the United States and its way of life was legendary. His favorite product was an idealized story of small-town life, the Andy Hardy series, with Mickey Rooney as the freckle-faced, devilish but good-hearted, Norman Rockwell American kid and his mom and pop and his wise old grandpa. L.B. truly believed the myth he was creating—and he loved the money it made for Metro.

I prepared myself as if for a stage appearance. I wanted him to see me as a young Katharine Hepburn character—East Coast elegant. I chose to wear a "new-look" navy suit, fitted jacket and flared skirt, flat patent leather pumps—and white kid gloves. My hair was clean and shining, my makeup discreet. I was twenty-five.

Gene was shooting *Summer Stock* on the lot that day.

I was ushered into the office. There behind his big desk he sat— sleek, white-haired, sturdy, and sharp.

L.B. Sit down, sit down, my dear. I want to have a talk with you.

Me. I want to talk to you too.

L.B. I don't understand you people. You live in the greatest country in the world. I had to talk to Spence and Kate too—what's wrong with you people? You look a very nice girl. [My outfit was working.]

You have a wonderful husband who loves you, a lovely little girl, and I understand you're talented— not just some Betty Grable . . .

So what do you want? Don't you appreciate the United States of America? I know many important people in the world [he gestures toward the banks of photographs—L.B. with the pope, L.B. with the president, L.B. with Churchill, and so on]. They would all love to be American, I can tell you.

Me. Mr. Mayer—it's not that I don't like America . . .

L.B. I should hope not. How can you even say that? And we're the richest country in the world—what's wrong with that? You're enjoying prosperity and the good life this country offers, aren't you?

Me. Yes, but there are others . . .

L.B. Ah—the others—what do you know about them? If anyone wants to succeed in this country, if they work hard they will succeed. If you care about the others as you say, do some good works. Don't try to change the country God loves best.

Me. But Mr. Mayer, some things need to be changed. My
   mother always said . . .
L.B. I knew you were the kind of girl who listens to her
   mother . . .

It was here I gave up and decided to go with the flow. I'd been about
to say that my mother always said that you must help others, you
must fight injustice, you must stand up for what you believe is right
even against public opinion or your own interest, but I could see it
was useless.

It went on for quite a while longer in the same rut.

There was one small diversion. He was back on the family, my
mother, Gene, my lovely daughter, when he suddenly looked at a
photograph of his two beautiful daughters, Irene Selznick and Edie
Goetz. There was a tiny pause—I looked too.

"It's true," he said. "I had to divorce their mother, Ida. But I settled three million dollars on her," here he slapped the desk, "in
cash."

His secretary came in. "Mr. Kelly is in the outer office." When I
hadn't appeared on his sound stage by three o'clock, Gene came up
to rescue me.

Mr. Mayer got up, escorted me out to Gene, put one arm
around each of us, and said, "You've got a lovely girl here—and
she's as American as you and me."

As we walked down the hall, Gene grinned at me and said, "You
with your white kid gloves—you must have given an Academy
Award performance in there."

Well, I did and I didn't, I guess. I *was* in *Kind Lady*, and we felt
triumphant. We laughed and made fun of L.B. and how I'd pulled
the wool over his eyes. But lately I've heard that he said to Billy
Grady, MGM's casting director, that Kelly should get rid of his
commie wife. And although I may have won that battle, I lost the
war. After *Kind Lady* I was blacklisted. It was four years before I
worked in the movies again, and ten years until a friend at CBS
went into the files, took my card out, and tore it up. The accusations listed on the card were:

With Ethel Barrymore and Maurice Evans in *Kind Lady*

1. Friend of Oona Chaplin
2. Spoke about *Red Channels* at the Actors' Lab
3. Met Paul Robeson at London airport
4. Spoke at a reunion of the Abraham Lincoln Brigade.

Yes, I was a friend of Oona Chaplin. Yes, I did speak about *Red Channels* at the Actors' Lab. Yes, I did meet Paul Robeson at London airport. I was there having a cup of tea when Robeson's friend, Ella Winter, swept toward me. When she heard that Gene's plane was an hour and a half late she said, "Paul is arriving now—in the next ten minutes. Come with me. You can be part of our reception committee. He'll be glad to see you." Ella Winter was a very forceful woman. She had been married to Lincoln Steffens, the great crusading journalist, and now, with her second husband, Donald Ogden Stewart, the blacklisted screenwriter (of such subversive films as *The Philadelphia Story!*), she lived in London.

Richard II at New York City Center, directed by Margaret Webster, 1950

Ella had visited the Soviet Union in 1923 and written a book about her trip. Some years later she advised the Soviet Ministry of Health to pay more attention to the needs of women. Specifically, she told them that using cloths for the menstrual period was medieval, and that they should skip sanitary napkins and go straight to tampons. A woman who could do that could easily sweep me away from my book and my tea. But the actress in me was the real reason I joined the welcome to Robeson. I knew he was coming to London to play Othello. Perhaps seeing me again he would decide that I should be his Desdemona.

And yes, I spoke at a reunion of the Abraham Lincoln Brigade. Or rather, I read the speech that Gene was supposed to give—but he had laryngitis.

So I think it was L. B. Mayer who pulled the wool over my eyes. They didn't want a public fuss about it all from an unimportant actress in an unimportant film. They just wanted to protect Gene, their star.

Playing my husband in *Kind Lady* was Maurice Evans, the English-born star of the New York theater. He was not political, but he was so horrified by the *Hollywood Reporter* story, so interested in the Actors' Lab, and so amused by my meeting with L. B. Mayer, that he said, "Forget them. Leave them behind you. Come to New York and play my queen in *Richard II* at the City Center. Rehearsals start a month after the film ends." And I did just that. So I won something after all.

19

IN 1947, GEORGE CUKOR asked me to play a very small role in *A Double Life*.

He telephoned to say that he and Garson Kanin, who had written the screenplay with Ruth Gordon, really wanted me for one scene—only two days, he said, as if to please me. He couldn't know that I'd abandoned my pretentions about "the theater." By now, I was dying to be in the movies. I jumped at the chance.

Garson Kanin, charming and witty, was also perceptive and good. He had read some early unproduced plays by Paddy Chayevsky and recognized his talent. He arranged a few days of work as an extra/bit-part player for Paddy so he could make some money.

Luckily for me, our days coincided. We met, we talked, and very quickly we fought about politics. I invited him home to dinner. He and Gene got on a treat—they were both left-wing Democrats, what the Europeans call Socialists. Neither one believed in the "dictatorship of the proletariat"; they recognized it as the dictatorship of the Party. I, of course, was still a true believer. At any rate we saw him a few times before he went back to New York to write for television.

Now Paddy and Delbert Mann were flying to LA in triumph as writer and director of *Marty*, their very successful TV drama. They were to make a movie of it. The producing company was Hecht-Hill-Lancaster for United Artists.

On the plane Paddy said, "I know a girl to play Clara—Betsy Blair."

My first movie role, only one scene, in *A Double Life,* directed by George Cukor

It seems that Delbert replied—and I only repeat it because they told me themselves—"No, she's too young and too pretty." (I'd been in a Kraft Theater live television show for Delbert, playing a college girl.)

Paddy said, "She can't be too young, she already had a kid when I met her."

They called me and asked if I would read for them—that is, audition. I said yes but that I'd like to have a script a day or two before, to work on the scenes. They sent it over.

Never before, nor in the years since, have I read a screenplay that I thought was so perfect. I was wildly enthusiastic. I jumped in my car and went straight to my acting teacher, my coach, the great Georges Shdanoff, known as Yura. He and Michael Chekhov had been young actors in the Moscow Art Theatre. They ran away and started a small theater in England, then another in Connecticut, and they ended up in Hollywood acting and teaching. I was in his class at the Actors' Lab, and when he announced that he was leaving because he believed he could do better work with actors as individuals, Patricia Neal and I left with him.

In those days, no one talked about "acting coaches"; their existence was a secret. It wasn't until Marilyn Monroe and Paula and Lee Strasberg that it came out into the open and created havoc for directors on the set.

Yura and I worked all afternoon that day and for six or seven hours the next day.

First we read the whole script aloud. Then we discussed the character of Clara—her background, her relationship to her parents and her work, her hopes and desires. We found "the beginning, middle, and end" of her part in the structure of the story. Yura believed, as Stanislavsky had taught (in person, in Yura's case) that the psychological understanding of the role, and the "factual" background of the character as invented by the actor, form the solid base on which to achieve the freedom necessary to act, to play.

Then we worked on Clara's scenes. Here, too, we pinpointed the beginning, middle, and end. We found a climax to work toward in each scene. We decided on the surface behavior and attitudes of this particular young woman. And, most important of all, her underlying and perhaps unconscious (for the character, not for the actor) emotions and aims for each moment. And where the humor lay, if any, and when the deep emotions might be revealed, and what a silence or a pause means—all this was to be explored. Ai-yi, we did work hard!

And still there was that important mysterious element to discover—where the character and the actor touch each other. How could my experience be used to create and illuminate this imaginary person—how to make her real for myself and the audience? Here we ran into a problem. The most obvious thing about Clara, revealed in all her behavior and dialogue, is her shyness. For whatever reason—probably because of my mother's love—I had never felt shy. So we set about finding a model. I had a good friend, Sylvia

Reading through *Marty* with Ernest Borgnine at home on Rodeo Drive, 1955

Jarrico. She was intelligent, witty, gentle, and self-effacing. She was soft-spoken but clear and kind—a perfect model for Clara. And so I used Sylvia, incorporating some of her manner into Clara and me.

And we worked, rehearsing every scene many, many times—trying things out—adding elements or taking them away, until my first audition. The bonus of this secret system was that once you'd broken down the scenes, you know exactly what you want to do, you know it by heart, and you go to the audition as if you had only read it through a few times.

The first audition was with Harold Hecht and Delbert and, as my acting partner, Paddy.

When I was called back it was the three producers, Hecht and Hill and Burt Lancaster, Delbert, Paddy, a secretary, and an actor to read with me.

The third time the group was the same except for the actor. Now

Paddy Chayevsky and Delbert Mann on the set of *Marty*

it was Ernest Borgnine. And it was suddenly enjoyable. There was no tension between us, therefore none in the air. We were "playing" in the sense of acting and as in a great game of tennis.

As the secretary walked me out she whispered, "I think you got the part. The Great Stone Face had a tear in his eye." She was talking about Burt Lancaster.

So far, no one had mentioned the blacklist.

Then, an apologetic phone call from Harold Hecht, the active producer—he was sorry, it was unimportant, it was his fault, anyone connected with him was suspect. Would I please write a letter that he could show them (the California congressman, or the HUAC, or Roy Brewer) that would clear me. I didn't have to name names, he said, at least not names that hadn't already been exposed. I asked him if he was crazy—why was he doing this now after these two intense weeks? Why did he let them start with me at all? He knew I wouldn't do it—he knew I couldn't. "Yes, yes," he said, "I'm

sorry—maybe you can just write a letter without names." Did I
want the role? Did I want to be part of this wonderful film?

There was only one answer to that—of course I did. So I said I'd
see, I'd try. Well, I tried, and the result was pathetic. My letter
sounded like a schoolgirl essay for Civics class. I went on about
freedom of speech and the American Constitution and the secret
ballot. I could say I loved my country—that was about all I could

say that would please them. But when I'd done it, both Harold Hecht and I knew it wouldn't pass muster. It didn't come near what the Un-American Activities Committee wanted—no, *demanded*. And Harold knew, because he had given them everything they wanted; he had named names.

At home, when friends teased me about working for him if I got the part, my answer was that I'd work for him, but I wouldn't have him in my house,.

I was miserable. I really wanted to play Clara. I knew it would be an important film, that it was new and different. It was about ordinary people.

And Gene rode to my rescue. The new head of MGM, Dore Schary, was a world and a generation away from L. B. Mayer. He was a liberal, an intellectual, and a gentleman. He and his wife, Miriam, were friends of ours—they were passionate charade players and part of our regular Saturday-night crowd.

Gene—with the kid gloves off—went raging into Dore's office: "You know her—you know she's not going to overthrow the government. You have to do something—she really wants this part. She read for them three times, and she got it. She tells me it's a great script—do something, Dore, or I'll stop shooting."

And Dore did. He called the American Legion in Washington right there and then in front of Gene, and he vouched for me.

And so I was in *Marty*.

Thank you, Gene. Thank you, Dore. Thank you, Delbert Mann.

And thank you, Paddy, for writing it.

So I'd escaped the blacklist. At least, I thought I had. But it turned out to be the same story as *Kind Lady*. I was allowed to be in *Marty* because of my connections.

20

THERE WERE two sailboats in my life. My father's partner, Mr. Ferguson, owned the first and very special one. It was special to me because on some summer Saturdays when I was eight and nine and ten, Daddy and I would go sailing with Mr. Ferguson. His boat was special, as was his car, because Mr. Ferguson was paralyzed from the waist down. He'd had polio when he was twenty-six, this gentle handsome man full of energy and wit. He was tall, too, although I didn't realize it, since I always saw him in his wheelchair. He drove his own specially adjusted car. We would meet him at the dock in New Rochelle. He would pull up, open the car door, and swing his wheelchair onto the wooden pier. Then he'd hoist himself into the chair, lock the car, and wheel down to the boat. I was greeted with a no-nonsense grin and told to jump on deck. He'd grasp the railing and lower himself to a sitting position on the slats of the pier, lifting his legs by his hands so his feet were on the deck, and then I was allowed to help. I was handed the things we would need for the day: two bottles of beer, a bottle of lemonade for me, a hamper with sandwiches and apples and cookies, his extra cardigan, and a captain's hat. As Daddy handed me the hat and I put it on Mr. Ferguson's head, he would salute. I'd salute back and say, "Aye, aye, sir," as he swung himself over to his place at the tiller. My father would untie the ropes, we'd cast off, and the outboard motor chugged us out on Long Island Sound to catch the wind in the sail.

Even as a child, or maybe especially as a child, I never felt any pity for him. He didn't want pity; he was too strong for that. I guess

A happy sailing day with my father

I could sense his spirit, but mainly I remember that I was intensely interested in the details of his ingenuity and skill.

And what I also remember is my solitary joy. I'd go to the front of the boat, lie on my stomach, get splashed by the spray, and dream. I don't remember thinking of anything at all. I just gazed at the sea and the sky.

In California I seem to have needed to find another sailboat. Or *boats*—they were rented, and I didn't always have the same one. Six or seven times a year I made sure that Lois and Bertha were there to see Kerry off to school, and I drove off to Balboa Beach on my own. For five dollars I rented a sailboat for four hours and sailed around the bay. I never went beyond the limits out into the Pacific. There was no danger, no particular adventure, just solitude. I never consciously thought, "I want to be alone," or "I need time to myself," but I was somehow driven to take this "time out."

Gene, as far as I could see, was smilingly bemused by this non-

Hollywood activity. I had one friend, Ethel Chaplin, who suspected me of some kind of tryst. She never said anything, but it was clear that she thought something was up, so I asked her to come with me one day. New York born and bred, she was perfectly dressed for sailing in white cotton slacks, sneakers, and a navy-and-white-striped T-shirt when I picked her up. When she saw the boatyard workers greet me and noted their surprise that I wasn't alone, she confessed her doubts with a Sydney Greenstreet imitation: "By Jove, sir, you are a character, you really are."

A character? Was I? Clearly I had some wish to get away. Why didn't I buy the whole Hollywood thing? Maybe there's a clue in my work as an actress. Why was I never cast as "the girl next door"? I thought I was a typical ordinary small-town American. But Teresa Wright, Phyllis Thaxter, June Allyson, or Dorothy McGuire played the parts I thought I should have. Now, if I happen to catch a film I was in on television, I can see quite clearly that, as an actress, I wasn't what I thought. From *A Double Life* via *The Snakepit* and *Another Part of the Forest* through *Marty* and the European films, I can see, I think objectively, a more offbeat, edgier quality than Hollywood wanted. Infuriating as it was, the directors who didn't cast me as sweetness and light were probably right.

And although I thought I was participating fully in my "perfect" life, I must have wanted something more and different. It took me a long time to realize this and to escape.

Why "escape"? I don't think of myself as Nora in *A Doll's House,* the play in which Ibsen examines the relationship between husband and wife—more specifically, between a paternalistic husband and a child bride in a prevailing masculine society.

Was I in nineteenth-century Norway? Was I in a bourgeois conservative household? No. Rodeo Drive was a casual, freewheeling, liberal home in twentieth-century Hollywood. So any comparison between *A Doll's House* and my life seems way off the mark. And yet when Stella Adler, in her book *On Ibsen, Strindberg and Chekhov,* says, "Somewhere a realistic, independent individual has always been there inside Nora. Her childlike pose was a pretence by which she herself was taken in," I recognize it. My own "realistic, independent individual" knew that to be a serious actress I should be in New York.

This is not the lament of an unfulfilled woman. I had an agent, I studied, I read, I was in plays and movies. I was an actress. But I was an actress subject to the convenience of my family life—and it was my own doing.

When Patrick McGilligan interviewed me for his book *Tender Comrades: A Backstory of the Blacklist,* I said to him: "I haven't had much of a career—I guess I always thought Life was more important." It was easy to say, but when I saw it in print it didn't ring completely true. Of course, life is more important—in a burning building, I'd save the child, not the Picasso. But I was choosing between two parts of myself, and it was the actress I put in second place. I don't regret it, except for never playing Mary Tyrone in O'Neill's *Long Day's Journey into Night*—and I admit that is the lament of an actress.

In the 1940s and '50s, it was a rare woman who could fight for herself and her work. They say necessity focuses the mind, sharpens ambition. I most certainly wanted to act, but I never realized the necessity of fighting for it, because in my case, there was no visible enemy—it was only me, myself.

I think it was the New Jersey in me. I'd gotten away lickety-split, but I took New Jersey with me. As my mother told me, I had to "brighten the corner" where I was. And it wasn't difficult. The corner I was in was already sunny (there wasn't even any smog in LA then). I never felt at a loose end, never wondered what I was doing with my life. I was too busy living to worry about my career. That was somehow for later.

Maybe I was always too young—the youngest in the family, the youngest high school graduate, the youngest in the chorus, in a play on Broadway and a wife at seventeen, a mother at eighteen.

The urge to act is powerful—even without any persistent attention from me, it pushed through. It said "actress" on my passport, but I had to get out of Hollywood before I could think of myself as a working woman.

21

THE TIME had come to grow up. It would have been lovely if I had been able to waltz right into an equal partnership with Gene. I was strong enough to change myself, but I wasn't strong enough to confront him and make him see me as a woman, not a little angel. For ten or eleven years I was in a gold silk cocoon nestled in my corner of Beverly Hills. But a cocoon has a chrysalis inside it—not a good or a bad chrysalis, just one that will emerge. It will burst open. It will emerge.

During those years I was a flirt of a particular kind—the almost innocent flirt. I can see now that I wanted every man to sort of fall in love with me. I was ready to be "soulmates"—that is, to have a special relationship in which I was adored. I gave back warm attention and intimate moments and sometimes a rueful "what might have been if I weren't so happily married" kind of smile. I'm sure this behavior was directly related to Gene and his fame. With the whole world admiring him, I had to find my own circle of admirers.

I don't think I was jealous of his success; I just wanted mine too. And rather strangely, I was never jealous or suspicious of him personally. He never gave me reason to be. Besides, most of me was still on cloud nine. Betty Comden—lovely, intelligent, sensitive Betty—asked me recently if I had been angry at how much time and space they all took in my marriage. She meant when she and Adolph Green, and Stanley Donen and Roger Edens would be at the house working. She was particularly aware of me since she was the only woman among them. I could honestly tell her that it never

The Glass Menagerie with Ann Harding playing Amanda,
in the summer theater at Taos, New Mexico

crossed my mind to be angry, or even to feel left out or deprived of attention in any way. What Gene and I had was what I knew of life and marriage. And in many ways, it was exceptionally good.

Gene never stifled me. My political activities were accepted as my own thing. I could go to meetings, work on committees, sign petitions, make public speeches, and give money when and where I chose. He never implied in any way that I had a position or special

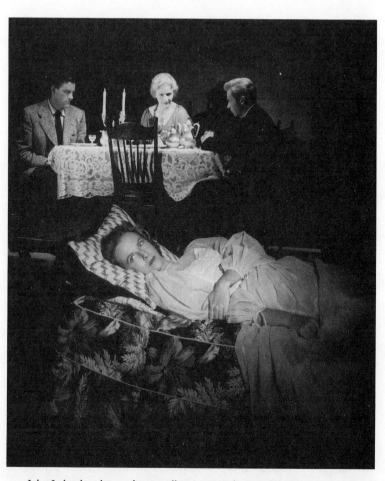

John Ireland as the gentleman caller, Ann Harding, and Richard Basehart,
all three wonderful, well-cast actors

responsibility as his wife to think of his reputation. I was a free
agent.

He also supported and respected my professional life. I was in
several plays in Los Angeles, from *Pamela* at the Eugenie Leon-
tovitch ninety-nine-seat house to *Deep Are the Roots,* downtown in
a big old vaudeville theater. I studied at the Actors' Lab. I did summer stock at Westport for *Sabrina Fair* and *The Rainmaker,* and

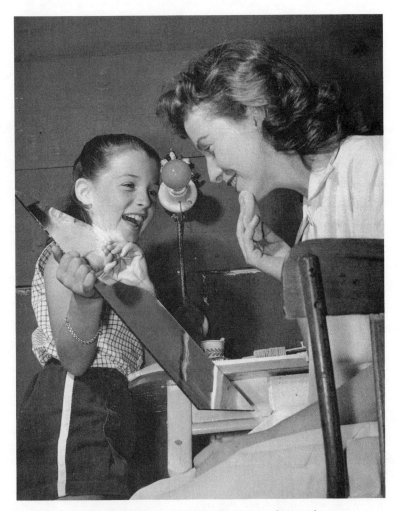

Kerry sometimes came with me for summer theater jobs.
Here we are in my dressing room in Taos, New Mexico.

took Kerry with me when she was seven or eight to Santa Fe and
Taos for *The Glass Menagerie*. I finally got to play Laura, with a
splendid cast: Ann Harding, Richard Basehart, and John Ireland.

It's true that our household ran perfectly—with me or without
me. So Gene was never the slightest bit inconvenienced by my

Rehearsing *Sabrina Fair* in Westport summer theater, 1949

absence. And he was attentive and enthusiastic. In LA, he came to my opening nights; elsewhere, there were flowers, telegrams, phone calls, and congratulations.

And we always had fun, alone together or with friends, and especially with Kerry. There was his work and success and premieres and recognition. There were trips to New York and Paris and London and Rome and Klosters to ski, by train and plane and ocean liner. We were happy in bed, at least as far as I knew. And yet, and yet . . .

I broke out of the cocoon. I don't remember being uneasy in the idyllic life I was leading. It was, after all, running in tandem with my left-wing beliefs. I was not clearheaded or clearsighted enough to see that there might be a contradiction there, that perhaps I was uncomfortable about my unearned luxury—unearned not by Gene, but by me. But I was looking for something. Given my image of myself, not to mention Gene's image of me, I couldn't believe what I found, what I was doing. I started to have affairs. I, who had always been a little puritanical about others, had to face myself. I also had to imagine that I was in love each time, or it wouldn't have been possible.

When I decided to write this part of the book truthfully, I had a dilemma. Should I name names? Well, I can't. I don't mean to be secretive or evasive, but "naming names" has associations for me in that other context, the Un-American Activities Committee, and therefore it's engraved on my soul as a sin. I see no difference here. Besides, I never slept with Frank Sinatra, or Aly Khan or Laurence Olivier—only with a few nice left-wing men who deserve their anonymity.

When I was in Paris alone for two weeks, working for Anatole Litvak, I stayed in the small Hotel des Saints-Peres, just off Saint-Germain des Pres. There's a time between day and darkness that movie cameramen call the "magic hour." It's magic because of the quality of the light. The sky gradually turns cobalt, the streetlamps start to shimmer as the stars come out. And then it's night. The magic hour is over. But that night in Paris, it wasn't over, it was just beginning.

Louis Daquin, a French director, and his wife had invited me to supper with Jean Lods, the head of IDHEC, the French film school. Jean had been to Madrid for the weekend and brought me a pair of espadrilles I'd asked for (in those days the only authentic ones were in Spain).

We were sitting outside a bistro a few doors down the street from the Café Flore. As we finished our perfect steak, pommes frites, two young men, beautiful—there's no other word—young men came strolling by. They joined us. They were both tanned, and lean, and neat in that particular French way, with their shirt cuffs turned

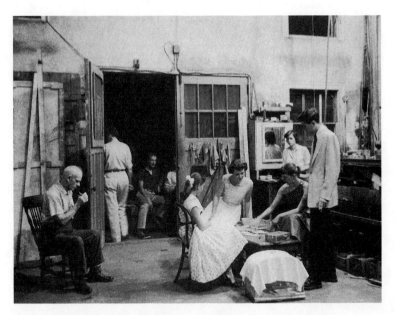

The *Rainmaker* rehearsal space in Santa Fe summer theater, 1950

back. One was an assistant director. I didn't quite understand what the other did, although they were trying to speak English for me. Let's say he was the hero of this episode. I learned later he had been a hero of the French Resistance, the communist part of it.

Louis ordered another bottle of red wine. I'd been drinking water, but now with a heady sense of adventure I said, "Me too, *s'il vous plait.*"

They stayed for about half an hour. Then, *"enchante"* as they were to meet me, they left.

We ordered cheese and crème caramel, coffee for them and mint tea for me. We chatted, we looked at the sky. The night cooled down. There were few people left in the street or the café. The waiters began to flick their napkins around and fold up chairs. I yawned. As Louis paid the check we heard running footsteps on the cobblestones. There was no one in sight. The two young men rounded the corner, backlit by the floodlights on the Church of Saint-Germain, and slowed to a saunter. They were back.

The hero pulled up a chair next to me. He gestured to ask if he could finish my wine. I smiled yes. He asked what I'd seen in Paris. I said I thought I'd seen everything, this wasn't my first visit. Had I seen the real Seine, the working river where the barges loaded and unloaded? No. Had I seen Menilmontant on a moonlit night like this? No. You must, he said, I'll show you, I'll get my car. Come with me.

I went. We said good night to the others. I forgot my espadrilles on the chair. I think I said thank you to Louis—I hope so. The hero took my hand as we walked to his car. We drove along the quais to the outskirts of Paris. I was no longer sleepy. We parked just above the docks, looking down on the stevedores in blue smocks, trucks, pulleys, ramps, crates, cartons, piles of timber, all brightly lit with steam rising from the river in the background.

He kissed me and I kissed him. We went back to Saint-Germain des Pres to his apartment. I stayed the night. We never did get to Menilmontant.

And I was from the generation where you didn't let a boy kiss you until the fifth date.

I remember it all, the courtyard of his building, the iron and brass cage-like elevator, the heavy paneled door, the darkened living room we crossed to the bedroom, the moonlight coming through the shutters, the white linen sheets. It was summer, we had very few clothes. As I slipped off my gold narrow strapped sandals, I had a fleeting image of the sturdy brown ones I'd so hurriedly put on in the bathroom of my childhood in Cliffside, to beat my brothers downstairs and win Uncle Sam's dime.

But of the twenty years in between I had not a single thought or image. I stood naked on the beautiful old parquet floor as if new-born. No guilt, no consciousness, no "what am I doing?"

His English was better than he thought, and my French improved spectacularly. We made love happily, we slept happily. Sitting naked in bed in the morning eating grapes I told him I have a wonderful daughter, my *petite fille*. He smiled at me and said, "Of course, *bien sur—et votre mari-husband—danseur—il est homosexual?*" I laughed in surprise, shaking my head no.

A year later, when it was over, I thought, what a strange question! I never figured out why it was strange, because by then I was thinking that I was even stranger. Why, even when his name was mentioned, did I never relate what I was doing to Gene?

Back in London and then Los Angeles, I couldn't face my betrayal. I made this escapade, which I felt as a great love affair, a separate thing. It was in a different country, we spoke a different language. I telephoned secretly. I wrote letters in my car and took them to the post office. I'd wake up without an alarm to run downstairs to get the mail first and hide his letters to me to read later. I did all the desperate ridiculous things one does in that situation.

I split myself in half—well, more in three quarters and one quarter, or even 90 percent and 10 percent. Ninety percent of me carried on as usual, wife, mother, actress, while 10 percent was passionately, romantically in love elsewhere. I have to admit that I loved it, the secrecy, the adventure, the danger, the sheer wickedness. I felt that I was striking out, doing something that was all my own. Not that I stopped to formulate any of this at the time.

And sadly I used this adventure to segue into another. I didn't confide in Ruthie, which would have been safe and traditional, to tell your best friend, another woman. Instead I turned to one of my mentors at the Black Watch.

He was an "uncle" figure, a wise and solid presence with soulful brown eyes. He listened to me. He was gentle and concerned. He consoled me. He implied that I wasn't bad. And soon I was in bed with him. This time was different. I didn't feel wild and passionate, I felt grown-up. We talked a great deal about his childhood and his Russian immigrant anarchist parents and how his politics had been imbibed with his mother's milk and what he wanted to achieve as a writer. Our lovemaking was tender and seemed to be part of our conversation. And it took place in odd locations—at least they were odd for me—his car, the empty apartment of a friend of his, even a cheesy motel on the corner of La Cienaga and Melrose. Of course, this was because we were both married, but we never talked about that. (Actually, my "hero" in France was married too, but in August French wives and children go to the country or the seaside.)

Out of these two experiences I made up a rule for myself. I wouldn't sleep with anyone whose wife was a friend of mine. I think everyone draws these phoney arbitrary lines—different ones in each case—in order to feel virtuous in some way. But deep down I knew I was no longer virtuous.

I can truly say that neither of these stories, nor the others, was about sex. On the quai in Paris, yes, I was excited and aroused. But I was even more in a state of exhilaration, of curiosity—I was like an explorer. I felt a stirring of independence—I'm free, I'm me, I can do this.

And when a few months later I was rehearsing a play with a handsome energetic fellow and gaily embarked on another affair, it was my "uncle" I confessed to and ended my story with him. My "uncle," not my dear husband, was the one I felt I was betraying.

And so it goes—and so it went. Until the morning I woke up. I'd been in bed for two days with the flu. Kerry had gone to school, Gene to the studio. The housekeeper was doing the grocery shopping, and Lois hadn't arrived yet. I was all alone. I wandered downstairs, pale and wan in bare feet and Gene's pajama top. I got some orange juice and went into the backyard. I looked at the avocado trees and Kerry's playhouse. I went back in. This was my house. I remembered it as I first saw it, with its sickly green painted beams, now stripped against the white ceiling.

I'm crazy, I thought. This is where I live. This is where I belong. But I suddenly couldn't hide the truth. That "I," the good little girl who lived there, was no longer me. "She" didn't have affairs, but the new "I" did. She didn't tell stories about where she'd been, while I had become quite skillful at lying. I was stricken. This can't be me. I told Gene that I didn't know why but I felt desperate, I needed to talk to someone. He was indulgent and concerned as always— whatever I needed, he just wanted me to be happy.

And so I managed to find the only marxist-Freudian psychoanalyst in Los Angeles. His first question was why did I think I should be analyzed. I burst into tears and blurted out, "I think I should get a divorce and I can't even mention that there might be a problem." In all my horrified soul-searching confusion, divorce was a word that had never surfaced. I was terrified. But I was impressed, too. Just saying the word aloud felt as if a great stone had rolled off my shoulders.

Gene didn't really believe in analysis, so he wasn't thrilled by mine. Like many partners, he probably felt threatened. But again, he didn't interfere. It seems I could do whatever I wanted as long as I was still his sweet dove. But I was no longer a sweet dove—if indeed I ever had been. Perhaps I was just very young and he was very powerful.

In my second year of analysis, I went to a sneak preview with Gene of *It's Always Fair Weather.* The next morning on the couch I found myself wailing, "How can I even think of resistance, and rebellion, I mean divorce, when he's up there in close-up, thirty-two times larger than life, and irresistible?"

I never wavered for an instant in my admiration for his work. I tried hard to get him to change or, at least, to see and understand the changes I felt in myself. I believe he wanted to, but it was impossible for him. His character, the creator, the patriarch, the boss in a way, was too set. He had what he wanted. He saw no reason to change.

And then in France in 1956, I really did fall in love. Now there was no escape; or, rather, I had found what I needed to give me the strength to escape. I asked Gene to meet me in a hotel in Paris. We sat on the balcony of the room I had taken overlooking the Champs-Élysées. He had a cold beer. I had a pot of tea. We talked until the sun came up. I told him everything; I cried. I thought about Kerry and felt that my heart was breaking. But I had to do it. I had to go. We had to divorce. Gene said he had known about my affairs but he thought since I hadn't had any adolescence, my wild period would pass. He'd wait it out. Even here, he seemed to think he was in charge.

Through my tears I kept to my resolve. I was angry at my tears; I thought they were childish, when I wanted to be calm and strong. I know now that they were legitimate, that I was crying because of what I was taking away from my darling daughter. I was breaking her family. I wasn't doing it lightly, or for fun or romance. I was doing it to survive as an "adult woman." I know it sounds pretentious to say "survive," given the life I was leading. But that life was so powerful, so seductive in its ease and pleasure, that I had to fight within myself not to fall back into it.

Three or four times during this long night, I said to Gene, probably to assuage my own guilt, to get him to share it, "But Gene, you can't have been faithful all these fifteen years. You're a sexy movie star. You must have had all kinds of women throwing themselves at you." "No," he said, and "No" and "No" and "No" again. And the fifth time I brought it up, "Come on, Gene," he did answer: "Never when you were there." Somewhere inside me I knew this was funny. At the time I only felt relief.

We agreed, naturally, to do our best for Kerry. We would share custody. We would be as gentle and civilized as possible. We would tell her together and assure her of our love for her.

We went back to Rodeo Drive. We planned to live separately in the house for the year a California divorce takes. We hired lawyers because Gene said we should. He had Greg Bautzer, the biggest lawyer in Hollywood. I found a young left-wing fellow who unfortunately was impressed even to enter Greg Bautzer's office. I didn't think it mattered. We didn't have anything to fight about.

I was wrong. The day came when my lawyer told me, "Mr. Bautzer says that Mr. Kelly doesn't agree to the community property division of assets." The law in California splits whatever was acquired during the marriage, fifty-fifty. He continued, "Mr. Bautzer says he will accuse you of adultery and of giving ten thousand dollars to the Red Chinese. Did you give ten thousand dollars to the Red Chinese?" I explained that I was a partner in a film company in Paris. We were planning a movie to be shot in China, a Franco-Chinese coproduction. Each of the three partners had invested. (More of this later—we did make the movie.) But this was not giving money to the "Red Chinese."

And then I saw red—New Jersey red, Beverly Hills red, and Chinese red. For the only time in my life I was so angry I couldn't think straight. I went home, and when Gene came in I told him to get out, I was ashamed of him. Wasn't he ashamed of himself? For money? Wouldn't he be ashamed in front of his friends? "What friends?" he asked. "Frank Sinatra—Mickey Rooney—I don't know—whoever's getting a divorce—they're obeying the community property law." "That's different—Mickey and Frank want out, so they pay—that's different."

Our assets in 1956 were said to be half a million dollars, including the "Betsy B" cattle ranch investment (named after guess who?) and various other things, oil shares and stuff to which, it's true, I had never paid the slightest attention. My legitimate legal share would have been $250,000. What I received was eighteen thousand dollars a year for ten years, at which time Kerry would have finished college. Long after I'd signed away my half of the house (I didn't care, I told myself—my politics were against private property anyway), and long after I'd accepted his terms, which amounted to less than the interest that $250,000 would have earned, I realized that I'd been bluffed and bamboozled. I don't believe he would have gone public with either of those accusations—not the adultery, for thirteen-year-old Kerry's sake, and his male pride—nor the Chinese one, for his self-respect. Or maybe I'm being too kind. He did supply the weapons to Greg Bautzer, after all.

I decided not to wait out the year. I went to Las Vegas for a quick divorce. One night during the six weeks I was there, Gene and I had a telephone conversation. I can't remember who made the call. I can't remember what we said. I only remember the end of it. I was sad and frightened and crying on the phone. And Gene said, "Well then, Betsy, just come back," and I sobbed out, "I can't—I promised."

22

THE INTERNATIONAL SCHOOL in Geneva was where Kerry wanted to be in this turmoil. Her suitcases were packed, and I packed my steamer trunk. Yes, I had one of my own now. It was a splendid white leather giant with wooden bars and brass fittings. I found it at a junk shop in Santa Monica for twenty dollars. It had belonged to Eddie Cantor, they said. I had come full circle, from the three-year-old sitting on the floor in Great-aunt Gladys's hotel room, and the ten-year-old "Climber" singing on the radio about wanting to be "the future Cantors, Kate Smiths, and Vallees too."

Here I was, at thirty-two: a mother, a recognized (and blacklisted) actress, and a divorced woman, moving to Paris. I had shipped my car to Billy's son, my nephew, in Connecticut. As I left, I looked back at the house, and I noticed the three silver birches we had planted in the front garden. I hadn't really thought of them as symbolic of us, but when I came back to LA two years later, one of them had died.

And I heard Gene's voice reading me a poem from Yeats, his favorite poet. Would there be another man who loved me as Gene said he did when he quoted the poem? "But one man loved the pilgrim soul in you, And loved the sorrows of your changing face." Now I wouldn't be "old and gray" in that house with him. And I silently thanked him, and I thank him now, for setting my "pilgrim soul" on its voyage, even though I've made most of that voyage without him. He gave me—and the world—an unforgettable legacy of joy.

Kerry stood on a footstool. I was behind her, arms on either side of her, grasping the iron railing of one of the open windows looking over Hyde Park Corner and up Piccadilly. It was 1952, during the shooting of *Invitation to the Dance*. We were in the London offices of Gene's agent, MCA, to watch the procession of the coronation of Queen Elizabeth. There were about fifty guests—visiting Americans, English clients, actors, writers, directors—having a great champagne and smoked salmon breakfast. Gene was cavorting around, being bumptiously Irish and antiroyalist, while I was telling Kerry seriously that we must absorb every detail of the historic event because this was the last time it would ever happen. I was speaking as a confident student of marxist history, of course. I had no idea how little I understood of Great Britain, or the British Empire.

It was a spectacular vision. The sun sparkled on caparisoned horses walking in perfect formation. Bands played, delegations from all over the world in native costume marched and danced. The Queen of Tonga, an enormous woman standing in an open Rolls-Royce, swinging her saronged hips and waving and smiling, stole the show.

But we had an even better memory of that morning. Our house was on the opposite side of Hyde Park Corner from Piccadilly. We had to cross the enormous square by seven-thirty, when the side streets would be closed off. We could see and hear the crowds gathering, so we set off at quarter of seven for what was usually a ten-minute walk. We found ourselves in a sea of people, five thousand, ten thousand—I don't know—but everyone was cheerful and good-natured. There were a few clouds in the sky and an occasional little shower. Someone spotted Gene. Someone called, "Good morning, Gene," and another, "Nice to have you here for our great day," and then gradually the song started. "Singin' in the Rain." It spread across the square until everyone was singing and waving and laughing and clapping. A path seemed to open in front of us, and we took Kerry's hands and skipped and ran the rest of the way. At the door to MCA's building, Gene did a little pirouette and bowed. A wave of love washed over us, and the song got stronger. We could still hear it on the sixth floor.

23

FRANCE, EUROPE, the earth, the universe. This is how children place themselves in the world. Well, the center of my world for the next five years was Paris. Even Hitler respected the beauty of Paris and didn't bomb it. To come from the United States to live in this ravishing old city was a gift.

I felt brand-new—spickety-span brand-new. New country, new language, new career (fingers and toes crossed), and a new man.

How lucky I was! I had struggled to break out of my fairy-tale existence in Beverly Hills. (Like all good fairy tales, it had its dark undercurrents.) Maybe I was a tiny bit brave to fly away from that safe nest. I know my good mother was appalled and frightened for me. But when I asked her whether she wanted me to be happy, she embraced me and my new life.

Not so Mom Kelly. Being Catholic, she was devastated by a divorce—and such a public one. But what was astonishing was that she blamed her own son. In her eyes, everything unfortunate in any of the Kelly lives was Gene's fault—it was heaven's retribution for his success. Suddenly I was glad I'd thrown away the doll dressed as a nun that she'd sent Kerry for her sixth birthday. (I bought a frilly little girl doll instead; when Kerry duly wrote her thank-you note, I had to stop her from mentioning its beautiful pink dress.) All that was behind me. I had no thought of what I was leaving, and certainly no regrets. I felt strong and confident, even more excited by this adventure than I'd been at fifteen going to my first call for dancers.

And I was madly in love for the second time in my life. The first time, Gene had chosen me; this time I made the choice. Of course, it wasn't simple. I struggled, I wavered, I cried, but something inside me was demanding that I strike out for a different life. I was leaving Gene, but it wasn't against him. Was it political? Maybe McCarthy and the blacklist did me a favor. Certainly the political atmosphere in Hollywood in the late 1940s and '50s was black. Someone told me when we first arrived in California that the visible roots of the palm trees lining the streets of Beverly Hills harbored the nests of rats. I never saw any, but I had begun to hate the palms. They were part of that world of pretty houses, powerful studios, and the beachfront. All of these harbored rats, too—the informers. It was time for me to go.

Moving to a new country is like being catapulted into the center of a kaleidescope. Everything is swirling around, making new patterns. But even a kaleidescope has the safe boundary of its tube. My safe boundaries had evaporated—no Gene, no MGM, no Beverly Hills routine. But I had a mysterious feeling of relief, of serenity even.

Most Americans respond to Paris—the noble buildings, the sidewalk cafés, the romantic atmosphere—but they complain about the Parisians. I thought they were great, just like New Yorkers, impatient, irreverent, funny, and smart. I felt at ease with them—welcome, as if I'd come home. But I wasn't at home. I was, and am, irrepressibly American, bred on my mother's democratic principles, and her applesauce.

Maybe my feeling had to do with the fact that the French love women—old, young, and in between. Even the country—*La France*—boasts the feminine gender. We have Uncle Sam as our national symbol. The English have John Bull. But France has Marianne, renewed and redrawn in the 1980s to a likeness of the beautiful Catherine Deneuve. And Paris is a city for women. It's full of flowers, gaiety, markets, and shops, all bathed in a soft, gray, sparkling light that makes everything beautiful. The streets are washed three times a day. They smell of peppermint or lavender, whatever the neighborhood chooses.

Language reveals a country's attitudes. "A woman of a certain age" is a phrase given to us by the French. They always say it with appreciation, implying not just that the woman is forty-five or fifty or sixty, but that she's a sensual being who has gathered warmth, tolerance, humor, even wisdom, on her way to this gallantly uncertain age.

Anna Magnani, the great Italian actress, had cosmetic surgery on her breasts. The young surgeon, seeing that she was pleased with the result, suggested that he could, with minor nips and tucks, do wonders for her face. He was answered with an amused but resounding "NO!" "This," she said, cupping her newly uplifted breasts, "this is *plastique,* this is anonymous, this makes it easier for the costume designer. But these eyelids, these bags, these lines—it's taken me all these years to get them. How could I destroy them? It would be to deny the great adventure that is my life."

How dramatic, how Italian! The story could also be French— but American? Probably not.

I sailed to France soon after entering my thirties, so I didn't really qualify as a *"jeune fille en fleur."* But my timing was perfect, as was my choice of man. I had been a "young girl in flower" for too long.

There's a good word in French: *"Epanouir."* The dictionary translation is "to make open, bring forth, open out, bloom, light up, beam." And *"une femme epanoui"* is a woman "in full bloom, beaming, wreathed in smiles."

All three expressions could be seen as the creations of male vanity. A young girl in flower is ripe for picking. A woman in full bloom is obviously beaming because she is sexually fulfilled. A woman of a certain age has gained her special quality through experience. But I had no sense of the battle of the sexes in France. Their old society seems to have found a way to enjoy the whole spectrum of gender and sex and age.

In the United States, we have the constitutional right to the "pursuit of happiness." The very words, so carefully chosen by the Founding Fathers, say that happiness is running ahead of us—that it's elusive. Our Puritan heritage insists that we should work to capture it. No, say the French. Happiness is pleasure. It's here and now.

It floats to you on a summer breeze. It's free. Eating, drinking, making love, reading a poem, lying under trees or walking on a city street, talking, arguing, playing with children, music, art, the movies—the things we all do every day *are* our life, and life itself is the pleasure.

The new man for this new life was Roger Pigaut, an actor, an aspiring director, and a socialist. I never was attracted to anyone who wasn't on the left. Roger (it's hard to write about him as "Roger"—it doesn't begin to convey my pleasure in his being foreign; think of him as *Rozhay,* please) was four years older than me, tall and strong with curly brown hair and gentle hands. He wasn't athletic but strangely graceful for such a solid man. He was from a working-class family, self-educated, poetic, and literary. And he was full of warmth and charm—not the Maurice Chevalier kind of hammy Frenchiness, but a charm that came from goodness and wit. His acting career had a brilliant start. At twenty-three he had played the lead in Claude Autant-Lara's beautiful film *Douce.* His most popular success was *Antoine and Antoinette,* by Jacques Becker.

By the time I met him, he had been in about twenty-five films and ten or twelve plays. He was well known and respected as an actor, though not really fulfilled in his work. But we had a plan. We would work together. We would make movies. We weren't just in love. Our lives would have a creative focus.

Roger had two adopted children: Sebastien, who was already a dark and dreamy adolescent when I appeared on the scene; and Poussine (meaning little downy yellow chick), who was nine years old, blond, and pretty. Neither of them lived with us, but they were part of our life.

Poussine was the daughter of the young actress Roger had married five years earlier. When her mother died of cancer three years later, Roger adopted Poussine and became her guardian. She lived with her grandparents during the illness, and afterward. We often had lunch there on Sunday.

Sebastien was the son of a Viennese-Hungarian couple who had fled to France as refugees from the Nazis. Near the end of the war

An arcade in Spain with Roger during *Calle Mayor,* 1957

they were rounded up and sent to Auschwitz, where they were killed. Sebastien's father was a writer, and Roger, as a very young man, was in love with Sebastien's mother. In the winter of 1945, as soon as it was possible to travel, Joe Pasternak, the MGM producer and a famous Hungarian, came to Paris on a mission to find any Jewish-Hungarian orphans and take them to the United States to be adopted by their compatriots in Hollywood. Roger, twenty-four or twenty-five years old by then, went to see him in his suite at the Hotel Georges V. He liked Pasternak and respected his mission, and he knew luxury and good intentions would have awaited Sebastien. But in the end he decided he couldn't send this beautiful, sad, dark-eyed boy to strangers; he couldn't take away everything the child knew when he'd already lost so much. He loved him. He adopted him himself.

Roger didn't pretend to be a saint, or even a do-gooder. It was just the way things fell out in his life. I admired his devotion to these two children. As John Guare wrote in his play *Six Degrees of Separation,* we're all connected. I didn't even need six moves to get from Gene to Joe Pasternak (who had produced *Me and My Gal*), to Roger and Sebastien.

For an English speaker, the French language is like a jungle of strange sounds. I took the total immersion course at the Alliance Française, and spent the rest of my time with Roger speaking French. At the end of three months I could even understand and join in the discussions. Argument is an intrinsic part of French life, one of the first cultural differences I noticed. In Paris you didn't just say what you believed was right or wrong about a political question, you didn't just like or dislike a film or actor or book or play, you had to defend and explain your position, listen to the opposing view, and respond. I found I enjoyed it all. I felt very Left Bankish, practically existential.

Because I imagined I'd live and work in France for the rest of my life, I hired a private tutor to get rid of my accent. Her name, Madame Coeurdacier, means "heart of steel," and it was fitting. She was old and tough, and when, after four months, she told me that she could do no more because I had the "lazy Anglo-Saxon tongue," I believed her. Fifteen years later, when I studied speech therapy, I discovered that there are physical properties to every sound that can be learned. I could perhaps have lost my accent. Alas, I didn't, but I was happy when I had my first dream in French. Maybe I *had* acquired a new language, since it had entered my subconscious.

New man, new country, new language; but of course, I wasn't

brand-new at all. All the strands of my life were present. Once Kerry was at the International School in Geneva, I flew there one weekend a month and she came to Paris one weekend a month, so we saw each other every two weeks or so. It was wonderful for me that she chose to go to high school in Europe. I don't think I could have been happy if I only saw her during vacations. I'd promised her in her crib that I'd let her go when she grew up, but this was too soon. Roger was gentle and patient. He was wise enough not to intrude on Kerry, just to be friendly and there.

With me he was a passionate and playful lover. And it was a different experience from any I had known. He loved me as I was. He didn't seem to have any preconception of how I should be. He delighted in discovering me, and I delighted in his discoveries—and made a few of my own.

I felt sexy in Paris. I was quick to absorb French ideas of pleasure. I began to drink wine. I appreciated food in a new way. And I reveled in my body and my intimate life with Roger. I know I wasn't suddenly transformed into Ava Gardner—I still looked like the girl next door—but boy, did I feel different. I don't subscribe to the myth that all Frenchmen are great lovers. But I had changed. I was what was different. I wasn't pleasing my mother. I wasn't pleasing Gene. I was free, just living, just being. It felt great.

Roger had been busy while he was waiting for me. He'd acted in a film. He'd had the legal papers drawn up to establish our film company, and he'd found an office on the Champs-Elysées that we could afford. And he found an apartment he thought I'd like.

Every big city has hidden corners. In the Fifteenth Arrondissement in Paris, just off a commercial boulevard, there are some little leafy streets, almost country lanes, with two-story wooden houses set in small gardens. In those days the area was home to a small colony of White Russian refugees from the revolution of 1917. One house was owned by the conductor of the Paris Opera, Igor Markevich. His tiny, extremely elegant mother lived on the ground floor. To reach the staircase leading to our flat above her we walked through her garden, bursting with clematis, peonies, and climbing roses. There were more flowers in her few square meters than in all of Beverly Hills when I lived there. (That was the time when the Japanese gardeners ruled the landscape, with their austere sense of beauty; now they're primarily Mexican, so there's a riot of color.)

Through that lovely Russian garden in Paris, up a short flight of stairs, was a porch and our front door. It was a modest apartment, compared not just to Beverly Hills, but even to Cliffside. And Roger was right; I loved it. The bathroom and kitchen were ramshackle. The two bedrooms were small, but there were old wooden doors and floors, a fireplace, and windows on all four sides. We moved in with bits of furniture from the flea market.

My French friends already knew and loved Roger; Alexandre Trauner, the Prévert brothers, Jacques the poet and Pierre the filmmaker, Simone Signoret, and Yves Montand. Roger's closest friend was Serge Reggiani, a very fine actor—an "actor's actor."

For Frenchwomen friends, there was really only Simone Signoret. There were other Frenchwomen I liked—I got along well with everyone's wife or girlfriend—but some cultural differences didn't melt away. I was mightily impressed by the meals prepared with such ease when we were invited for dinner. But I could never get a straight answer as to where a particular prosciutto or gateau had been bought or how the salad dressing was made. When we were hosts I fell back on that old standby, baked ham with brown sugar and pineapple rings studded with cloves. This was so American, so weird and unheard of in Paris in those days, that I think I got away with it.

I noticed the elegance and grooming of every woman that I passed in the street. I knew that it was often accomplished without the resources of plumbing and money that we took for granted in Beverly Hills. How did they do it? Perhaps given love and appreciation, women flourish and blossom like flowers—even if they do keep their culinary secrets. Oh, and proving my claim that the French love women, they invented and gave us the most useful of loving tributes ever—the bidet.

Although Beverly Hills seemed as far behind me as Cliffside and School No. 6, I couldn't deny what was a big chunk—almost exactly half—of my life. I had such riches from it. Kerry, Gene, writers, musicians, designers, directors, and I'd established myself as an actress. I could work. I could get jobs. I could pay my way as an independent woman.

Besides, I wasn't in Timbuktu. I was in Paris, so a great many good friends passed through. Adolph Green and Sydney Chaplin visited often, Robert Capa and Anatole Litvak were based there. The Bernheims came back to live, Madame and Michel to their old Art Deco apartment in the elegant Sixteenth Arrondissement, Marjorie and Alain and their sons to the even more elegant Palais Royale. Danny Kaye took me to dinner once when Roger was on location; I think he was disappointed not to meet the man who had lured me away from Beverly Hills (where he was none too happy himself).

Carol Matthau, whom I'd first seen, with a stab of envy, in 1942 in a newspaper photograph captioned "This year's three most beautiful debutantes, Gloria Vanderbilt, Carol Marcus and Oona O'Neill, at El Morocco last night," came from Madrid and stayed with us for a few days. I met her when she was married to William Saroyan and they lived across the street on Rodeo Drive. She was irresistible, lovely, and ultrafeminine on the surface, camouflaging her sharp intelligence and wit. She and Saroyan were divorced, and before she met Walter Matthau, she came to Paris with a slightly broken heart—or so she said—after an interrupted love affair. Her tryst had been with Kenneth Tynan, the English writer and critic. His wife, Elaine Dundy, had sent a private detective after them. This bowler-hatted, dark-suited spiv confronted them with a camera in their hotel room. Carol fled from Tynan, the hotel, and Spain. Now, a bit weepy, she was curled up in a corner of our couch as she recounted the story. Roger was supplying cups of tea, I was supplying the sympathy and lots of Kleenex. After a final sniffle she looked up with a gleam in her eyes and leapt to her feet. She glided slowly into a tango and sang out, "The pain in Spain comes mainly from Elaine, the pain in Spain comes mainly from Elaine," and collapsed, laughing. The crisis was over; her sense of humor drowned it.

After her divorce, when she went back to acting, she needed

photographs. She wanted the best, so she asked her dear friend Richard Avedon to take them. "Dick, I can't pay you now, but I promise when my ship comes in, I will. I promise, cross my heart." A year or so later at a New York party, the news came of the sinking of the *Andrea Doria*, all lives lost. Carol, with a tragic face, flew across the room to Avedon and murmured, "Oh Dick, that was my ship."

My beloved Salka Viertel invited me to lunch with Helene Weigel and Stella Adler. Weigel was no longer the subdued refugee wife of Brecht I'd seen in Santa Monica but reestablished once more as the great actress and star of the Berliner Ensemble. And Stella was magnificent, just back from her annual visit to the mud-bath spa in Italy. They were some years older than I was, and I was aware that I was with three extraordinary women. In Hollywood, when George Cukor included me in lunches with Garbo, Hepburn, and Ethel Barrymore, I felt a childish glee at having been chosen, and I behaved like a well-brought-up child. This was different. We were women together having a good meal. There was conversation, political, arty, and gossipy, with lots of laughter. I was wearing my favorite pale blue denim flared skirt, black silk shirt, and black espadrilles. Salka, always casually elegant, was in beige linen; Helene Weigel was in a navy tailored suit and a pillbox hat. Stella the magnificent was in a black-and-white-print silk dress, very high heels, and a broad-brimmed black straw hat. When she swept off to the ladies' room, Salka and Helene turned into catty sixteen-year-olds—"Yes, she looks wonderful, but does she have a little too much makeup for the daytime? Aren't her heels too high? Does she think she is still thirty?" When Stella was back and Helene excused herself, it happened again. "She's a great actress, but why does she wear those severe clothes? Why no makeup? One doesn't have to look so plain." I didn't dare leave the table.

Gene called whenever he was coming to Paris, and Roger and I were invited to the premiere of his ballet at the Paris Opera. And strange though I now think it was, for the first few years I went to Klosters for Christmas. According to Gene, I was the "Christmas

Fairy"—he and Kerry couldn't have Christmas without me. I believed him, and Roger made it easy, so I went to a tiny single room and put a happy face on the awkwardness I felt.

I never felt awkward with Simone Signoret. She was a mass of contradictions, an actress, a star, but without pretension. She was a woman of strong, left-wing conviction without the formulaic rhetoric that too often comes with it. She was eager to listen to other ideas. She might answer them with that Gallic shrug, but there was always humor and compassion too. She was loving and generous, but also critical and demanding. Quintessentially French, she was at ease anywhere in the world. I saw her in New York, Hollywood, London, Saint-Paul-de-Vence, and Berlin, but it was at home in Paris that I got to know her. She had the gift of intimacy. First came Catherine, her daughter, and Yves Montand, her husband. But right up there in importance were "*les copains*," the pals, the mates, the comrades—her chosen friends. Roger and Serge were among them, and soon I was too.

Simone loved to laugh. Yves made her laugh. She once told me that it was this that carried her through the stormy parts of their marriage. And it *was* stormy. I'm not talking about the Marilyn Monroe kind of thing, I'm talking about everyday life. They were completely engaged with each other. I'd never seen a loving couple who fought so well. From the outside it seemed that it was Yves who shouted and slammed around the house. He was narcissistic (a Mediterranean man); she was more intelligent. They were both powerful. She always held her own as an equal. Karen Blixen once wrote that a real couple must be "worthy opponents." That they were. It was a revelation to me. My mother and father never fought. Everything happened behind closed doors. Gene and I didn't even fight behind closed doors. Knowing Simone was a crash course in feminism with a great teacher. Unwittingly she gave me a different perception of what a woman is. Not as a separate sex, and certainly not as the "second sex" Simone de Beauvoir so brilliantly diagnosed, but simply as a being. Alone or with a partner, self-reliant and loving, giving and taking, my Simone embodied a "worthy

Simone Signoret, London, 1960

opponent" in all her relationships. I owe her a lot, not as an ideal to emulate, but as a friend who opened my eyes to a stronger reality and sense of self.

Yves and Simone were both gigantic stars in Europe. But we were lucky in those days. There was no entourage surrounding them—or Gene, for that matter—no need for bodyguards, press agents, managers, trainers, and hairdressers who traveled with you. Kidman and Clooney and Madonna should envy us our freedom from all that. But then as now, S. J. Perelman's phrase "In the aristocracy of success, there are no strangers" applied. Weekends at the elegant and casual Montand house in the country were for us, the pals, but might include Picasso or Buñuel.

So there I would be in the friendly company of great men. Buñuel was easy. Quite old, quite deaf, by then, he sat calmly in the sun or by the fire, never missing a trick. Alert and mischievous eyes, deep pleasant voice, as solid as an Incan god; and for an actor, he *was* a god, one of the great filmmakers.

His long career took him from the Surrealist days in Paris, the time of "L'Age d'or," to Mexico for *Los olvidados* and *Robinson Crusoe, Viridiana* in Spain, and back to France and *The Discreet Charm of the Bourgeoisie*. Some of his many other films were perhaps not masterpieces, but he was always the great Buñuel. Simone was in one of the others, *La Mort en ce jardin*. She didn't really like the scenario, but the producer said he wouldn't make the film if she wasn't in it. How dare a mere producer refuse a Buñuel film if he didn't have a star?—she signed the contract.

Halfway through shooting, she and Buñuel sat in silence while the cameraman lit the next shot. Suddenly he turned to her and said, "Someday you and I must make a Buñuel film, not this crap."

Naturally, as an actress I wanted to be noticed, to please him. But I was too much in awe to make even the slightest gesture in his direction. Then Yves suggested charades. And surprisingly, Buñuel liked charades. My inhibitions flew out the window. I was playing "the game" just as I had in Beverly Hills. And we connected after a few rounds; Luis Buñuel and I were in cahoots. He was a brilliant guesser. I was soon acting to him, and he to me. I can't say I ever forgot he was the great director, but I did forget that I wanted anything more than victory for our team. I relaxed, I could joke and insist, as one does in a game. We communicated through mime. So it was charades that made it easy for me to be friends with Buñuel.

Picasso was another story. He moved in his own field of energy. There seemed to be a charged space around him, filled with his male force. I didn't like it. I was conscious of pulling against it. My reaction surprised me, because there was something of Gene in his physicality, the same compact muscular lightness of foot. (Picasso may even have been a good dancer, for all I know.) I'm not equating their talent, only noting the similarity in the inherent confidence of their bodies, the ease with which they occupied their space in the world. It made me realize that I had ignored, or perhaps denied, one side of Gene, the "manly" stuff. I think this is why I never warmed to John Huston or Irwin Shaw, talented and charming as they were. I don't think I would have liked Hemingway. The idea of a bunch of guys sitting around drinking, proving their manhood by hunting or deep-sea fishing, is a real turnoff. Of course, I didn't see Gene like that; the only place he had to prove himself was in his work (and, I admit, on the volleyball court or the ski slope). I knew best the tender indulgent side of him. For many years I forgot there was anything else. I recently came across a card sent to me by David Selznick with some flowers. It says, "To an unretouched angel for her courtesy to drunks at dawn." Then I remembered several nights in Beverly Hills when, as a matter of course, I would jump out of bed, put on a robe, throw water on my face, and run downstairs, happy as a lark, to make scrambled eggs and toast. Putting this together with my unexpected reaction to Picasso, I suddenly understood that I'd taken an equal part in the fantasy Gene and I shared. For Gene, I was still the perfect little angel girl, when I'd grown way past that; and for me, he was Gene, who could do no wrong. I guess I blotted out anything that would spoil the picture. So thank you, Monsieur Picasso, for opening my eyes to a part of my own life, even if we never said much more than *"Enchante"* and *"Au revoir."*

I was beginning to understand a lot of things, to be aware of vital changes in my life—not only the lovely "new man, new country" stuff, but the strength and energy you have when your work is equally important to you and the people around you. For the first time since I was seventeen, my work didn't have to fit in so it wouldn't disturb my life with Gene and his movies or our holidays. I hadn't known that my last few years in Hollywood, the years of lying and floundering around in love affairs, had been hard on me. I was too busy feeling guilty about Gene. Of course I was right to feel guilty, but guilt is destructive, I was glad to be rid of it.

Now I could relax and breathe freely. I was no longer divided in any way. Love, work, politics, friends—everything was open and together.

Our best friends (apart from Simone, for me) were Serge Reg-

With Serge Reggiani and Roger, 1957. We were the entire staff of Garance Films.

giani and Jack Berry. Serge was our partner in Garance Films. We had an idea for a movie to be a coproduction with China (my connection with the "Red Chinese"!). I admit the word *"garance"* describes a certain shade of crimson, as in the shrub *garance*. But we chose it as a tribute to Jacques Prévert and Arletty. It was the name of the character Arletty played, with her mysterious gaiety, in *Les Enfants du paradis,* written by Prévert. But we didn't dislike its connotation of red, the color of passion and fire and revolution—in fact, it amused us.

I already knew Serge. He was the second lead in the Litvak film in Paris, the actor Tola Litvak had asked me to work with on his English. And he was the subject of the first conversation I ever had with Roger. Gene and I were invited to the Cinémathèque for one of the cultural gatherings the French are so good at organizing. When I was introduced to Roger, he said he felt he already knew me, that Serge had told him about me. And when he suggested a lunch one day—perhaps with Serge—I said yes, we're at the Hotel Lancaster. He called the very next day, and asked me to lunch with him alone. Again I said yes, but don't pick me up at the hotel, I'll meet you on the corner of the Champs-Élysées. Obviously, we'd both felt that stirring, that frisson of attraction. Whichever word best describes the feeling, we had it. It turned out to be serious.

Serge is a fine actor on stage and screen, and an odd, whimsical, electrifying character in life. He has the singularity and intensity of Hamlet, a role he played with distinction at the Avignon festival. His most important international success was *Casque d'or,* opposite Simone Signoret. I think Serge, Roger, and I made a good combination for our company. We were alike in our aims and enthusiasm, but three very different sensibilities. Roger was the dreamer, intelligent and poetic in his approach, but also the most persevering and practical for the day-to-day work. Serge was anarchic and quick, sometimes harsh, sometimes brilliant, always impatient. I was the optimistic one. I was always sure we could do it, we could make movies happen. I think now I was exactly what Roger and Serge needed—I had enough confidence for all three of us, and also a bit of American know-how and can-do.

It seemed I'd learned a bit about filmmaking in those California years. Gene was a natural teacher, and in his excitement about his work he explained a great deal to me in passing. Gene thought of the arc of the whole movie, where a song-and-dance number should be, and what kind of number would be right to illuminate the character and advance the plot. His medium was the musical, but the underlying principles are the same for any film. And my work with Shdanoff was never limited to my character and my scenes. We always dissected the entire play or screenplay. So now in Paris, I discovered that when I read a scenario I got a sense of the whole, an understanding of the structure. And I was more practical than I could have guessed. I was quick to grasp the cost of things, their relative importance, and where economies could be made without damaging the project. The little squirrel who hoarded her dimes in New Jersey came back to life.

But I thought I also knew where money should be spent. In this area I had a lot to learn. My only reference was Hollywood studios. Even in their heyday of wealth and power, they were never profligate. They controlled every penny. Europe was a different matter altogether. I gradually understood through our own productions, and as I acted in films in Spain, France, and Italy, that it wasn't a question of controlling the money as much as a case of finding more of it to be able to continue shooting. I don't know if this uncertainty added to the excitement. At the time I attributed the great atmosphere on all these films to camaraderie, to a "we're all in this together" attitude. Staunch union supporter that I am, I was thrilled by the small crews and the absence of lines of demarcation over who did what. The cameraman himself might help lay a rail for a tracking shot. There were no bored electricians standing around. I imagine the small American independent films of the last few years share this atmosphere. But the comparison I was making was with the golden age of Hollywood, the big studio years when the studio apparatus was too cumbersome for the joyous, creative-together experience I found in European moviemaking. On the other hand, in those days, the greatest stars, even the glamorous or difficult—Marlene Dietrich, Bette Davis, Robert Mitchum—were friendly on set, and democratic. There was none of the vanity, or, rather, stupidity, that I read about today, where popinjays demand that no one speak to them or even look at them as they walk through the crew. Are they mad? We're just actors, after all.

Our first production was about Paris and the Seine. We were lucky. Joris Ivens came to us with his idea. He'd written it down in two pages. But if you knew his work, two pages were enough.

Joris was one of the great men of documentary film. Born in Holland in 1898, he had a long, adventurous, and productive life. His round boyish face, intelligent eyes, and warm smile didn't reveal the warrior soul inside him. But his work did. After twenty years of distinguished filmmaking—including, in 1937, *The Spanish Earth,* his film about the civil war, and *Four Hundred Million,* shot during Mao Tse-tung's Long March—the Dutch government appointed him film commissioner of the Dutch East Indies. What he saw there forced him to resign his post, and to make the film *Indonesia Calling.* The call was for independence, and it cost him a lot. Forever after Holland made difficulties for him. For example, they gave him a passport for three months at a time, which meant that every twelve weeks, wherever he was, he had to spend hours standing in line in the Dutch embassy to renew it.

He came to Paris with his new young Polish wife, Ewa Fiszer, a

A preview showing of *La Seine a rencontré Paris,* directed by Joris Ivens,
written by Jacques Prévert, produced by us, Garance Films—
Gérard Philipe talking to Joris Ivens, 1957

poet and translator. She was intelligent, delicately pretty, with old-world manners and education and a certain rigorous morality. Once, when I complained about the plumbing in Paris, she gave me a mini-lecture on the need to "adjust" when one moves to a new country. I'm afraid I snapped back, "Easy for you to say, Ewa, you're adjusting up from Warsaw. Me, I have to adjust down."

Joris was the old pro. We were his producers, but mainly we were eager and enthusiastic supporters. We all went location scouting, Serge, Roger and I, Ewa, the cameraman, Andre Dumaitre, and Sebastien, working as an assistant. We had fun. We saw everything anew through the vision of Joris. We watched him expand his original idea, seize unexpected moments, wait for the light for a particular shot.

Joris was a communist. In film-history books, he'll always be known for the political content of his work. But he was also a poet

Joris Ivens, Julie Dassin, and me

with the camera, and his film for us, *La Seine a rencontré Paris,* is a poem addressed to Life and Work and Paris.

When Joris had finished shooting and assembled the material, we showed it to Jacques Prévert. I think it was Roger's idea to ask him to write the commentary. Jacques responded brilliantly, with his own poem. It was a perfect match. Serge recorded it with music by Philippe Gérard, and the film was finished. We were wildly proud to have helped it get made, to be part of it. Garance had produced its first film.

And my first European movie was set up and ready to go. I was off to Madrid to earn some pesetas in a really good scenario with a great part and a fine director.

24

I ASSUMED the Spanish film came to me because of *Marty*. But I was wrong. Juan Antonio Bardem, the director of *Death of a Cyclist* (which made him famous), had spotted me in my first movie, the bit in George Cukor's *A Double Life*.

Our paths crossed at the Cannes Film Festival; Bardem was a member of the jury. United Artists, the distributors of *Marty*, decided to send me to represent the film. It was an official American entry in the competition. I was practically unknown as an actress, so it wasn't a case of flying in for two days with all the hoopla surrounding a star. I was to be there for the whole two weeks to build up as much attention as I could for *Marty*.

Television and newspaper journalists from the whole world come to Cannes. I did every interview, every photo shoot, every TV appearance the publicity machine could arrange. In the first week there were nine or ten a day, plus lunches, cocktail parties, dinners, and then the appearance at the formal evening film, where the photographers line the steps up to the Palais du Cinema. My four evening dresses were supplemented by gowns from MGM's wardrobe department shipped directly from Culver City to the Carleton Hotel. I'd bought a few new things for the festival. One, from Elizabeth Arden on Sunset Boulevard, was a white organdy shirtwaist with spring green overchecks. It had a full skirt, long sleeves, and a high neck with ruffled edgings. Every morning I'd look at it hanging in my closet and decide—no, it's too girlish. People will think I'm trying too hard. Then one day on the Croisette I

The glory that was the Cannes Film Festival for *Marty*, 1955, with flowers and photographers

saw a storm of photographers running and shouting—they'd obviously spotted some great star. It was Marlene Dietrich. And what was the much older epitome of elegance wearing? My "too girlish" organdy dress!

On the red-eye flight from LA to New York, en route to Cannes, Marlene was a fellow passenger. I had left my new, chic makeup case on the floor in front of the airline desk in the airport. In those days, the airlines only handed out earplugs and hard candy for take off and landing. Alain Bernheim went up and down the aisle asking all the other Hollywood folk, including Marlene, if they had an extra toothbrush or would lend me a comb and lipstick in the morning. The stewardess supplied a toothbrush and toothpaste and Alain had a comb—but no lipstick. As we landed at LaGuardia Airport, standing in the aisle waiting to get off, Marlene was directly in front of me. She bent down, looked out the window, and saw ten or twelve photographers and journalists waiting on the tarmac. She turned, gave me a once-over and said, "Nobody knows I'm on this plane. They must be for you." And she fished out her lipstick and handed it to me—not a "sister" in the feminist sense, but a true professional.

I was never the center of a storm of photographers, and I was realistic enough to recognize that all the reporters showering me with questions, listening to my answers, taking my picture, were using their film and filling their notebooks while waiting for Marlene or Sophia. I didn't care a bit; I was having a ball.

Once before I'd almost been in the spotlight. Anatole Litvak had invited me to the New York premiere of *The Snake Pit*, because Olivia de Haviland, the star of the film, couldn't come. Gene and I went and sat in a box with Litvak. As the film ended, just before the lights in the theater came up, when Litvak and I would have taken a bow, Gene grabbed my hand and said to Litvak, "Tola, we have to run, I'll be mobbed. See you at '21.'" And we ran. I was used to this. We always left a concert at the Hollywood Bowl, or a basketball game, or even the Ice Capades with Kerry, before the end. It was years later in my analysis that I allowed my anger for that moment I'd missed to come to the surface, the moment when I would have stood up to the sound of applause. I didn't mention it to Gene even then.

Marty was shown at the end of the first week. It was an over-whelming success. The sophisticated European audience was touched by its simplicity and by the authenticity of its story—that of a butcher and a schoolteacher, characters who don't usually fig-ure in the world according to Hollywood. The audience sponta-neously burst into applause four or five times during the film, and at the end I stood alone in the box while they got to their feet, turned toward me, and clapped and cheered for what seemed like ten minutes.

I suddenly became a sort of favorite of the press. The second week is when the most famous directors and stars pay their fleeting visits, but everyone from Swedish television to *Paris Match* asked for another interview. I just smiled and said, no, you've got millions of photos, and I've already said what I have to say. I didn't want to do it all again, because the most important part of a film festival is to see movies. It opens your eyes to the art of cinema. In Cannes there are filmmakers from Japan, Israel, Argentina, China, Africa, and all the countries of Europe. I'd worked hard for United Artists and *Marty*, but now I needed every minute I could find to see as many movies as possible, including the unofficial ones shown in projection rooms and small cinemas away from the festival. I had good friends there to steer me in the right direction: Jules Dassin, who had a French film in the competition, and Gene Moskowitz, the *Variety* correspondent in Paris. He was an astute guide—a true cinephile. He had used his GI Bill money to go to Institut des Hautes Etudes Cinématographiques in Paris, then the only film school in the world, and he could write *Variety*-speak reviews. He knew which "art" film could have a commercial life in the United States. He always raised the level of discussion and pushed the work of the more serious directors. He would see the beginning of a new trend in a national cinema, write about it, and point it out to the heads of festivals. He did it for the Polish cinema at the time of Wajda and Munk and the very young Polanski. It was thanks to him that *Variety*, the show-business trade paper, was also for a time a champion of the avant-garde.

I don't remember eating or sleeping during that week. What I remember is saying a proper good night in the lobby of the Carleton to whoever my escort was and then ducking out the side door of the hotel to meet Mosk and the Russians or Swedes or whoever was showing a film at midnight or two a.m.—sometimes both.

One morning, a pale, bookish Frenchman in a linen suit, looking like a minor functionary in the State Department, asked to speak to me as I came out of the elevator. He was bringing an invitation from the Chinese delegation, who were not staying in a hotel but on a boat anchored just off the beach. They wanted me to come for tea. They understood the delicacy of my situation as an American. (In the 1950s, U.S. passports carried a notice that they were not valid for travel to mainland China—but they didn't think to mention an offshore yacht.) But the message was that everything would be arranged very discreetly. The Frenchman and a woman companion, complete with cameras, would pick me up as if for a photo session. We would board the ship on the far side, out of sight of sunbathers and swimmers—or the FBI, if they were watching. Of course I went.

There were four Chinese men; two of them spoke very good English. They were full of smiles and politeness. We were served jasmine tea and almond biscuits. After some mundane chat and pretty compliments they came to the point. Would I take a message to the great Chinese-American cameraman James Wong Howe, who had photographed over a hundred films, including *Body and Soul* and *Sweet Smell of Success*. They wanted him to visit China. They would welcome him as an honored guest. They would greatly appreciate it if he were willing to impart his wisdom to their filmmakers. And as a token of their esteem, would I carry a gift to him, a precious scroll painting? I didn't know him personally, I said, but yes, I would call him when I got back to Hollywood and deliver the invitation and the painting myself. They brought out a slender wooden box about twelve inches long, opened it, untied the cord, and unrolled a silk scroll. It was a traditional scene, a hut in the mountains with two fishermen in front of it, the trees and hills behind and water in the foreground. They entrusted it to me, and I delivered it. I don't know if James Wong Howe ever acknowledged it or went to China. But in Cannes the morning after my excursion to the boat, when I opened my door, there was a present for me on the threshold. It wasn't wrapped, and there was no card, but there was Chinese writing on it. It was a small can of pineapple exactly the size of the thousands of Dole cans on the shelves of every market in America and in most pantries. I had a million reactions at once. How sweet to leave me a present—and so discreetly. For them, this is a present, this is what they have to give. Therefore, I appreciate it. But what does it mean about their vast country? What does it mean about their economy or their knowledge of the United States? And does it say something about our abundance?

The festival was almost over. There was only the last evening of prize-giving and the formal party. Apparently there was a buzz in the air—*Marty* might win something. It must have reached New York and Hollywood. The United Artists executives and the producer, Harold Hecht, had flown in for the last weekend. I was too excited and having too much fun even to notice the rumors.

It's true that Anatole Litvak, who was on the jury, had given me some friendly and knowing grins, but I assumed they meant something like, "So there you are—I gave you a small part in *The Snake Pit*. I recommended you to Orson for *Othello*. You coached one of my French actors in English. And here you are starring in a film at Cannes." Members of the jury don't socialize with the competitors during the festival, but you do cross paths day and night. In the 1950s the jury was driven into the hills above Cannes to the splendid house of the Begum Aga Khan for their final deliberations; Robert Favre le Bret, the director of the festival, was fanatical about secrecy.

The jurors were sworn to silence, but they had to be allowed back to their hotels to dress for the evening. I had a note delivered to my room. It was from Anatole Litvak. It said, "Look beautiful tonight. Love, Tola." Oh my, I thought—and gee whiz—can this mean . . . ?

And it did.

Jules Dassin won best director for *Rififi;* Vasiliev, the Soviet director, shared the prize for his own film.

And then the announcement: "For the beautiful humanity of the film and for the performances of Betsy Blair and Ernest Borgnine, the Golden Palm to *Marty.*" It was tremendously thrilling.

There is a mystery. For the only time in the fifty years of the Cannes Film Festival, there were no separate Golden Palms for the actor and actress. We were treated as winners. *Paris Match* had me on the cover under the title "Winner at Cannes."

Through the years, I've been on the jury of film festivals at Berlin, Locarno, and Tours, so I can tell you how it works. There are no outside influences, no bribes offered. Behind the closed doors, though, adjustments are made and some trade-offs negotiated. Delicately phrased guidelines are handed down by the festival directors. Because of the international spirit of these occasions, there is an understanding that the prizes should be distributed with consideration for both political and geographical factors.

I thought Ernie and I had won. I didn't notice the absence of a personal ornament to take home. But a few years later, Anatole Litvak told me that because some jurors thought three Golden Palms were too many for one film—especially an American film—it was decided to include Ernie and me in the announcement, but our supporters would not allow any other actors to be honored. *"Tant pis,"* as the French say with a shrug of the shoulders. It means "Too bad." I think of it as "Who cares?" There is no "best" anyway.

It was one of the most wonderful times of my life. My adolescent dream of my own theater putting on plays to change the world became a passion for the movies. Film could be the greatest influence for understanding and beauty for everyone. It was probably as naive as my first dream. At any rate, it doesn't seem to have worked out as I thought it would. Fortunately, there are always young men and women from Delhi or Dublin or Detroit with their own ideas and visions. All power to them—and good luck. I'm sure they'll need it.

That glorious night we, the winners, walked along the beach, barefoot in our evening clothes; a Soviet director, a communist or two, some fellow-travelers, a blacklisted director and his wife, a formerly blacklisted actress (me—who would be again but didn't know it yet), and Juan Antonio Bardem, a member of the jury. Laughing, full of champagne and success, we felt the Left was invincible, that taking the prizes at the festival in Cannes was only the beginning. Most of us crashed to earth with a giant thud the very next year. The Twentieth Congress of the Supreme Soviet exposed the villainy of Stalin, and the Russian tanks rolled into Hungary. But for this night, we were happy.

At some point, Julie Dassin, who had played charades with me in Hollywood and Paris, announced that I must do one in Russian for Vasiliev, who spoke neither French nor English. It was to be easy, just one word, and the word was *"kolkhoz,"* collective farm. To explain the game to him, Julie did Chaplin as the Little Tramp, and we guessed it. Gene Moskowitz did Hitler, and Vasiliev smiled and understood. So there on the sand in the light of the moon, the Russian director installed on a chair filched from the beach restaurant, I launched into what may be the most epic charade ever performed. Whatever I did first just didn't work, so I had to go back to the beginning. I was the downtrodden peasant, I was a troop of Cossacks slashing through a ghetto, I was the czar and czarina in elegant furs, their daughters, and their hemophiliac son. I was Lenin on the train from Switzerland, I rushed the steps in Odessa as in the scene from *The Battleship Potemkin,* the wretched farmer again, putting down his scythe and straightening up to express his hope, the brave Red Army helping the peasants, and finally I was the tractors rolling into the vast fields while one farmer, then another, then another and another surveyed the luxuriant crop and sat down with their families to celebrate. And Vasiliev suddenly laughed and shouted *"kolkhoz."* We all danced about, linked arms, and kissed on both cheeks.

The glorious night was ending. As we started walking toward the hotel, Bardem stopped me. The others went ahead as he said, "Betsy, I want to give you my scenario. I want you to come to Spain and be in my next film, please." It was so sudden, I was very direct: "Juan Antonio, you're a wonderful director. But I can't come to work in Spain while Franco is there." It's funny how some moments stay in your mind, as clear as a photograph. I can still see

Bardem standing on the beach, the gentle waves of the Mediterranean behind him, his black tie undone, his big horn-rimmed glasses. All he said was "Betsy," but with a gesture and an intonation that made me understand him. In the moment of silence between us I saw a man who was living the battle, who was antifascist and anti-Franco to his core, while I was a girl from New Jersey, Hollywood, and Paris. My objection to working in Spain became superfluous.

I flew from Paris to Madrid for the filming of *Calle Mayor*. I remembered flying from Hollywood to Rome to be in *Othello* for Orson Welles, my excitement at being alone and my fears and hopes for that adventure. This time I had no mixed emotions. I was eager to start. I was clearheaded and prepared. I was just a working actress going to work.

Manuel Goyanes, the Spanish producer (it was a French-Spanish coproduction—the French producers were Serge Silberman and Georges de Beauregard), Bardem, and my costar, José Suárez, met me at the airport. The usual whirlwind started, press interviews and photographs, makeup and hairdressing consultations, costume fittings, new pages for the script, dinner at the producers' house to meet the other actors.

I met the two people who became my friends on the film, Ricardo Muñoz-Suay and his wife, Nieves. Ricardo was Bardem's assistant and friend; Nieves was the script supervisor. This job is vital to ensure the continuity of every detail—the movements of actors, the costumes, the props, and the dialogue—and also to record the directors' comments on each take.

Nieves did it all with charm and complete precision. She was always calm and smiling. When chaos reigned on the floor, the area around her chair was an oasis of order.

Nieves and Ricardo spoke English. Bardem tried, but we mainly communicated in French. It would be reasonable to assume that language would be a problem in European films, but everyone was matter of fact about it. I don't know how it is now, but in the 1940s and '50s most European films were dubbed, the dialogue recorded in the studio after the film was shot—which is how two French

At Madrid airport with José Suárez,
my costar in *Calle Mayor*

actors, Dora Doll and Yves Massard, and I could all be Spaniards in
a provincial town. Bardem engaged a really wonderful Spanish
actress to dub me. I was lucky. I remember seeing *Anchors Aweigh* in
Italy with Gene. In musicals they didn't dub the songs, only the dialogue. So Gene, with his lovely thin Irish singing voice, was speaking with a reedy high-pitched sound they thought matched his
songs. (He didn't like it much at the time, but eventually it became
a funny story.)

The shooting of the film was demanding and difficult. I was on
a high of energy and commitment. Roger came to visit several
times. It was lovely and romantic. And when he left, I loved him
even more. I was really working, and it was all I had time for, all I
could give myself to for those months.

On the set of *Calle Mayor* with Juan Antonio Bardem, the director

It was my first movie without Georges Shdanoff, my coach in Hollywood. When I was preparing for it in Paris, it was as if he were there. I approached it exactly as I would have done with him. He had taught me for six or seven years, through seven films and perhaps fifteen plays, some of which I actually performed. Others, *The Seagull, Joan of Arc, A Doll's House,* and *Our Town,* may have had some of my finest moments as an actress, but they were seen only by him in his little studio. I realized he had done what the best teachers do—he'd prepared me to do it without him.

Calle Mayor (Main Street) was an original screenplay, inspired by *La Señorita de Trevelez,* by Carlos Arnishes. One can also find a trace of *Doña Rosita la Soltera,* by Federico García Lorca. In each of these stories a young woman is trapped in a society where her only future lies in marriage. She can never be independent. Isabel, my character, is the center of the film, but Bardem's particular gift was to show this society as a whole. The plot revolved around a trick played on Isabel by a group of young men. The handsomest of them courts her, pretends to be in love with her, proposes to her, and, when she accepts, drops her in public. She retreats behind her window to watch life pass her by. The Catholic Church was a reactionary force in Spain, but it is in the cruelty of the men, in the barren harshness of their emotions, that one sees a direct reflection of the real villain, the regime of Franco.

After several weeks on location in Cuenca, a mountainous mining town in northern Spain, with an old plaza surrounded by beautiful arcades at its center, we came back to the studio in Madrid. The work was going well. We were on schedule. The crew was enthusiastic and warm. I sometimes had dinner with Nieves and Ricardo. Most nights I just checked over my scenes for the next day, said good night to Roger on the phone, and went to bed.

And then a bombshell. I quote my FBI file:

From a report in the *Herald Tribune:*
The film director Juan Antonio Bardem was arrested in Spain on suspicion of having leftist tendencies, and as a result, Betsy Blair, star of the film *Marty,* has been sitting in her Madrid apartment doing nothing. For the information of the Madrid office, subject [me!] has been reported to have been associated with several Communist Party fronts.

I came into my hotel to find Nieves and Ricardo waiting for me. The concierge said I had an urgent phone call from Señor Goyanes the producer. Nieves took my hand, Ricardo my script and bag. They came with me to pick up the call. Señor Goyanes said, "Betsy, don't worry. We won't be shooting tomorrow—Juan Antonio has been arrested. But don't worry. I'll arrange everything. It might take two, or even three days, but don't worry." I somehow answered, "Okay, all right, call me anytime, I'll be here." I was stunned. I was in Spain. I had images of Falangist police.

I was grateful that Nieves and Ricardo had come to give me this news. We ordered tea in my room. They didn't know any more than the fact of Bardem's arrest. But they reassured me by their readiness to take on this problem. I must tell them anything I heard from Goyanes, and they would let me know whatever they could find out elsewhere. Did I want to come to their house? No, it was better I stay here. When they left, I called Roger. He offered to fly to Madrid in the morning, but I said no it might be all over by then—a bit of New Jersey optimism coming to the rescue.

For two weeks I heard a different story every day. There was nothing I could do to help except stay and support the idea that the film would be finished. But finished how? Señor Goyanes suggested another director, he mentioned René Clair or Jules Dassin. I knew Julie Dassin would never accept such an offer when his colleague was in one of Franco's jails. But I didn't know René Clair or his political attitude. I understood the producer's dilemma. He was doing his utmost to get Bardem released, but his investment was disappearing down a black hole. He was allowed to visit Bardem. He came to see me afterward to give me a message: Juan Antonio wants the film to be completed, even without him.

But I couldn't do it. It wasn't that I didn't believe the producer, exactly; I just couldn't. The reason I'd come to Spain was Bardem and his scenario.

So I said to Señor Goyanes that I could only resume shooting if Bardem himself told me to. It took him two days to arrange my visit. We were escorted to the prison by a man in a dark suit and a high-up policeman in a costume that would have made me giggle under other circumstances, a tricorne hat with a cockade, high boots, epaulets, and a strap diagonally across his chest leading to his holster—perfect for an operetta.

But this was real. I think it was the main police station in Madrid. The entrance and the foyer were like a palace. There were large dark oil paintings on the wall, a vaulted ceiling, and a marble floor. We went down a flight of steps to a small bare reception area outside the cells. Bardem was waiting between two policemen. In my memory, I see him in a white open-necked shirt and dark trousers, but logic tells me he must have been in a prison uniform. But about his eyes behind the horn-rimmed glasses I'm not wrong. Goyanes was urging him to tell me to go ahead, but as he said the words, "Betsy, I want the film to be completed," his eyes were desperately telling me that I mustn't do it, I must hold out.

I had almost checkmated myself. By the time we got back to the hotel I had worked it out. My only weapon now was the bad reputation of actresses. I would be "temperamental." I wouldn't discuss it, I wouldn't answer the phone. The only thing I said was that I wouldn't shoot a single frame without him.

Roger, in Paris, had spoken to some Spanish exiles, including the writer Jorge Semprun. The consensus was I must continue to be temperamental. It could be Bardem's best hope. The producer might only continue to fight for him if the film couldn't be completed. In Madrid, Ricardo and Nieves said the same. So I stayed difficult and incommunicado.

During the week, in a moment of caution—or in my idea of a strategic move—I called the American embassy and made an appointment to see the cultural attaché. It was a bit like when I went to see L. B. Mayer about the blacklist. I didn't have white kid gloves, but I was at my most conventional and correct. And so was he. My act was nothing compared to his reality. I explained my position—American actress in film, director arrested. He asked if it was an American movie. When I said no, it was a French-Spanish coproduction, that was the end of it. Please call him at any time, thank you for coming, good-bye.

In May and June 1998, I received letters and several pages of files on me from the U.S. Army, Navy, and Air Force—or, more precisely, from the U.S. Army Intelligence and Security Command, the U.S. Naval Criminal Investigation Unit, the Air Force Office of Special Investigations. Before they arrived, I had just about recovered from the effects of receiving my FBI file; I had even begun to see the humorous side of the whole operation. These new files reignited all my feelings. I was angry again, and then I thought it was even funnier. I found myself singing at odd moments, "The army! The navy! And the air force! They will set us free!"

Our great services. To think they had nothing better to do than spy on me. And to think I was appealing to the same people who were doing the spying.

These files were sent—pursuant to your request under the Freedom of Information Act, and referred to us by the F.B.I.

It was in the air force pages that I found what must be a reference to my visit to the U.S. embassy in Madrid.

Your letter dated March 5th, 1956, furnished information concerning the arrest in Spain of the director of a film which the subject was then making.

You should take appropriate action at once to resolve the extent and nature of subversive activities of the subject. Your inquiries should resolve also the question of identity between the Betsy Blair referred to by Colonel Dunnington and Elizabeth Winifred B. Kelly.

At the bottom of this page they repeat, just as in eight pages of the FBI file:

Betsy Blair and Elizabeth Kelly are probably identical with Mrs. Eugene Curran Kelly, better known as the actor Gene Kelly.

I seem to have confused them all yet again. I don't know what I expected. Maybe I thought it could help Bardem if someone from the U.S. embassy questioned the Spanish authorities about an American citizen being stranded. It was a completely foolish idea.

And then one late afternoon Ricardo called. Bardem was being released that night. We would be shooting in the morning. Joy to the world—at least, to the little world of our movie.

There was a tremendous welcome for Bardem from everyone on the set. Serge Silberman, the French producer, had come during this crisis. I have a feeling he may have had more influence in the French embassy than I had in mine.

Bardem didn't say anything. He started work, as concentrated and passionate as ever. We soon moved to our final location, in Logroño. As Juan Antonio called "Cut and print" for the last time,

A Balmain dress for *La Seine a rencontré Paris*

there was a deep communal sigh in silence, then a few *"Olé"*s, some laughter, and a lot of embracing. We had done it.

For me, the work itself had been tremendous and the adventure amazing. I felt that I was in the real world. And in fact, I *was* in the real world. You can't get much more real than jail.

I was offered a French film. The star was Robert Lamoureux, often described as the French Danny Kaye. The director was Georges Lampin, a lovely old man and a very respected filmmaker. His latest movie was *Crime and Punishment,* with Jean Gabin. Our script was definitely not based on Dostoevsky. It was a bit silly— rich American girl and poor French artist fall in love in a light-hearted way. My new agent, Andre Bernheim, thought that it would be good for my European career, and we decided I should do it. It was pleasantly uneventful. There was no drama off the set, and not much drama on it. Lamoureux was a big star, but completely cooperative and agreeable. I don't remember much else about the film, only that my mother loved it because I had beautiful clothes by Pierre Balmain, and I wasn't a victim (as in *Calle Mayor*) or a wallflower (*Marty*) or mad (*The Snake Pit*).

Life in Paris was wonderful. Roger and I were happy. Kerry was growing up splendidly. Garance Films was preparing a second documentary, *Paris mange son pain,* by Pierre Prévert. And Roger and a young writer, painter, and mime, Antoine Tudal, were working on the feature-film scenario for Roger to direct in China.

And sunny, ravishing Italy beckoned me.

25

MICHELANGELO—the only one most of us had heard of at that time was the great Florentine. But now my agent said there was an offer and a scenario for me to read from an Italian director, Michelangelo Antonioni. I was to look at the role of Elvira.

Il Grido (The Cry) baffled me. I thought I could read a screenplay and understand it. I read and reread the poor English translation and was vaguely intrigued. If it had been in French, I would have asked Roger to read it for his opinion. I told him I didn't really think it was for me, but Roger could see that I was somehow reluctant to say no. Let's talk to Serge, he said. (Annie Noël, Serge's wife, had been in Antonioni's first film—this would be his second.) Roger knew they had a high opinion of him, but we were surprised by the force of Serge's reaction. He didn't want to hear the story, he didn't want to know about the role. He simply insisted, "You have to do it. He's a great director." I guess those old angels had followed me to France and were smiling on me again.

I sent the following telegram: "I would love to work for Mister Antonioni, but I find the role vague and disconnected." I was immediately invited to Rome for the weekend.

They met me at the elevator of the Hotel Excelsior, a tall man, a short man, and a nice-looking woman—the director, the producer, and the translator. Antonioni was the tall one, incredibly elegant as only the Italians are, nervous, and shy—or so I thought. The producer, Franco Cancellieri, made the introductions, bustled us into a secluded corner of the lobby, ordered tea for me, espressos for them, mineral water for all, and left us. We discovered we could communicate in French. I gave Antonioni Serge and Annie's greetings, and we put our scripts on the table. The discussion started. My tea got cold, he gulped his espresso and shoved it aside. The words, vague and disconnected, that I'd chosen so lightly for my telegram were spoken in English. "*Pourquoi* [why] vague? *Comment* [how] disconnected?" I felt in his questions, not anger but something finer and more ferocious—a kind of artistic outrage. My mind was racing. I was alert but a bit lost. I fell back on what I knew, on the way I worked with Shdanoff. I said I found it difficult to explain, that perhaps I hadn't grasped it all, maybe we could go through the screenplay together so I could question him when I didn't understand.

And that's what we did. For the next two hours I thought we were having a fruitful discussion. I can see now that my very American combination of naive confidence in my opinion and the Stanislavsky approach to acting were completely alien to him. His art is so personal and mysterious. I'm very glad—and lucky—that he didn't decide to drop me there and then.

The only thing that redeems me is that I went straight to my room and telephoned my agent in Paris. I said we had had a good meeting. I made a lot of suggestions, we argued about some, he seemed to agree about others. He said he would change a lot of things, but I know, I really do know, that he won't change anything. And I don't care. I want to be in his movie.

Il Grido is the story of a thirty-five-year-old worker in romantic despair who goes on a journey in search of his future. He defines his exploration by the women he meets. There were five of us: Alida Valli, Gabriella Palotta, Mirna Girardi, Dorian Gray, and me. (Of course, this framework made the characters "disconnected.")

The Elvira section was shot in the north of Italy, in the Po Valley. It was bleak and desolate and cold, perfect for the scenes but miserable for the cast. I remember one midnight standing near a bonfire, my hands pushed up into my sleeves, stomping my feet to warm them, and explaining to the producer, through chattering teeth, why actors had trailers in Hollywood. It wasn't because they were

The magisterial Michelangelo Antonioni, 1958

spoiled stars, I said, the studios were never indulgent; it was because it saved time and therefore money. Just at that moment an old woman from the nearby hamlet hobbled up to me, smiled, and offered me a present. It was a hot, charred baked potato in a scrap of cloth. I was sort of smiling back and gesturing that I wasn't hungry when she made me understand that it wasn't to eat, it was to warm my hands. It was such a comfort physically and emotionally that Hollywood and its luxuries flew out of my head.

I think that was the moment I became one of them. This was my third European film. I'd been aware at the beginning of each one that the makeup, hairdressing, and costume people, the cameraman and crew, expected a Hollywood creature, a demanding egotist or a spoiled brat. I made a conscious effort to be the opposite of

With Steve Cochran in Antonioni's *Il Grido*

what they dreaded. It wasn't hard. I'd never been a star. I'd played the lead in a low-budget movie that won lots of prizes and made millions of dollars. At heart I was still a high school basketball player, a member of the team.

Under the best circumstances, with a good director, a movie *is* a team effort. On *Il Grido* we had this extraordinary captain, Michelangelo Antonioni. I didn't get to know him personally, we didn't become friends—but he evoked in everyone, including me, a passionate loyalty and desire to please him.

The daily schedule of European films is most civilized. In France shooting starts at noon or one o'clock and goes straight through to seven or eight—no getting up at six-thirty to be on set at nine. In Italy it was more haphazard. On *Il Grido* the call was usually for eleven. The actors and camera crew were ready. Then we would wait for Michelangelo. It might be eleven-thirty, or twelve, or twelve-thirty, when the elegant figure slipped into his director's chair. The atmosphere quickened. There was electricity around his silence. He lit a cigarette. The assistant handed him the first of three or four tiny espressos. There was not the slightest trace of pretension or aggression in this ritual. We were seeing an artist preparing to work, and we somehow knew it and respected it.

When he beckoned the cameraman, the great Gianni di Venanzo, there was a palpable surge of energy. We were ready, and Antonioni knew exactly what he wanted. He was patient and tenacious, gentle and calm in his contact with the actors, wittier and more autocratic with the crew. Once we started the pace was fast, and Antonioni was the quickest of all. He was everywhere, moving a prop, adjusting a costume, checking through the lens, huddled next to the camera, looking, watching, demanding. All directors do these things; it's their job. But it seems to me now that the finished film was already embodied in his presence. Perhaps the comparison is with the painter who faces his canvas, makes his first brushstroke with the whole structure of the picture already at his fingertips. No one else can see it, no one else could have done it.

The producer, Signor Cancellieri, was a small, charming man, friendly and apologetic for the poor accommodations. The hotel was cold, the telephone was often out of order. He was devoted to Antonioni and the project but increasingly frantic. I didn't quite understand why, but I worried about him. His eyelids were always pink. I thought he might have conjunctivitis. Then my agent managed to get through on the phone. The second part of my fee was overdue, and there was only a secretary in the production office in Rome. The system in Italy was that you were paid a third when you signed the contract, a third on the first day of shooting, and a third when the film wrapped. I told my agent not to worry, Signor Cancellieri was almost always here with us, and I'd speak to him. Again our producer was apologetic and promised to see to it right away. Another ten days passed. My agent called three or four times to tell me to stop shooting—there's no other way, the Italians are impossible—just refuse to shoot, or you'll never get paid. Finally I said, "Listen, I can't stop shooting. It might kill the director, he might die."

Of course I knew this was not literally true. But the power of Antonioni's intensity was so strong that when I said he might die, I almost believed it.

I never mentioned money again. The producer sensed that I wouldn't and was grateful. We finished shooting. I'd had another difficult and exciting acting experience. We said our farewells, and I flew back to Paris.

Everyone agreed with my agent that I would never see a penny. Roger and Serge were the only ones who understood, who didn't think I'd been foolish. But even they assumed that was the end of it.

Lo and behold, it wasn't. Six months later Signor Cancellieri telephoned. He was in Paris, he had the money for me, would I meet him for a drink at Fouquet's? And there I found a different man. I'd nicknamed him "the Rabbit" because of his pink eyes. Now he was smiling and genial. There was nothing at all rabbitlike about him. I realized it wasn't conjunctivitis, rather that he probably did a lot of crying during his desperate struggle to find the money to finish the film. We had a joyous meeting. We were both triumphant, but we didn't mention it. It's obvious why he felt like that—he'd made the movie against the odds. My feelings came from the fact that the Italians weren't "impossible." I never thought they were, and here was this big fat envelope of cash to prove it.

About fifteen years ago, Antonioni gave a long interview to *Cahiers du Cinéma*. When asked what was the worst time of his professional life, he replied, "The first two hours I spent with Betsy Blair."

By then I was living in London with my second and eternal husband, Karel Reisz, a film director himself. I was practically in tears when I showed it to him. He read it and smiled at me. "Don't be silly—think of it as a kind of great honor."

26

THE SKIES of Paris were dazzling blue. There must have been gray days, but I don't remember them.

There had been two cars floating around Europe, left over from Gene's film *Invitation to the Dance*. Given my choice, I'd taken the convertible Hillman Minx. It was small, economical, already in France, and blue and white, like my first Pontiac in California.

One afternoon I was tootling around in the car. I knew my way from my early explorations of Paris. I liked driving in Paris; I liked the challenge of keeping my head among the wild French. Not for them the stately procession of cars in Beverly Hills, with its stop signs on almost every corner. Here it was every man for himself. The worst spot was the Etoile, the circle around the Arc de Triomphe. There are six main roads, including the Champs-Élysées, leading in and out of it. The cars, four or five deep, race around it, missing each other by inches as they change from lane to lane.

And that day in that spot a tiny black cloud scudded across my blue horizon. I managed to slip into the mad circle and move inward, since I needed to make almost the complete circuit. But I couldn't get out to the edge where I needed to exit. I missed my street and went round again. I signaled, I waved, I made begging faces, I smiled, all to no avail. On the third lap I gritted my teeth and cut across. I made it to a chorus of honking horns. The last car in my way was a taxi. As he jammed on his brakes and I mouthed my thanks, he shouted at me, *"Conasse!"*

Now this is a rude word, and somehow it hit me hard. I found my hands shaking. I pulled into a side street and parked, locked the car, left a note on the windshield, and went home. Roger collected the car. And I recovered to joust on the roads again.

Then in the dead of winter, when it's dark by three-thirty in the afternoon, I was Christmas shopping. The lights were brilliant, but my whole view of the sky suddenly turned black. I stopped in a café. As I sat down, the sentence burst fully formed into my mind: "I don't live anywhere." I, the radical who scorned private property, the one who had blithely, without a second thought, signed away her half of the home on Rodeo Drive, was suddenly scared to death. "I don't live anywhere. Women need to have something. What about my little girl? She must never feel like this. I have to buy an apartment for her to have when I'm not here. She must never feel like this." Obviously, I'd forgotten for the moment that she had a father, and, even more, that she'd grow up and be independent. And maybe that's just what I was doing. My sudden terror was probably an acute growing pain. At last, a sense of responsibility!

Just off Saint-Germain, we found a beautiful apartment on the Rue du Bac. Our neighborhood bistros were the Café Flore and the Deux Magots, where every day of the week you could drink your coffee, not exactly with, but in the same room as, Simone de Beauvoir, Sartre, James Baldwin, sometimes even Picasso. I was more impressed than I'd ever been in Hollywood.

Our building, Number 77, was not one of the grand ones built around a courtyard. It was a solid bourgeois apartment house circa 1800, made of gray Parisian stone. There were five floors and an attic with servants' rooms, one for each of the residents. We had the fourth floor—only one flat per floor—but the staircase was wide and the steps were shallow. Now there's an elevator, but then we were young—we bounded up and ran down the four flights.

We had to buy it. My Christmas-shopping moment had been so powerful, there was never even any discussion. Having found it, the problem was how to pay for it.

World War II had been over for twelve years, but France, maybe Paris especially, was still a financial wilderness. There were no mortgages as we know them, and two actors with uncertain incomes couldn't get a bank loan. In every real estate deal, cash was paid under the table disguised as "key money." The black market for currency was flourishing.

I knew a money changer in a tiny room on the Champs-Élysées, Pop Landau, a Polish concentration camp survivor. Gene and I had been introduced to him by John Huston. All the American show-business visitors to Paris—and probably anyone else who had dollars to change into francs—found their way to Pop. I don't know if the French authorities knew about him and simply turned a blind eye, or if he really was clandestine. I do know that if you went to him with cash you got twice as many francs as at the official exchange rate.

Pop Landau was a small tidy man, very neatly dressed in shirt-sleeves and a brightly colored tie. His hands were spotless and perfectly manicured, his face and balding scalp looked as if they'd been cleaned and polished. His French, English, and Yiddish were fluent, and I'm sure he knew enough to get by in every European language. He lived and worked in one tiny room that could only have been rented as an office. It had no bathroom; Pop used the public one on the next floor. I don't know if he ever left the building. You could call him at any time, day or night, for an appointment. When you arrived, you heard the key turn in the lock, the three bolts slide back, and then the door opened a crack with the heavy chain across the gap. When he saw you there was a big smile, especially if you were a young woman.

But there was nothing creepy about Pop. He was like an impish uncle that you had never met as a child. He greeted you, sat you down, and disappeared into a curtained corner to bring out two glasses of tea and sugar. His pen and pad were on the table. You took out your dollars and sipped your tea. He counted them quickly and skillfully and wrote two figures on the pad—what the official rate of exchange would give you, and how many francs he would give you. As you looked and smiled acceptance he sipped his tea. Then he was off behind the curtain again to come back with the pile of francs. He counted them out for you and asked you to count them again. Then and only then would he take your dollars, put them in his wallet, and burn the piece of paper in a brass ash-tray. There wasn't any small talk, until one day I couldn't resist asking him about the only weird thing in the room.

His furniture consisted of a table, four chairs, two lamps, a cup-board, and a single bed. Above the bed there was a shelf that ran around three sides of the room. And it was full of dolls—little dolls like the ones you find in souvenir shops for tourists all over the world.

I didn't realize what I was doing when I asked about them. His face went white, he screwed up his eyes, hunched his shoulders, his elbows on his knees, his hands clasped tightly in front of him, and said, "When I finally make my way home, the only thing I find is my baby girls' little doll." His wife and three children had been killed in the concentration camps. I put my hand on his; I said I was sorry to bring back his pain. It was all I could think of to say. He waved away my apology, shook his head, and turned away to blow his nose with his immaculate handkerchief. And then it was business as usual. It was never mentioned again, but we had a more personal relationship after that. Before, I'd been the wife of a movie star; now I was someone to whom he had shown a glimpse of that terrible time in his life.

I hadn't seen Pop Landau since my move to Paris. Now I thought he might somehow know how we could borrow the money for the apartment. I told Roger about him and called and made an appointment for both of us. He let us in, looked Roger over, looked at me, saw my happiness, shrugged, and smiled at us both. He brought us tea, and I told him our problem. He couldn't help us in France; but then he said, with a conciliatory nod to Roger, that he'd seen Gene when he'd last passed through Paris, and from what he'd observed in Gene's attitude about me, he thought I could borrow the money from Gene.

Of course, I couldn't bring myself to ask Gene. The last thing I wanted was to be dependent on him again, and I didn't think I deserved his kindness. Besides, after my experience of the divorce, I wasn't sure he was capable of generosity toward me.

I had one other source. There was a Swiss bank. I imagined they would lend me the twenty-five thousand dollars we needed.

Some weekends when I went to see Kerry in Geneva, I would spend Sunday night with Oona and Charlie Chaplin. It was a short train ride to their house in Vevey. I didn't know Charlie well in Hollywood, although we went to parties there, but Oona and I were friends. She was an extraordinary woman in every way. Extraordinarily intelligent, extraordinarily pretty, extraordinarily sweet, and she was full of fun.

I have a trophy, a thick pottery mug we won together. Its inscription says, "First Annual Cockamamie Tennis Tournament. Chaplin—Wyler Courts. Women's doubles." Oona and I had been the victors.

It was the first and only tournament. Before the year was over, Charlie had been driven out of the United States. When they were settled in Vevey, Oona flew back to California one last time. She sold the house, closed the bank accounts, tucked the bonds and stock certificates in her handbag, and flew back. And then she did this wonderfully loyal thing. She handed in her American passport, renouncing her citizenship. Her life was with Charlie. If they wouldn't have him, they couldn't have her.

On my first visit I began to understand why she loved him so. In Hollywood when I saw him he always seemed to be "on." He was the life of the party. He did old routines—even the Little Tramp. He tried out new ones. He played his latest composition on the piano, giving a running commentary with the plot of a possible scenario. And he was brilliant. He was Chaplin, after all. Along with every other woman in the room, I was entranced. But I did marvel at Oona's reaction. She giggled as if she had never seen or heard any of this before. The men were less patient. Perhaps they felt a bit of envy.

At home in Vevey, Charlie was adorable—there's no other word. Sunday night and Monday morning were very good times to be there. He had the British Sunday papers flown in for him. Charlie loved gossip. He pounced on the papers. I know he was well informed, he must have read the serious articles, but first it was the scandal. He would read out loud the most extreme bits—and he was particularly pleased if the subject was an aristocrat. The poor, clever Cockney boy that I'd never seen in Hollywood was there with us in the white-haired man. And when you came down to breakfast on the terrace or in the conservatory in winter, Oona, in her beautiful silk dressing gown, and Charlie, in his white toweling robe, would be huddled together, talking and laughing.

On my first visit Charlie suddenly asked me a personal question in the middle of dinner. "How are you for money?" I said I was fine. From the divorce settlement I had eighteen thousand dollars a year for ten years. In ten years Kerry would be a college graduate, so she was safe. I was about to be in a movie, and I had ten thousand dollars in the bank. "Ah," he said. "You must promise me something. Oona, take her to the little bank tomorrow morning. And Betsy, you must deposit your ten thousand dollars there, and this is the promise I want. You're not to touch it for the next ten years. Will you promise?" I was not simply surprised, I was astonished. Charlie insisted. Finally I said, "Okay, I promise." I didn't know if I meant it or not, but I was swept away by his unexpected concern for me.

The next morning it was a fait accompli. As Oona and I, in the backseat of the chauffeured car, were driven down the mountain to Geneva, I'd adjusted to the idea so well that I asked her why he'd said the "little bank." She laughed and said not to worry. Charlie had six million dollars in the little bank.

In those days a private Swiss bank was like a fine townhouse. A liveried doorman ushered you in. You were shown to a small, extremely elegant drawing room with paintings on the wall and antique furniture. You were served tea, and in this charming unbusinesslike atmosphere you did your business. It may be the same today, for all I know. Back in Paris, Gene Moskowitz informed me that an American citizen is not allowed to have a numbered bank account. I wasn't about to break any laws, so I couldn't keep my promise to Charlie.

But before I found this out, I paid the bank one more visit, to ask for a loan for the apartment. Even without Oona, and with what must have been an infinitesimal deposit in their eyes, I was given the same welcome by Monsieur Pierre, one of the owners of the bank. Over tea, I explained what I wanted. "I see," he mused gently. "And what security can you offer?" Confidently I replied, "Why, the apartment on the Rue du Bac." "Oh my dear Miss Blair, an apartment in Paris does not constitute security for a Swiss bank. But may I suggest that we handle it for you? The Bank of America would surely lend such a small sum on the guarantee of your ex-husband. Would that be possible?"

So many things went racing through my brain that I couldn't answer. I said I seem to need a few moments to think. He left me alone for ten minutes. I paced around on the Aubusson carpet, sat and closed my eyes. I saw myself at seventeen or eighteen, saying I supposed my $1,800 dollars got mixed in with all the other money, and at thirty-one, telling Gene to get out of the house if he could threaten me with accusations of adultery and the "Red Chinese" connection just for money. But the overwhelming feeling I'd had in the café in Paris drowned these visions. I needed this apartment. I needed it for Kerry in the future and for me now. When Monsieur Pierre came back, I said quite calmly, okay, yes, how do we go about it?

And Gene came through for me. He did call first to make sure I was putting the apartment in my name only, and I realized that was what I wanted anyway. I could have started a new political party, "Independent Security for Women"!

Well, almost independent. I was learning that the real world must be confronted with more careful thought. My feelings, my reckless temper, my childish belief that everything would come out all right because I was a "good guy," were not the only elements in the equation of life. There were compromises to be made—not important ones like cooperating with the McCarthy committee, but compromises to do with my pride and foolishness. We got the wonderful apartment, and I paid off the loan in two and a half years from my own movie earnings. I was proud of that. I still am.

Bea Dassin told me that moving to France I was allowed to import one "household" without paying customs duty. Even I, mad as I was about everything French, jumped at this chance. I didn't own anything. I'd left Beverly Hills with photographs of Kerry and my clothes. My grandmother's silver and my childhood books had been shipped back to Cliffside. So my dear mother was sent on a grand shopping spree.

Percale sheets and pillowcases, a big American refrigerator, a washing machine and dryer, a toaster oven, a Waring mixer, and anything else she thought I'd need, duly arrived at Le Havre, and everything was trucked to Paris.

Today, European machines are as good as American ones, but this was 1957, when for comfort and convenience we were on top of the world. The refrigerator, in particular, was an object of wonder—as well, no doubt, of a bit of shoulder-shrugging derision. French women go shopping every day; they wouldn't see the need for such a giant.

The apartment was a beauty. There was an enormous living room with a big old marble fireplace and windows from floor to ceiling with their original wooden shutters, a small bedroom for Kerry and a large one for Roger and me, a library with another fireplace, a bathroom, and a kitchen we could eat in—we had a long table in one corner of the living room for more formal dinners. Naturally, being American, I had to have another bathroom. I enlisted my great designer friend Trauner to help us. He knew a just qualified young architect who turned out to be perfect, enthusiastic, and open to any ideas I had, but careful—and economical—about the basics, the heating, plumbing, and electricity, and the solid construction of the building itself. And what a building it was. I watched Trau examine it for at least two hours. He did the usual things, looking for cracks, tapping the walls, opening and closing doors and shutters. He measured the height of the ceiling and checked it against the depth of the stairwell from the third floor to the fifth. He then politely visited the apartments above and below us. I stayed behind to listen when he was overhead. I heard nothing. Then he went down to the third floor. I had instructions to stomp around and jump up and down while he was there. And he heard nothing. He came back jubilant to tell us how lucky we were.

It was just as he'd expected. He drew a diagram to explain. There was a five-foot space between each ceiling and the floor above. The layers were first the plaster we could see, then solid oak beams running from back to front, then a diagonally crosshatched floor holding a two-foot-deep layer of stones, another group of beams from side to side, and finally the parquet floor above. No wonder there were never complaints from neighbors about noise.

I asked if we could expose the beams in the library. We did, and the young workmen were as excited as I was to see that Trau was right. They carefully took out and replaced a small corner of the crosshatching so we could see the stones—they were as big as ostrich eggs. The whole experience that's reputed to be a nightmare was a joy. Even the language difficulty made it more fun.

We moved in two weeks before Christmas. We had very little furniture, but we had a party. I'd forgotten it until forty years later, in December 1999, when I went to Paris for the funeral of our dearly beloved Jack Berry. His children and the children of Julie Dassin brought it back to me. Kerry was in Paris for the holiday, and all the American blacklisted families were there. It was memorable for the kids because not only did we have a turkey with stuffing and cranberry sauce, but Roger and I had furnished the living room with cushions to sit on and fourteen Christmas trees decorated with anything and everything, from the traditional baubles to socks and kitchen utensils and scarves.

Jack Berry—John the director, Jack the friend. With Serge Reggiani, he was our closest friend. Jack's incredible breadth of spirit embraced Roger for my sake, but very quickly it was for Roger himself. Jack managed somehow to get a house for his family in St. Cloud, outside Paris. He was scrambling around to make money to live on, to get a film project off the ground, to get a job in the theater as an actor or director in London or Paris. He came to our apartment several times a week for lunch, a corner to work in, the telephone for contacts, occasionally bed and breakfast.

Jack encouraged Roger on our French-Chinese production. Roger was talented, imaginative, and knowledgeable, but sweet and modest—a doer, not a go-getter. His idea for the film was a dream from his childhood—a Parisian boy who finds a kite, and floats away on it to a far distant land, to China—a kind of Aladdin and his magic carpet. Antoine Tudal, who wrote the screenplay, was also a painter, though he earned his living by doing a mime at the Crazy Horse. The Crazy Horse was an enormous nightclub show, a bit like the International Casino, but French, therefore much raunchier. It was mainly for tourists, so ooh-la-la, the showgirls were bare-breasted and the dancers were strippers. Quite often we picked Antoine up after the show, and I, the ex-puritan from New Jersey, discovered that I enjoyed the sexiness of it all.

With Jack's pushing, my enthusiasm, Serge's impatience, and Roger's steady persistence, we were ready to contact the Chinese embassy. The script was sent to Peking. The minister of culture expressed great interest. Diplomatic discussions, to which we were not invited, took place. Our little project was approved in the highest circles. The French government's "Aid to the Cinema" is very generous, especially for a first-time director. In our case it covered two thirds of the Parisian part of the budget. Air France would contribute the transport of personnel and equipment and fly the rushes back every day to the laboratory in Paris to be developed. The Chinese would pay for everything in China and have distribution rights for Southeast Asia and China itself. We seemed to be in the home stretch.

Then our friendly French money man coproducer had to withdraw. He'd realized that this could not be the usual film-financing game. We had two governments and Air France involved. So his investment had to be on deposit in the bank two weeks before the first day of shooting. It was impossible for him. Serge, Roger, and I sort of slithered out of his office. The three of us held hands without speaking as we crossed the Champs-Élysées to our own office. As we well knew, movie projects collapse all the time, but we weren't ready to give up on this one. It was about seven at night. We had three days to find fifty-five thousand dollars to meet the deadline without our official partners knowing we were in trouble. At some point we stopped to get something to eat—no, we didn't stop, we just stoked up to be able to continue racking our brains and making our lists. I was worried about Roger. It was to be his film, but he was calmer and cooler than we were. By about three in the morning we had our top four possibilities and a plan to approach the first one—Monsieur Morgenstern. We went home to bed and, surprisingly, slept like babies.

Morgenstern was the biggest, most solid, independent producer in France at the time. Serge and Roger knew Madelaine, his sweet and lovely daughter. She was married to Francois Truffaut, still an influential critic, not yet the famous director. If we had them on our side, we could get to Morgenstern immediately. Calling for an appointment might take a week, and we didn't have a week.

It worked. Serge came to our apartment at eight-thirty a.m. At nine he called Madelaine. At ten we delivered the script to her. She and Francois read it that day and called at six. We had supper in a café and explained what we needed and how urgent it was. They were both enthusiastic, so although we had contacted our producers number two and three, we relaxed and didn't follow up on them. Morgenstern couldn't see us all day—the second day of the three we had—but Madelaine delivered the screenplay, a synopsis, and copies of the budget and the financial setup to him at home that first night. All five of us, Madelaine, Francois, Serge, Roger, and I, went to his house at eight-thirty the following evening. He was serious and benign, but very sharp. I think he must have decided beforehand that it was a promising project and a well-constructed deal. If he liked Roger and thought he could do it, he would join us—or, rather, save us. And he did. He was generous, too. He took the French distribution and 25 percent of our share; our first coproducer had wanted 40 percent. We signed the contract in the morning, and his check was in the bank at noon. Roger and Garance Films were making a feature film.

A few weeks earlier, the Chinese had asked me to come to their embassy. The cultural attaché received me with one of the men who had been on the yacht at the Cannes Film Festival when I went to tea. In Cannes they had sneaked me onto a boat. Now they were offering to sneak me into China for the shooting without my passport being stamped. For a few days I was wildly excited at the prospect. Then I had a vision of me at the top of the steps from the plane, in the spot where presidents and pop stars stop and wave, and there I was, tall, pale, and redheaded. If the FBI could spot me at London airport greeting Paul Robeson among the thousands of people there, I was sure to be seen arriving in Peking. I thought of Kerry and newspaper reports. I was scared off—I didn't go. I was too fond of my American passport to risk losing it.

We saw Roger off at Orly Airport with the boy actor and his mother, an assistant, the cameraman, the great Henri Alekan, and the sound engineer. It seemed such a small crew to go so far to make a movie. But they did it. The Chinese had prepared everything, and in ten days the rushes started to arrive in Paris.

Serge and I went to see them at the lab every day and sent messages to Roger that all was well.

And all *was* well. Kerry was lovelier every day. Roger was coming home after almost a month in China. I had an offer to be in a play in London. The apartment was perfect. Adrian Scott was writing a scenario for Jack Berry to direct with the leading role for me. I may not have been employable in Hollywood, but in Europe for a few years after the success of *Marty,* I was bankable. That means that if I were in a film, the money to make it could be found—naturally, not only on my name. Adrian had a wonderful career as a writer and producer in Hollywood before the blacklist, and Jack's American films were much appreciated in France, especially *He Ran All the Way,* with John Garfield. And I wanted to work for Jack. I'd been in a play, *Deep Are the Roots,* for him in Los Angeles and San Francisco in the late 1940s. I think that for me as an actress, he was the best director I've ever worked with.

Jack always had several scripts going at once in the hope that one of them would get made. Almost every independent filmmaker or theater director does the same. He was working on a thriller with Ben Barzman. He was trying to mount an Odets play, and there was a project with Haya Harareet, an Israeli actress. She was working in the Kameri Theatre of Tel Aviv, where the English director Thorold Dickinson discovered her for his film *Hill 24 Doesn't Answer.* She came to Paris with an idea of her own, a movie about

Hannah Senesch, an Israeli poet and heroine of World War II. Haya was young, lusciously beautiful, enterprising, and intelligent. Someone sent her to Jack, and he was instantly smitten—"nuts about her," in his words. She was irresistible to him, and Jack, I quote from one of his obituaries, ". . . he had one side Blaise Cendars [Surrealist poet], a touch of Verlaine, a sliver of Saint-Just [revolutionary moralist], a vision of *The Grapes of Wrath,* a zest of Voltaire and several drops of Casanova." So we began to see quite a lot of Haya. Then she and I were each invited for the second week of the Cannes Film Festival. Roger was cutting his film, so he couldn't come. Jack wanted to come with us—for Haya, and to hustle his projects. Haya wanted him to come, but no one had any money. I suggested that she and I ask the festival to give us a suite at the Carleton to share—then I'd sleep in the living room. It worked. We ordered enormous breakfasts every day, English and American with croissants on the side. Jack would leap across the bed to hide in the bathroom while the waiter laid the table. When we set out for the day, Jack would go downstairs first and call us to join him in the lobby. I don't suppose we fooled the sophisticated staff at the hotel for one second, but the three of us laughed all week.

Neither of Jack's films, the one for me or the one for Haya, was ever made. But he soon did a French movie, *Give 'Em Hell,* that was an enormous hit in Europe. It was a detective thriller, starring Eddie Constantine, an American who lived in Paris by choice and made a successful career there. (It was he who suggested Leslie Caron when Gene was looking for a dancer for *An American in Paris.*) Jack's movie had all the verve and excitement of the Hollywood film noir so loved by the French. And Haya was discovered for a second time by William Wyler and chosen to star opposite Charlton Heston in *Ben-Hur.* This led to a contract with Metro, and off she went to Hollywood.

Before leaving, she asked me for phone numbers of good people, possible friends. I said she needed only one, my darling Ruth Conte, and I was right. Her best memories of her time in Hollywood are of Ruthie. And it was in Hollywood that she met Jack Clayton, the director of *Room at the Top, The Innocents,* and *The*

Cannes, 1955: an official from the film festival and Chukrai, director of *The Cranes Are Flying*, gazing adoringly at Haya Harareet

Great Gatsby, among others. They fell in love. So in the early 1960s, when I moved to London, Haya was already there. And for the last forty years, she and Ruthie and I have been a solid triangle of best friends.

Roger finished *The Kite from the Other Side of the World.* It was a smash in China, a reasonable success in France, Scandinavia, and Hungary, but was shown for only two weeks in New York. Garance Films went into a pause. Serge and I were both working, and Roger decided he would take acting parts while we looked for other subjects.

The play I was offered in London, *The Trial of Mary Dugan,* is an old American warhorse, reputed to be the first "courtroom drama." It would never have made it into my list of great plays to enlighten the world. But it was a leading role on the London stage and a limited run of three months. The Savoy Theatre, adjacent to the Savoy Hotel, was home to the D'Oyly Carte Gilbert and Sullivan Opera Company. While they were on tour, the theater put on a play rather than shut down. I remember that I worked hard to make Mary Dugan more than a self-sacrificing martyr. The critics were tolerant of the play and welcoming to me, but it was not serious material and therefore not a really satisfying experience.

The stage manager asked me if I'd like tea served in my dressing room between shows on matinee days. It duly arrived in all its English high tea glory—white linen, silver teapots, china cups, cucumber sandwiches, scones with clotted cream and strawberry jam, and various cakes. It took two waiters to deliver it from the hotel. At the end of the run I went to the hotel desk to pay, since the waiters had never presented me with a bill. The cashier sent a bellboy for the maître d'. "Oh no, madame, there's no charge. We always send tea to the leading players in our theater."

My closest English friend was the theater director Lindsay Anderson (he hadn't yet made any films). When he heard about this bonanza on matinee days—even before we knew it was free—he arranged his life to join me, sometimes on Wednesday, almost always on Saturday. I'd met him in his capacity as journalist when I was in Europe with Gene. His quizzical, iconoclastic attitude appealed to me, and I think he saw something other than a movie star wife in me. His opinions—no, his *pronouncements*—were shocking and exciting. I laughed with him, sometimes at him— with his grudging admission occasionally that I might be right in this or that particular case. I don't think many people in his circle ever laughed at him. It may have been one of the reasons we were friends. And I learned a lot. He was a natural teacher, leader, revolutionary thinker about art and life. He was bitchy and disdainful, but with the courage and audacity of mind of a true artist.

One day Lindsay brought Karel Reisz to my dressing room for tea. Karel had written a book on film editing, and was now making documentaries. There should have been a fanfare of trumpets, or a thunderbolt from the skies, but there wasn't. I met an intelligent man with a lovely sensitive face, amazing blue eyes, and better teeth than I had noticed on any other Englishman. I've never asked him what he thought that day, but I think he met a lively American actress who was a friend of his friend Lindsay. And that was that— at least as far as we knew.

Lindsay Anderson and Karel, 1963

Roger came from Paris most weekends and several times for a week. It was always like a wonderful holiday—not like in Spain, where I was living and breathing the movie. Here we would walk by the Thames, have long lunches, visit museums, go to the movies. Only at four in the afternoon I'd sleep for an hour then get myself ready for the play. I realized that I loved doing it even though I knew it wasn't great. It was the challenge I was sharing with the other actors to involve the audience in our story, to make them care what happened to our characters, that brought it to life for me.

Roger and I were both working. Our finances were in good shape. As part of our wonderful apartment we had a maid's room on the top floor, and we decided we should have a maid. I'd seen the attic room when we first looked at the apartment but I hadn't really taken it in. Basically it was okay. Painted, dormer window repaired, washbasin under the eaves replaced, some shelves and curtains, and it would be livable. But the communal bathroom was a nightmare. It had what is called in France a Turkish toilet. This is a tiled two-foot-square, ten-inch-deep indentation in the floor, a bit like a shower pan. The sides slant to the drain in the middle. There are two foot-sized raised bits, strategically placed for standing on while squatting down.

There was a meeting of the coproprietors that week. I blithely proposed that we modernize the bathroom upstairs. There was a sharp silence. I looked around quickly, registered the widow and the old couple, and thought perhaps they can't afford it. I offered to pay for it myself. The mild disapproval turned into antagonism. They saw me as the Ugly American throwing her money around to get her way. I retreated and asked my builder to patch up the tiles surreptitiously and give the bathroom a quick coat of paint while he was doing our work. And no one complained—it was never mentioned. I didn't get my way, but I'd had a lesson in international relations.

Jeanette arrived from the country. A friend who came from a village near the French Alps had asked his parents to find someone for us. We were lucky beyond belief. She was nineteen, intelligent, pretty, cheerful—even cheeky, and with a mind of her own. I could be ready to dash out when she'd look me over and say, "No, no—I must press your skirt." She was also a good cook. She'd brought with her a jar containing an ugly straggly brown blob, about the size of a golfball. This was her "mother of vinegar." Leftover wine, tea, occasionally flat mineral water was poured over it, and made the best salad dressing I've ever eaten. She was happy with us, too. She'd been working since she was fifteen in a high-bourgeois house with a staff of six. Her only time off was for church on Sunday and Sunday afternoon. The family and guests ate lavishly, but the servants had meat only twice a week and no butter. The mistress of the house doled out the supplies herself and kept them under lock and key. Jeanette was glad to join us in the twentieth century. And I learned that there were aspects to my beloved France that I didn't know.

27

AND THERE WAS another Italian film: *Senilità*, from the novel *As a Man Grows Older*, by Italo Svevo, to be directed by Mauro Bolognini. He had made *Il Bel Antonio* with Mastroiani, a film that deserved its worldwide success. Mine was a wonderful role—not the lead, which was Claudia Cardinale, at her most beautiful—but a really good part to explore. I wanted to work for Bolognini; the great Tosi was doing the costumes, and I loved Italy. But mainly I was in a kind of exaltation all the time. I was finally making an independent living doing something I loved.

At home in Paris with Roger I thought I was completely happy. There was never any friction, the lovemaking was all it should be. I wasn't aware that our life together had gradually begun to revolve around me—what I was doing, what I needed to do, what I wanted, was paramount. We drifted into the opposite of my life with Gene. Perhaps it was just what I needed to counteract those years in Hollywood. I didn't see danger lurking, that it might be destructive, that I might not like to be the dominant partner. Our life was full and interesting: working, playing, loving, just being alive and in Paris.

There were other more serious events out in the world. The Algerian conflict was hotting up. We were all on the side of the Algerians in their fight for independence. The novelist Vladimir Pozner, who, when he was a refugee during World War II, had been a factory worker and then a screenwriter in Hollywood, was one of the leaders of the Parisian part of the battle. He organized meetings,

Gala FILM DISTRIBUTORS LTD. present
MAURO
BOLOGNINI'S   SENILITA 'x'   Starring ANTHONY FRANCIOSA · CLAUDIA CARDINALE
BETSY BLAIR · PHILIPPE LEROY

raised money, and wrote powerful polemics in the newspapers. As a result he became a target for the right wing in France, which supported the *"pieds noirs,"* the French settlers in Algeria.

Gene and I had met the Pozners—Ida, Vladimir, and their baby, Andre—at Salka Viertel's house in 1943. Andre and Kerry were almost the same age, so there were a few family picnics, but I got to know them better during the Sunday afternoons when I escaped the volleyball for what I thought of as my European education. Ida was a lovely woman, dark-eyed, slender, gentle, and quite without malice. What she had was courage and wit and grace. Vladimir was another story, mysterious and almost unknowable. He was seductive, with his black hair and sort of crumpled face, but I think now that his inner life was consumed by his political dream of a better world.

In Hollywood in 1947, Vladimir was writing the scenario of the

Going mad in *Senilità*

Lillian Hellman play *Another Part of the Forest,* about the early life of the characters in *The Little Foxes.* I had made a screen test to play the young Birdie. Oh, how I wanted the part. And at a party at Salka's, Vladimir was the one who told me that I got it. I was to be Birdie.

No one would have chosen the circumstances in which I was able to repay him for the joy I felt that night ten years earlier.

On the set of *Another Part of the Forest,* 1948.
Foreground: Michael Gordon, the director, and Dan Duryea.
Behind: Jerry Bresler, the producer; Fredric March; and me

Vladimir picked up his mail one morning and opened a letter
bomb. It blew up, gravely wounding his hands, his chest, and his
face, luckily leaving his eyes intact. He was in the hospital for two
months under armed guard provided by the same French government he was attacking over Algeria. They obviously didn't want
him dead. But when the doctors said he could go home to conva-
lesce, they withdrew his protection. Ida asked Roger and me if he
could possibly hide out in our apartment. Of course, we said yes.
We had an extra room, Kerry would sleep in the study when she
came for the weekend, Jeanette would be there when we weren't,
and the apartment was only a few blocks from where the Pozners
lived.

It was a period of great tension in Paris, and now we were part of
it. Ida came every morning, waving blithely as she passed the window where the concierge peered out. She was so elegant no one

could have suspected that she was carrying special foods and medicine to her ailing, endangered husband, hidden on the fourth floor.

Jeanette was trustworthy. We didn't even have to explain why our friend's presence was a secret. It was enough for her that he'd been hurt, that he was just out of hospital, and that he'd arrived in the dark of night. She embraced the extra work and cheerfully went about her business. Roger and I did too. But I admit, I looked up and down the street I now knew so well every time I went in or out. I told myself that there was no way I could recognize anyone suspicious, but nevertheless, even on our staircase I scanned each face.

After three weeks Vladimir was strong enough to move. He and Ida went to the country to the house of another friend, where he made a full recovery and lived a long and productive life.

And Algeria won its independence.

28

THE FRENCH MINISTRY of Culture decided to start an annual Festival of Documentary Films in the city of Tours. The French take documentaries seriously, as the jury chosen for this occasion indicates: Eugene Ionesco, Louise de Vilmorin, Marguerite Duras, Claude Mauriac, Jules Romain, me, and four others, ten in all. I was thrilled to be included. Except for me, the jury was French. I know festival juries usually have an actor as a sort of decoration, but what it meant to me was that I was being accepted as part of French life. I wasn't dropping in from Hollywood.

Marguerite Duras asked me if I'd like to drive to Tours with her in her "jalopy." She actually said "jalopy" in English. I don't remember who introduced us, but we knew her in a casual way from our neighborhood, Saint-Germain des Pres. She would sometimes beckon to Roger and me to join her at her table in the corner of the Café Flore, where she sat smoking, surrounded by papers and journals. She was as intriguing and mysterious as her writing. She wasn't at all pretty, not even handsome or striking and certainly not elegant. I only remember her in dull, unmatched shades of brown, thrown together without thought. But shrouded in her brown clothes, and her cigarette smoke, as well as weariness, she exuded an earthy intelligence and warmth that made her unforgettable— especially to a girl from New Jersey. When I accepted her offer of a ride, I thought, good, I'll really get to know her. The truth is, she got to know me. Without any obvious questions she drew out the story of my life and elicited nuances of my feelings that I'd never

The unforgettable Marguerite Duras

examined. Somehow I understood that a bit of her mystery came from the belief she had that the surface of a life is not a true picture of it, that life is not logical, that real existence is to be found in subterranean currents, in the clash of experience and the individual personality. She didn't say any of this. It was conveyed in quizzical looks, French shrugs, and acute judgments on every subject. We didn't become close friends. After the festival we reverted to our casual sociability—Roger and I went to her apartment for drinks a few times, she came to us, or we ran into her at the Café Flore. But in the years since, I'm occasionally aware of a fleeting insight or an odd reaction to something that I think comes from having known her.

Tours is a beautiful little city, the weather was sunny, the jury both serious and convivial. Everyone seemed to be on holiday from Paris and their usual preoccupations.

The late 1950s was a very good period for documentaries. We saw twenty-nine films, and there wasn't a single dud among them. We had boisterous jury meetings and rowdy wine-fueled lunches. It soon became apparent that there was a sharp division between two groups, with a couple of jurors occupying the middle ground. I tried to understand why. It didn't seem to be a matter of age—there were young and old on both sides. It wasn't divided strictly by politics or religion, although the other side tended to be on the political right. It wasn't until we reached the final meeting, when there were only two contenders left for the first prize, that the major difference became clear: there were those who spoke English and those who didn't. The two films were the English entry, *We Are the Lambeth Boys,* and a linked trio of very short Italian films, shot in color in churches in Naples, Florence, and Turin. The churches were beautiful, the camera work was beautiful, as art history or superior travelogues they were fine films, and they had strong advocates. The English film was the final one to be shown. It had been rushed to Tours—there was even uncertainty as to whether it would arrive in time. We settled down for the last projection on Saturday evening with a completely sold-out house. The jury was to deliberate during and after supper and Sunday morning if necessary. The prize-giving ceremony was Sunday afternoon, when the winning film would be shown again.

It started well—working-class teenagers from a housing estate all spruced up to go clubbing, music by Johnny Dankworth, black-and-white photography by Walter Lassaly. The director was Karel Reisz, the man Lindsay Anderson had brought to my dressing room for tea—the one with the amazing blue eyes. Five minutes into the film, the audience realized there were no subtitles. A murmur ran through the cinema. Five more minutes, and they got restive and a bit noisier. After fifteen minutes, a small group left, banging their seats.

The film lasted an hour. By the end, half the public had gone. But the jury knew we had a real contender. The film was marvelous. By the end of the evening we'd decided unanimously (the English speakers having won the fiery argument) that *We Are the Lambeth Boys* would have the first prize. There was no need for a morning meeting.

But the director of the festival summoned me to a meeting at ten a.m. He was distraught. Personally, he agreed with our choice, but he was extremely worried about the public's reaction and the future of the festival. He had the idea that I, the Anglo-Saxon, might be able to clarify what the film said, what the young people in it conveyed of their life and dreams, how specifically English and yet universal it was. Would I please speak before the showing? I couldn't refuse. I believed in the film, and perhaps the public, who had been denied the experience of the film's truth by the lack of subtitles, could gain an understanding even through my first extemporaneous speech in French. I said yes, apprehensively.

The British ambassador to France came from Paris to accept the award on behalf of Karel, who wasn't at the festival. The audience whistled and booed the announcement. When the ambassador came onstage, foot stomping and rhythmic clapping joined the boos. His graceful speech in perfect French was completely drowned out. The prize was a sculpture by Germaine Richier. The ambassador was disconcerted enough to hold it upside down, the plinth on top. He said later that he hadn't had such a hostile reception since Palestine.

Then it was my turn. The stomping stopped, and the applause was genuine. I was a woman. I was an American who had chosen France and a Frenchman (they all knew this from the glossy magazines), and I was a movie actress. I suddenly felt good and confident. I took the precaution of beginning by quoting Churchill on his first visit after the war. On the solemn occasion of laying a wreath on the Tomb of the Unknown Soldier at the Arc de Triomphe, he said, *"Prenez garde! Je vais parler le français."* I got a laugh. I spoke off the cuff, but I had thought of what I wanted to say. I made a comparison with *Marty,* the reason they knew me and accepted me so warmly. *Marty* was a fictional version of this documentary. The boys and girls of Lambeth would grow up to be Martys and Claras. One of the boys was even an apprentice butcher. I asked them to look at the faces, the dancing, the cricket playing, the surroundings, to listen to the music and think of their own adolescence.

My French must have been okay. At this second showing they were quiet for about forty minutes, and they stayed until the end. Gene Moskowitz wrote about it for *Variety* as the "Battle of Tours" and cast me as a Joan of Arc.

Film festivals have always been good experiences for me, but I've also seen firsthand how cruel they can be. The year of *L'Avventura* at Cannes, Antonioni and Monica Vitti, elegant and romantic, swept into the star box. And then the audience hated the movie. There were catcalls, boos, stomping, and departures—the whole shebang. At the end, when the beautiful couple stood valiantly in the spotlights to acknowledge the cheers of a few of us, they looked as if they'd been in a road accident. Ravaged faces, his tie askew, his hair rumpled, her mascara streaked down her cheeks, her lipstick gone, her dress crumpled. And at the second festival in Tours the following year, when the name Karel Reisz appeared on the screen simply as the producer of one of the documentaries, I was glad he wasn't there to hear the leftover uproar.

Karel had sent me a still from the film with his thanks on the back. It's now framed in our house in London. There were still no trumpet fanfares or flashes of lightning, but life was creating one of its mysterious things, underground streams that might someday flow together to make a river.

29

THE HELL of being an actor and the heaven of being an actor are one and the same: you never know what will happen next—or if anything will ever happen again.

I had a phone call in 1958 from a fellow I'd known for years. Bob Joseph was a writer, a journalist, a publicist, maybe even an agent at one time. He was a wit and a good guy. I knew he'd written a play that was being produced for Broadway starring Jack Lemmon, and I was glad for him. Bob had always been a fast talker and a bit of a mumbler. Now I heard a loud staccato machine gun of a voice. "Betsy, it's Bob Joseph. We're in trouble. Would you be free—if we send you the play by courier and you like the part—it's Jack's wife—could you fly to New York on the weekend [in four days' time!] and join the rehearsal on Monday? We've been at it for two and a half weeks and we have to replace the actress. Can you come? Are you free? Jack's contract is for four months—you can have the same. The director is Sandy MacKendrick. Please be free." I said, "Bob, calm down. Yes, I am free. Of course I'll read the play and call you immediately. He's a wonderful director. Do you think I can do comedy?" There was a beat of silence, then, "The play is out the door on its way to you," and he sort of trailed off. "It's not exactly a comedy. . . . Call us," and he was gone.

Jack Lemmon, Alexander MacKendrick, New York—I think I accepted the part as I hung up the phone, or even sooner.

Alexander MacKendrick was the director of several fine British films, the Ealing comedies, *The Ladykillers, Whisky Galore, The*

Man in the White Suit, and, in Hollywood, *Sweet Smell of Success.*
This was his first theater production. He was a brilliant, exceptionally handsome man and very charming. Unfortunately, in the
beginning I found him almost incomprehensible. It wasn't only his
Scottish accent—that was hard enough—it was his metaphysical,
conceptual mind that was elusive. So I had a problem.

And it was a serious problem too. There were only ten rehearsal
days left before we went to Philadelphia for a week, then Boston for
two weeks prior to the Broadway opening. Of course, I was way
behind the other actors. Not for me the calm read-through of the
whole play on the first day of rehearsal, no time to get to know the
other actors, the play, the director, no lunches or coffee breaks—I
had to catch up with them onstage.

The producer had foreseen all this. He assigned a very bright,
ambitious young actor who had a supporting role in the play to
help me. Whenever we weren't in a scene, we were in a dressing
room together running my lines, discussing the part, the play, the
relationships onstage and off, and eating apples. The assistant stage
manager would call us when we were needed, and bring us sandwiches for lunch.

On the second or third day something switched over in my brain
and suddenly I could understand Sandy MacKendrick, brogue and
all. I even began to enjoy his oblique approach to every question
that arose.

And I had a lot of questions, as every actor does during rehearsal.
But since I was concentrating so desperately to be ready myself, I
wasn't aware of the graver questions hovering over the production.

Jack Lemmon was a movie star, a fine actor, and a lovely man.
He had chosen this play, *Face of a Hero,* to come back to Broadway
in a straight role. He knew better than anyone what he was facing;
the critics and the public who adored his cinema persona were in
for a shock. He knew it was up to him to grab them, to make them
forget his delicate wit and charming modesty on the screen, and
accept him as a corrupt and potentially dangerous man. My character was an intelligent, thoroughbred, New England "public wife,"
with all the nervousness and frustration that "public" implies hid-

den deep within her. The role was not long, but my scenes were with Jack. He was wonderful to work with, adventurous as an actor and considerate of the other actors, especially me, the latecomer. So with Sandy and Jack—and, let's not forget, my young actor—I began to have fun, to feel the excitement of the opening night of a new play.

Philadelphia—the train ride, the hotel, the theater, the first time on the real set, my costumes, by the great Ann Roth, the run-through for the lighting rehearsal; I was rarin' to go. Then crash! Bang! A meeting with the producer, Sandy, and Bob Joseph. Tonight, the first performance with an audience, I was to play her as an alcoholic. Everything else was fine, there were no line changes, I just had to convey her alcoholism, just factor it in—it would help Jack's character and the whole play. I ran to the hotel, my head in a whirl, and called the young actor. He arrived in my room with two apples, and we worked on it for an hour or so. Then I had to be alone. I thought I'd sleep for a half hour, but I couldn't keep my eyes closed. I went to the theater, did my makeup, and dressed, and the play went on, somehow. I've never been able to remember anything at all about that performance. I think it must have been okay. The audience didn't rise up against me—but the whole evening is a blank.

We all calmed down—or, rather, I calmed down. There were a few rewrites, and the rest of the week in Philadelphia went well. We were sold out there and in Boston, and had a huge advance sale in New York, all based on Jack's name.

I hadn't been to Philadelphia since my wedding day. I stood in front of the church and realized that in about two and a half years it would have been our twentieth anniversary. I closed my eyes and tried to picture Gene and me on that happy day. We looked wonderful, and as I felt the tears start, I opened my eyes and walked on—briskly. I hadn't planned to go into the church anyway.

Across the alley from our stage door was the stage door of the other tryout theater. The play there was *The Wall*, John Hersey's drama about the Warsaw Ghetto during World War II. One of the leads was Marian Seldes. Marian was a tall, dark-haired, vibrant

girl, wildly enthusiastic about the theater. She has kept those qualities intact, but as a woman she's been able to reveal what was surely
always there, her wit and intelligence. And she was then, and is
now, an exceptional friend. She and I, and usually the young actor,
had supper most nights after the show, and went to museums and
movies in the daytime.

And on to Boston, where everything changed.

They fired the director and called in Harold Clurman, one of the
founders of the Group Theatre—the legendary Harold, director,
critic, idealistic theoretician, a great man in the American theater. I
already knew him from my Actors' Lab days. The Harold I knew
was awkward but delicate, bumbling but brilliant, rather like the
boy in high school who gets straight A's but doesn't know how to
talk to girls.

Now I saw him at work. As is often the case, he was a different
man. Calm, fluent, confidence-inspiring, he took us on a renewal
journey through the whole play. To me he suggested the word
"recovering." It was exactly the kind of illuminating direction an
actor can use. A recovering alcoholic is a character with hope. I had
a through line for my role.

Alexander MacKendrick did the most unexpected and admirable
thing. He didn't pack his bag and slink away. He sat in the theater
and watched us work, and watched Harold work. This enormously
successful movie director revealed his true nature, his lack of petty
vanity, his largeness of spirit and intellect. He didn't desert us,
and we loved him for it. Between them, they got us through the
hell of an out-of-town crisis—the producer, the director, and the
writer holed up all night in hotel rooms rewriting, the actors cop-
ing with new scenes, and the terror of the approaching opening on
Broadway.

And amid the tension—and without the presence of Marian
Seldes—the young actor and I fell into bed with each other. He was
a lovely fellow and a lovely lover. We had a fleeting but real experience. I knew I'd remember him and a hotel room that smelled of
apples.

What I didn't yet know was why this affair was different. I

thought I was wholeheartedly committed to Roger. I was adamant that I would never marry again, but I saw the rest of my life in Paris with him. He was coming to visit in six weeks, his first trip to the States, and I couldn't wait to be in his arms, to show him New York, and for my mother to get to know him.

It was a wonderfully successful visit in every way, and when he'd flown back, and I was writing to him, I stopped and thought about it. It was then I realized what was bizarrely missing in this story—it was *guilt*. I was sorry to have something in my life that I didn't tell him, but I didn't feel guilty. I wouldn't tell him because I wouldn't hurt him, but I didn't feel wicked or guilty. I felt free—I owned my own body. I loved Roger, but I didn't belong to anyone. I would choose to be faithful because I preferred it, but I couldn't be sorry for the experience that gave me this insight. So not wicked, or guilty, or sorry, or even very nice, but maybe a bit more grown-up. You could say it was high time, at thirty-four. Even without a normal adolescence I think it was more than high time myself.

30

BEFORE GOING HOME to France, I went back to Los Angeles for a week to see my dearest friend Ruth Conte. Oh, it was strange to be there as me, not Mrs. Gene Kelly. I told myself I was a visitor, an actress in plays and movies in Paris, London, Madrid, Rome, and even New York, and I lived in a wonderful apartment on the Rue du Bac in Paris. But every time we drove through Beverly Hills we passed 725 North Rodeo Drive. It was then I saw that one of the three silver birch trees we'd planted in the front yard had died, the birch trees that had seemed to represent the three of us, Gene, Kerry, and me. Now there were only two, for Gene and Kerry. We didn't have to take that route each time, but I wanted to. I think I needed to confront my feelings: "This is my house—I found it—I bought it—I made it our home—and I left it." I felt it was as much my house as the one I grew up in, in Cliffside. I finally understood that nothing goes away, you can't leave it behind or erase it, everything you live is forever part of you.

I'd come to California to see Ruthie but also to have a meeting with my agent, the all-powerful Lew Wasserman, head of MCA at that time. I had a simple question. Why, in the almost three years since *Marty*, since my Academy Award nomination, since the Golden Palm at Cannes, since the worldwide financial success of the film, and, more recently, my European films and the play in New York, why did I not have a single offer from Hollywood? He expressed surprise; he said many of his directors and writers had given him the impression that they were thinking of me for roles, he would check on it immediately. He called me that very afternoon. I must come back into the office, to see "Captain" Something-or-other and straighten out the problem. It was the same old story—the publicly unacknowledged blacklist. The captain (so-called from his days in the army—probably the OSS) informed me that I must simply write the cringing, betraying letter (those are my words, not his), or meet one of the congressmen and clear my name. I went straight back to Lew. I'd known him for many years. He was Gene's agent almost from the beginning. He and his wife, Edie, had been to parties at our house. He was rather shy at parties, for all his success. I remember him preferring to be in the kitchen with me drying the glasses I was hurriedly washing when there were more guests than glasses. So we could be honest with each other now. When he said he'd try to find a solution without my "cooperation," I trusted him.

A couple of months later I had a telegram in Paris. A screenplay was waiting for me, to be picked up at the concierge desk of the Hotel Georges V with a letter from Lew explaining everything. His strategy was simple. Even if I didn't think it was a great part or a great script, I had to do it. The billing would be "JOSEPH COTTON— VIVECA LINDFORS—BETSY BLAIR." The director was Joseph H. Lewis, who made stylish, effective movies, not B movies exactly— more B+ ones. The featured actor was Ward Bond, a regular in John Ford's films, a big, burly, good actor—and one of Hollywood's noisiest reactionaries. He was in favor of the Un-American Activities Committee and passionate about cleansing Hollywood of "Reds, communists, pinkos, and fellow-travelers." He was the reason why I must be in the film. Lew said if I appeared in a movie with Ward Bond, the studios would assume that I'd been officially removed from the blacklist. And the wonderful roles would follow.

The Halliday Brand was a good little story—politically liberal, even—and a good enough part for me. I said yes. I was surprisingly excited to be going back to Hollywood to be in a movie.

I had lunch with the director, and we talked about my character for all of ten minutes. I could see his energy and that he knew what he wanted. I guessed, correctly as it turned out, that the filming

With Joseph Cotton and Bill Williams
in *The Halliday Brand,* 1958

would be fast and efficient. There would be no waiting around on the set in a creative silence as there had been while Antonioni gulped his espressos.

On the first day of shooting I was eagerly looking forward to the moment when I would meet the Man, Mr. Ward Bond, my enemy. There was a kind of glee for me in the thought that he would be unwittingly helping me, *his* enemy. I expected him to be crude, and not very bright. I had no idea what I'd do—just a feeling that I should dazzle him, and make him envious of a liberated left-wing person. Well, he confounded me and my expectations. Seven o'clock, in the makeup room—I already knew Viveca and Joe Cotton, I'd met the hairdresser and the makeup man. There was only Mr. Ward Bond to meet. He was already ensconced in one of the reclining barbershop chairs in front of the long row of mirrors. The assistant made the introductions. Did he just look up and nod? No, he straightened his chair, stood up, shook my hand properly, and welcomed me aboard. I was playing his daughter in the film, and he gave me a fatherly smile. And that was it. He was unfailingly polite, on time, ready to run through scenes if any of us wanted to, always knew his lines. There was no cause for complaint. I had to remind myself that I hated what he believed. I couldn't hate him as a fellow actor.

The film opened, ran, and closed without having any particular effect. No one noticed it, as far as I know, except perhaps a few film buffs. Recently the French director Bertrand Tavernier described to Karel and me the opening tracking shot—but then, he's not only a wonderful filmmaker, he's also the most knowledgeable film buff in the world.

As for its effect on me, the blacklist, my "Hollywood career," it was zilch, nada, zero. I never again had an offer for an American film. Twenty-five years later, I was in a few episodes of *Thirtysomething*. One of its writers, Richard Kramer, is a friend, and he suggested me. And thirty years later, Costa Gavras gave me a part in his American film *Betrayed,* starring Debra Winger and Tom Berenger. I'd known Costa in France with Yves Montand and Simone Signoret. When I arrived at the location, he said, "Welcome—I always wanted to work with you, but I never thought you'd be playing a grandmother in our film together."

Hollywood had really said farewell to me when I left in 1956. My farewell to it took quite a bit longer.

In 1983, I was in Hollywood with Karel, staying at the Chateau Marmont. He'd been finishing a film, and we were going to Michigan for Christmas with Kerry and Jack and the grandchildren. On December 23, the phone rang at two in the morning. It was Kerry. The house on Rodeo Drive was burning down. They called her so she wouldn't be shocked when it was on the morning news. She called me for the same reason. I lay in bed for about an hour, then I said to Karel, "I have to go there." He offered to drive me, but I said no I had to do it myself. There were hardly any cars on the road. I turned off Sunset Boulevard and saw the fire engines with floodlights, the blazing house, the rotating lights on the police cars cordoning off the approaches. I parked, said to the policeman, "Friend of the family," and he let me through. Gene was standing in the road with a lady friend and Lois, his secretary from my time. Tim, Gene's son with Jeannie, had been downstairs when the Christmas tree ignited into a fireball and shot up through the house. He ran through the fire to wake Gene and take him down the back stairs to safety. Now Tim was dodging the firemen, trying to get in and out of the house to save things, but the firemen finally stopped him. Gene was standing there in his pyjamas with hat, overcoat, scarf, and slippers brought by neighbors, just watching the flames, as were Lois, with her sweet helpful face, Tim, with his young smoke-blackened face, Bridget, pale and beautiful, and the lady friend, looking stunned. Gene said, "Oh Bets, oh Sweeney." I said, "I had to come." The lady friend said, "I'm pleased to meet you, I've heard so much about you." Lois and Gene and I had a tiny conspiratorial smile at that, and then came the tears and embraces. Eventually we went to the lady friend's house for a drink and tea. Then I went back to the Chateau Marmont. The 725 North Rodeo Drive that was part of me was gone. It was no longer "mine," but in its proper place, as a memory.

31

BACK IN PARIS, I was struggling through Proust. It seemed necessary to me. I can see now that I was driven by a foolish desire to be able to say I read *Remembrance of Things Past* in the original French. Pride goeth, etc. . . . the fall is that it's only a hazy memory. And I'm still waiting—like many others—for that mythical holiday when I'll tackle it again, in English this time.

During what Roger jokingly called my Proustian period, I haunted the English bookshops, the Librairie on the Rue du Rivoli and Shakespeare and Co. on the Left Bank. I zipped through many a book for the sheer pleasure and speed of reading English. But one stayed in my mind. I had to go back and read it again.

A Walk with Love and Death, by Hans Konigsberger, is a love story of adolescents caught in the tragedy of war. Even as they discover in each other the joy of passion, they are doomed by hatred, by the politics of great powers. Konigsberger tells the story simply and beautifully. I was entranced by it. I carried it with me wherever I went.

One of the trips we—that is, the book and I—took together was to London. I had a part in a movie, written by my blacklisted friend Paul Jarrico and directed by Basil Dearden. *All Night Long* is a modern version of *Othello* set in a jazz milieu. Finally, I was to be in *Othello,* not with Paul Robeson at Stratford-on-Avon, nor with Orson in Morocco and Venice, but at Pinewood Studios outside London. And not as Desdemona (in this case, the lead singer with

David Storey, Karel, and Richard Harris during the filming
of *This Sporting Life,* 1963

the band) but as Emilia, the wife of the drummer, Iago, played by
Patrick McGoohan. The film was okay. Dave Brubeck was in it, so
the music was great. And for me, it turned out to be the most
important job I ever had.

Lindsay Anderson, Karel Reisz, and David Storey were preparing *This Sporting Life* at Pinewood, with Lindsay directing, Karel
producing, and David, who had written the book, writing the
screenplay. Through my friendship with Lindsay, I usually had
lunch with them. Most days they drove me back to London after
work. The assistants on *All Night Long* knew where to find me if I
wasn't on the set or in my dressing room.

With Gerard Blain in *I Delfini*, directed by Francesco Maselli, 1960

Karel and I were getting to know each other. He'd already directed his first film, *Saturday Night and Sunday Morning*. He was producing this one for Lindsay while recovering from his success.

I woke one morning with a "visual" in my head, a sequence of shots for the opening of a film—not any old film, but *A Walk with Love and Death*. I saw barren rocky peaks covered in snow, the pale sun emerging from gray clouds to melt the ice and snow, the camera descending the mountain, dripping rocks, crumbling snow drifts, dark muddy earth, rivulets running together to become a stream, tender green shoots appearing, then a forest glade opening to a meadow filled with spring flowers, where we see our young antihero. I lay in bed and wondered if it was presumptuous to imagine that my unconscious was thinking like a film director.

At lunch that day, I revealed all this to my chums. In this context they seemed to me to be an august triumvirate. Lindsay, never one to show surprise, raised a quizzical eyebrow. The impossibly hand-

Maselli with Haya Harareet

some David looked at me with a gentle smile. But Karel said, "Go for it—find out about the rights to the book." That may have been the moment when I fell in love. But if that is what happened, I wasn't aware of it for many months.

From Paris I contacted the publisher and made a deal with Hans Konigsberger's agent, ten thousand dollars for a year's option and a first-draft screenplay. Roger and Serge agreed that it was the next project for Garance Films. Since Karel had encouraged me, I kept in touch to report each development. It all took longer than I expected. When I spoke to Hans on the phone, he was enthusiastic but deep into his new book. He could only come to Paris in about six months to work with me. It turned out to be perfect timing. We all three had movies to make: Serge in Paris; Roger a French film shooting in Africa; and me, my third Italian film.

I Delfini (The Dolphins) is a story of the wealthy young establishment in a provincial city, a small-town *Dolce Vita*. The director was Francesco Maselli, "Citto" to his friends. Joris Ivens had brought him into our lives about a year earlier. He was slight, wiry, irresistibly lively with an audacious wit, most often at his own expense and followed by his engagingly manic giggle. He told me recently that our American expatriate community in Paris had been a revelation to him and to other Italian communists. They saw themselves as sophisticated, bloodied warriors. They'd lived through Fascism, World War II, and now the struggle within their party after the disillusion with the Soviet Union. In the Americans they found the earnestness and naïveté they expected, but they also saw the idealism they'd lost along the way, and a true camaraderie. The blacklisted writers and directors were pooling any money they earned and dividing it according to need. And, more surprisingly for the Italians in our cutthroat movie business, they were helping each other professionally. It seems we were also better read than their European snobbishness had assumed we would be. And besides, we were fun. The homey Jewish warmth of New York—just like *"la mama's cucina,"* said Citto—coupled with the informal California style of entertaining was extremely appealing to them.

And I, in turn, when I got to Rome, was enchanted by Citto and his circle. The late 1950s and early '60s was a golden time for Italian cinema, and Citto's group was the golden youth of that period. They seemed to inhabit Rome as if it were their own back garden, a place in which to run around and play. Most days there were eight or ten people at lunch at the table kept for them by the owner of the restaurant Bolognese, in the Piazza del Popolo. And, as in Paris, whoever had money paid. But there was never much money. I remember a day when Citto said, "I have a little advance on the film—lunch is on me, but no dessert or coffee, okay?" At eighteen, Citto had been an assistant to Visconti and then to Antonioni. After he'd made his first film, *Gli Zbandati,* he was interviewed by *Cahiers du Cinéma.* Asked which directors had inspired him, he cited Mizoguchi and Renoir. So one day—as the story is handed down—Monica Vitti and Antonioni were part of the group at the regular table. Citto called for the bill, and was embarrassed to find he didn't have enough cash. Quietly, he asked Michelangelo to help him out. Antonioni paused, waited for a moment of silence, and then said, "Of course, but as a matter of interest, why don't you ask Mizoguchi?"

The heart of this circle of friends consisted of Citto, Goliarda Sapienza, his loving companion, and his sister Titina, two of the most intriguing women I've ever met. Goliarda, a delicately slim Sicilian with enormous gray eyes, seemed wise beyond her age, as if thousands of years of ancient Mediterranean knowledge of men and women, art and food, had culminated in her. She often dressed in a twinset and a pleated skirt, which made me realize that what would look horsey on an Englishwoman and collegiate on an American was transformed by Italian femininity and style into pure elegance. Besides, she could made a different, delicious pasta sauce every day for a month.

Titina Maselli is something else altogether. Raven-haired, with a Garboesque beauty enlivened by her intelligence and wit, Titina holds your attention effortlessly. The first time I saw her she was wearing a simple white shift and an interesting jacket, navy blue with narrow white stripes—I assumed it was from a great designer. "No," she smiled, "it's a busboy's jacket. I picked it up for pennies in a restaurant supply shop."

Goliarda became an author; Titina is a painter and stage designer. Marco, Titina's partner, worked in the Foreign Office and was later the Italian ambassador to China. There was a striking girl called Piera with the painter Eduardo Arroyo. Citto's assistant, Gigi Vanzi, became a director. They truly were a sparkling group in their early thirties, and they fulfilled their promise.

I Delfini was an ensemble film, and Citto assembled an exciting cast: Claudia Cardinale as a working-class girl, Gerard Blain, the beautiful Antonella Lualdi, Tomas Milian, Anna Maria Ferraro, Sergio Fantoni, and me as the *contessina,* the little countess. We had a ball. This schoolteacher's daughter relished playing a member of the Italian nobility.

Citto is a wonderful director for actors. He was different with each of us: he cajoled, he flirted, he pleaded, he was tough or analytical, whatever was needed. The great cameraman Gianni di Venanzo shot the film, and it was beautiful.

Karel, 1985

Given that I was planning to direct my own movie, I watched everything and asked endless questions, particularly of the camera crew. As I began to see the complexity of lighting and angles and which lens to use, I retreated. I decided, as I think many first-time directors do, that if I had a good cameraman he'd take care of all that. I could focus on the story, the acting, and the atmosphere.

I knew who I wanted for my two leading actors: Tom Courtenay and Geraldine Chaplin. I'd seen Tom on the stage as Billy Liar, directed by Lindsay Anderson. And I'd watched Geraldine grow up to a beautiful sixteen, delicate and sensitive and witty. I wrote to

Oona and Charlie and sent them a copy of the book. They replied that in principle they had no objection if Geraldine wanted to do it. Oona added a P.S. that she loved the book herself and thought Geraldine would be thrilled.

Everything was falling into place. Hans Konigsberger had written the screenplay, and it was good. We could raise the money. The movie was as sure to be made as any film ever is—that is, not sure at all. But we were confident and determined. I think it would have happened.

But my life was changing wildly. Those discreet underground streams joining together to form a flowing river that I described earlier, turned out to be a roaring torrent.

Karel and I had started slowly. From the first tea in my dressing room at the Savoy Theatre, through occasional meetings when he came to Paris for the opening of *Saturday Night and Sunday Morning*, or I came to London to see plays directed by Jack Berry or Lindsay Anderson, we became friends but we didn't yet know we were embarking on a voyage together. At the film festivals in Cannes and Venice I began to wonder about us. After a few Bellini cocktails in Venice, his story slowly emerged.

Karel arrived in London in 1939, aged twelve, in the Children's Transport organized by the Quakers and by a young English stockbroker, Nicholas Winton, a "Righteous Gentile," who saved the lives of 632 Jewish children. Karel was one of them. They were sent from Prague on sealed trains through Germany, to the Hook of Holland, and then on ships to England.

In 1936, Karel's parents had sent his older brother Paul for an English education to Leighton Park, a Quaker school. Their Uncle Franz had chosen it over Harrow and Mill Hill "because they don't beat the boys." It was a fortunate choice. In 1939, with the Nazis already in Prague, Karel's mother and father had the courage to send him to England. The school accepted Karel as a refugee and found the sponsor required by the British government. On the day of his arrival the headmaster welcomed him. Karel's mother had sewn name tapes on his clothes as "Charles Reisz" to ease his acceptance by English boys. "No," said the headmaster, "you'll have

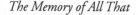

With Daniel Gelin in *Tchin-Tchin*

enough changes to cope with. You must keep your own name—Karel." And, in a gesture that seemed miraculous to a child used to the more impersonal disciplines of a Central European school, this same headmaster, this English Quaker, Mr. Edgar Castle, took Karel to the nearest bicycle shop and bought him a bike.

I can't claim to understand the complex emotions of that twelve-year-old boy. Nor of the eighteen-year-old who learned the fate of his parents in Auschwitz. But I know that whatever formed Karel, the sorrows, the losses, the struggles—and the joys—all that made him the man he is, made him the man for me.

But first we had a tempestuous six months with quite a few flights from London to Paris, and Paris to Manchester, where Karel and Lindsay were shooting *This Sporting Life*. One week it was impossible for Karel to leave his life; the next, it was impossible for

With Kerry and Karel in London, 1962

me. I was aware that what I was contemplating would be repeating my first move, leaving a whole way of life and a good man about whom I had no complaints, just because I wanted to do so. Could I trust my instinct that was telling me that I must?

I also realized that going to get what you want includes leaving behind not only good elements of that life, but even parts of yourself that flourished there. And you can't get them back; they don't fit in your luggage.

And in the middle of it all I was to be in a play, *Tchin-Tchin,* by Francois Billetdoux. The costar was Daniel Gelin, and my son was played by Claude Berri, now the successful director and producer. A French play, in Paris, in French!

Roger came back from shooting a film in Yugoslavia. He overheard a phone call from Karel. I admitted my confusion. He behaved unbelievably well. With assurances of his love, he moved out to give me time to think. *Tchin-Tchin* was opening in three weeks, and Roger continued to work with me on my accent every morning before I went to rehearsal. My character was an Englishwoman, so my accent was acceptable, but I needed his help, and he gave it. Still, it's hard to act in another language. I think I take more pride in that performance than any other. Gian Carlo Menotti invited us to the festival in Spoleto, and Karel came to see the play and me. My cup of joy ran over.

But my friends in Paris—Jack Berry, Serge Reggiani, Trauner, Simone Signoret—didn't understand, because I couldn't seem to explain. Then one day in Paris, Simone asked me what it was about Karel, and it was suddenly clear. It's not just a case of falling in love, I said. It's not just his intelligence, his integrity, his gentleness, his charm and wit, and his blue eyes—it's beyond all that. It's because I know I'll always be interested in him, intrigued by him.

And it's true. I still am. To this day, I don't know how I was smart enough to see it.

And Karel brought me an extra gift—his three young sons, Matthew, Toby, and Barney. And they've brought gifts too as they grew up. I'm now part of an enormous tribe, Karel, Kerry and Jack and three grandchildren, sisters-in-law, nephews and nieces and great-nephews and great-nieces in the States; in London, three stepsons, three lovely stepdaughters-in-law and four step-grandchildren. "In-law" and "step" are such dull words. The French have it better; they just say beautiful. So *"belles-filles"* and *"beaux-fils"*—I'm lucky to have you all in my life.

I left Roger, the Rue du Bac, and my French friends, and moved to London and Karel. Sono Osato once told me she envied my courage and daring to take off for Paris and then London. I had to confess to her that it wasn't bravery that spurred me on, it was plain old love.

I was sure I'd never get married again—but when Karel said, "We won't do this living together, we'll get married," my conviction disappeared, just blew away.

I paid a price for my good life. I never did make that movie. When I'd been with Karel for three or four months, watching him and Lindsay Anderson work, seeing films with them, listening and talking to them, I quietly and ruefully decided that I wasn't a director. I didn't discuss it with Karel, who had encouraged me. I needed

With Karel on our wedding day, 1963

to decide for myself. I didn't agonize over it; not a tear was shed. Tears at that time were as far from me as the moon.

About two years later, John Huston made *A Walk with Love and Death*. If such a master of cinema didn't quite succeed, my version might have been a disaster. I'll never know, and it is my only regret. Alas, I wish I'd done it before I fell in love. But it was a small price to pay for the happiness I found.

And for that happiness I thank my mother, Frederica, and my daughter, Kerry. And Gene. And Roger. And Karel.

Acknowledgments

My most heartfelt thank-you to Victoria Wilson, my editor at Knopf. In the cleverest and gentlest way she took me on this literary voyage.

I thank my family and the friends who helped me. Among them I must name Karel Reisz, Mary Kay Wilmers, John Guare, Antonia Fraser, Pamela Ransley, Kerry Kelly Novick, John Lahr, Louise Stein, Robert Tractenberg, Clare Moynihan, Mary Pat Walsh, Haya Harareet Clayton, Simon Ransley, Norma Barzman, Kevin Brownlow, Ellen Chenoweth, Arabella Weir, and Lynn Nesbit.

Francoise, Matthew, and Julian Reisz checked up on my French when it was rusty.

I used the friendly resources of the British Film Institute, the Motion Picture Academy of the Arts and Sciences, the Lincoln Center Library of the Performing Arts, and the Library of Congress.

And, not to forget the FBI—I thank them for complying with the Freedom of Information Act.

Index

A Note on the Type

This book was set in Adobe Garamond. Designed for the Adobe Corporation by Robert Slimbach, the fonts are based on types first cut by Claude Garamond (c. 1480–1561). Garamond was a pupil of Geoffroy Tory and is believed to have followed the Venetian models, although he introduced a number of important differences, and it is to him that we owe the letter we now know as "old style." He gave to his letters a certain elegance and feeling of movement that won their creator an immediate reputation and the patronage of Francis I of France.

Composed by North Market Street Graphics,
Lancaster, Pennsylvania
Printed and bound by R. R. Donnelley & Sons,
Harrisonburg, Virginia
Designed by Anthea Lingeman